WEDDED STRANGERS

THE CHALLENGES OF RUSSIAN-AMERICAN MARRIAGES

EXPANDED EDITION

Lynn Visson

Hippocrene Books
New York

The author gratefully acknowledges the permission of publishers to reprint excerpts from the following copyrighted material:

Excerpts from *Breaking Free: A Memoir of Love and Revolution* by Susan Eisenhower. Copyright © 1995 by Susan Eisenhower. Reprinted by permission of Farrar, Straus & Giroux, Inc.

From *A Journey for Our Times* by Harrison Salisbury. Copyright © 1983 by Harrison E. Salisbury. Reprinted by permission of HarperCollins Publishers, Inc.

.From *An American Engineer in Stalin's Russia: The Memoirs of Zara Witkin, 1932-1934* translated and edited by Michael Gelb. Copyright © 1991 The Regents of the University of California. Reprinted by permission of University of California Press.

From *Defector's Mistress* by Judy Taylor and Jack Viter. Copyright © 1979 by Judy Taylor and Jack Viter. Used by permission of Dell Books, a division of Bantam Doubleday Dell Publishing Group, Inc.

From *Me and My American Husband* by Tamara Gilmore. Copyright © 1968 by Tamara Gilmore. Used by permission of Doubleday, a division of Bantam Doubleday Dell Publishing Group, Inc.

From *Of Love and Russia: The Eleven Year Fight for My Husband and Freedom* by Irina McClellan, translated by Woodford McClellan. Copyright © 1989 by Irina McClellan. Reprinted by permission of W.W. Norton & Company, Inc.

From *Russia: A Long-Shot Romance* by Jo Durden-Smith. Copyright © 1994 by Jo Durden-Smith. Reprinted by permission of Alfred A. Knopf, Inc.

Reprinted with the permission of Simon & Schuster from *Pizza in Pushkin Square* by Victor Ripp. Copyright © 1990 by Victor Ripp.

From Wettlin, Margaret. *Fifty Russian Winters: An American Woman's Life in the Soviet Union.* New York, Pharos Books, 1992. Copyright © 1992 by Margaret Wettlin.

Copyright ©1998, 2001 Lynn Visson
Expanded Edition in Paperback first printed 2001.

All rights reserved.

For further information, address:
HIPPOCRENE BOOKS, INC.
171 Madison Avenue
New York, NY 10016

ISBN 0-7818-0832-4

Cataloging-in-Publication Data available from the Library of Congress.

Printed in the United States of America.

For Boris

PREFACE TO THE
EXPANDED EDITION

Since the publication of this book in 1998, the collapse of the Soviet Union has run its course, the fledgling industry of matching Russians and Americans who are seeking transoceanic marriage has mushroomed in both Russia and the United States, and the Internet, e-mail, chat rooms and list servers have given intercontinental romance a new electronic charge. Gone are the years of visas denied, phone conversations cut off, letters intercepted and families harassed because a man and a woman born on opposite sides of the globe wanted to join their lives together. Today, Russians can speak and travel freely; their fear is of poverty, unemployment and unpaid wages rather than American nuclear bombs, while for Americans the view of Russia as the enemy is becoming a relic of the past. And for thousands of American men the image of Soviet tanks rolling on Red Square has been replaced by the vision of blond Russian beauties looking for American mates.

The response to *Wedded Strangers: The Challenges of Russian-American Marriages* has been overwhelming. I have received hundreds of letters and phone calls and a flood of e-mail from Americans married to Russians or wishing to be, and vice versa; so has my publisher, Hippocrene Books. These husbands, wives, suitors, fiancées and lonely singles, people of all ages from all walks of life in both countries, wanted to share their experiences, their problems, their failures and successes; they wanted to ask questions, comment, complain, joke and tell their stories. The Russian edition of *Wedded Strangers,* published last year in Moscow, also sparked some heated debates.

In view of these expressions of interest, I felt that *Wedded Strangers* should be updated and expanded to take account of the boom in the Russian-American marriage market in recent years. Moving easily between the two countries on business or for study or work or some other reason, many more Russians and Americans have met and married, and are learning to cope with their cultural differences—or failing in the attempt. Though part of an increasingly homogenized world, they are still very Russian and very American. And when these couples start families of their own, as many of them are doing, their problems multiply.

For this expanded edition I have interviewed, talked to and corresponded with dozens more Russian-American couples. I am deeply grateful to everyone who has responded to the book, with praise or criticism, with suggestions, or with a story to tell. As in the first edition, some names and identifying details have been changed in the interests of privacy, but all the stories are true.

Lynn Visson
New York, 2000

ACKNOWLEDGMENTS

❧

This book is the result of a collective effort, for it is the story of several hundred Russian and American men and women who decided to spend their lives with each other— and with each other's countries. Some of these couples are longtime friends; others I interviewed in Russia and America, met through friends, or through their writings about their marriages. Considerations of space and privacy prevent a complete listing, but I am most grateful to all these individuals for their interest in this story of cross-cultural lives and loves.

Research and interviews in Russia were made possible by a short-term travel grant from the International Research and Exchanges Board (IREX). I am particularly grateful to Dr. Andrei Brushlinsky, Director of the Moscow Institute of Psychology of the Russian Academy of Sciences, Dr. Valentina Levkovich, and the eminent sociologist Dr. Igor Kon.

I would like to thank Antonina Bouis, Paula Garb, Elisavietta Ritchie Farnsworth, Colette Shulman, Mary Ann Szporluk, Professor Deborah Tannen, Joyce Toomre, Joanne Turnbull and Nikolai Formosov for their assistance and encouragement. Yale Richmond, Cornelia and Michael Bessie, Dr. Robert Bosnak, Professor Maurice Friedberg and my mother, Mirra Visson made valuable critical comments on the draft manuscript.

My friend Anthony Austin, a former editor of the New York Times Magazine *and Moscow correspondent, slashed at the text with an unsparing editorial pencil and an intimate knowledge of Russian life. I will be forever indebted to him for so generously sharing his wealth of editorial experience.*

Wedded Strangers was made possible by the determination of the publishers, George Blagowidow and Jacek Galazka. I am deeply grateful to them, to the staff of Hippocrene Books, and in particular to Carol Chitnis for her gracious editorial assistance.

Most of all, I am grateful to my husband, Boris Rabbot. While Wedded Strangers *is not a story about our marriage, in a larger sense it* is *our story, the story of the experiences we have shared with the other Russian-American couples on these pages. Literally and figuratively, Boris has been the driving force behind this book. It is dedicated to him.*

Author's Note

All translations into English are mine unless otherwise noted. Names within the text are spelled according to a modified Library of Congress transliteration system, with preference given to commonly accepted usage, e.g. Dostoyevsky rather than Dostoevskii. The standard Library of Congress system is used for the spelling of names in the footnotes and bibliography.

L.V.

TABLE OF CONTENTS

꧁꧂

INTRODUCTION

She was a beautiful and famous 44-year-old American dancer. He was a handsome, idolized 25-year-old Russian poet. She spoke no Russian and he no English. From the moment they met in Moscow they began sharing their passions, their art, and their tempestuous lives. "We fell in love immediately, as souls," she later said. "Not only was ours a love marriage, but it was also a marriage which united Russia and the United States."[1]

He was a young American engineer drawn to Russia by the socialist dream of building a new world. She was a Russian movie star. He fell madly in love with her screen image and left for Moscow to try to win the heart of his "Dark Goddess," a living symbol—he wrote—of Russia's tragic destiny, of "Russia of ecstatic joy, of incredible suffering . . . Russia of heroes and martyrs, bearing like her, in their glowing, unconquerable spirits, the undying fires of the future."[2]

He was a brilliant 57-year-old Communist physicist, the director of the Soviet space research program, and an adviser to the Russian President. She was a 38-year-old Republican businesswoman, director of an American world affairs institute, whose grandfather had been the President of the United States. "Strange as it seems, we're very similar people," he said.[3]

Extravagant and impassioned, the images of Isadora Duncan and Sergei Esenin, Zara Witkin and Emma Tsesarskaya, rise up out of the 1920s like overblown heroes and heroines of romantic visionary novels. Realistic and contemporary, Roald Sagdeev and Susan Eisenhower symbolize the state of Russian-American relations in the 1990s. Hundreds of ordinary American and Russian journalists, diplomats, performers, students, scientists, businessmen and tourists have sought—and continue to seek—romance and marriage on the other side of the ocean. Though few of them lived such wildly colorful lives as the two couples in the 1920s, they shared the experience of falling in love with a stranger who they had been told was their enemy, and of leaving their homeland to make their lives in the stranger's country.

Despite decades of mutual suspicion and stereotyping, Ivan and Mary have been falling in love and marrying. American socialist idealists, black activists, and children of Eastern European immigrants who went to build the USSR in the 1920s and 1930s married Russians. In later decades an American President's assassin and a Soviet tyrant's daughter would each tie the knot with the "enemy." Ballet dancers, hockey players, interpreters, publishers, doctors and Congressional aides, photographers and professors have all acquired spouses from each other's countries. They met them at work, in universities, on vacation, through friends, at parties, on beaches and on the streets in Russia and in America.

Prior to *glasnost* and the collapse of the Soviet Union, couples who decided to marry took enormous risks, for the Soviet regime's policies, the fluctuations of the political barometer, and bureaucracies on both sides that denied exit and entry visas kept many couples apart for years on end with no hope of being reunited. The men and women who finally succeeded in leaving did so with no assurance that they would ever again see their native land or the families they had left behind.

Now all has changed. During the late 1970s Kevin Klose, the former *Washington Post* correspondent in Moscow, was branded a "bourgeois pen-gangster" by the Soviets. In the summer of 1993 he and his wife Eliza traveled to Moscow to attend the marriages of both their son and daughter to Russians.[4] In that year 350 special U.S. visas were issued by the American authorities for Russian spouses, while only 11 had been granted in 1988.[5] A more open Soviet society, relaxed travel restrictions and the collapse of Communism have facilitated contact and fostered romance. As a result of the rapid development of cultural and commercial ties between the two countries, Americans living in Russia have been dating and marrying Russians, and during the last few decades many Russians who emigrated to the United States have found American spouses. Dating and marriage bureaus specializing in matching Russians and Americans have mushroomed, and the search for love has created a flourishing business in both countries.

Why are these Americans and Russians so intensely attracted to each other? What do they expect from romance and marriage? For better or for worse, how do they live together? How does a Russian deal with his American wife's money in the land of capitalism? Why do Sergei and Muriel have frequent misunderstandings even though she is fluent in Russian? How did the contents of Mark's refrigerator change after Svetlana moved in? How can Irina's views turn an evening with friends into a verbal brawl? Why does Pyotr wrap a scarf around his daughter's throat during an August heat wave? The ups and downs in the relationships between the Russian and American partners often mirror the relationship between their countries.

Since I have always lived on the border between the two cultures, I have a strong personal interest in the answers to these questions. Raised in New York in a Russian-speaking household, I taught Russian literature, participated in many bilateral projects and exchanges, interpreted at international conferences, and lived in Moscow for a year doing research. My interest in Russian-American couples is by no means academic, for I have been married to a Muscovite for more than twenty years. In talking to our many friends and colleagues who are partners in Russian-American marriages, I became increasingly aware that we shared many of the same joys and difficulties. My interest in these microcosms of Russian-American relations prompted me to explore how these couples met, what attracted them to the "other side," and how they lived together in America and Russia, coping with the problems of adapting to each other's country as well as to the manifold aspects of married life.

The stories recounted here of the lives of such couples are the result of ten years of conversations and interviews with nearly a hundred Russian-American couples in the United States and Russia, library research, and consultations with Russian and American psychologists and sociologists.[6] My reading included memoirs of Russian and American spouses, sociological studies of intercultural marriage—since Russian-American marriages reflect some of the same issues and problems found in other intercultural marriages—and even the Russian edition of *Cosmopolitan* magazine. Many challenges, however, are particular to unions between Russians and Americans. I was fortunate to meet fascinating, infuriating and charming individuals aged twenty to eighty who lived in places ranging from Moscow to Los Angeles, couples who were blissfully content and couples who were miserable. Their stories have different endings—some happy, some tragic, some pathetic or even comic. Some endings have not yet been written. But one thing no American married to a Russian seems to have complained of is boredom.

In some cases, to protect the couples' privacy, only first names are given, and names and identifying details have been changed. I am immensely grateful to all of these couples, for they have taught me a great deal about Russians, Americans, myself and my husband, and about the age-old mysteries of human nature, love, and marriage.

BREAKING THE ICE

Building the Future

Whenever a Westerner meets an Easterner, each is to some extent confronted with the unknown. And the unknown is at once an enticement and a challenge; it awakens in us both the lover and the would-be conqueror . . . Each finds himself drawn to the other, yet mystified; each projects his romantic hopes on the stranger, as well as his designs; and each pursues both his illusions and his vested interests with a curious mix of innocence and calculation that shifts with every step.[1]

This description by the Anglo-Indian essayist Pico Iyer of the complex attraction between East and West is equally applicable to Russian-American romances. Forbidden fruit is tantalizing, and the exotic can be erotic. The short-lived union in the 1920s between the American dancer Isadora Duncan and the Russian poet Sergei Esenin was a striking illustration of the glamour and attraction of two opposing cultures, and was billed as the dawn of understanding between "the soul of Russia and the soul of America."[2] From the moment they met in a Moscow painter's studio, the aging dancer and young peasant poet—both slaves to their art and their bottles—were infatuated with each other:

Suddenly the door burst open and the most beautiful face she claimed ever to have seen, crowned with golden glittering curls, and with piercing blue eyes, stared into hers. She needed no introduction. She opened her arms, and he fell on his knees clasping her close to him, shouting 'Isadora, Isadora, mia mia.'[3]

"Zolotaya golova"—golden head—exclaimed Isadora, repeating two of the few Russian words she knew as she plunged her hand into Esenin's golden curls.

For two years the couple's stormy romance was conducted through gestures, tears, insults, embraces, quarrels and drunken reconciliations. Isadora had fallen in love not only with Esenin but with the Russian revolution, the dream of a new world of artistic experimental freedom. Esenin was in love with Isadora's fame and with his ability to captivate her. Their trip to America in 1923 proved disastrous, for the American press described him only as Isadora's crazy Russian husband, and Esenin failed to win the recognition he sought as a poet. Drunken binges and bouts of furniture smashing did not help to achieve his goal, and upon their return to Russia the two parted company. Both died tragically, Esenin by committing suicide in 1925 and Isadora by suffocation when her long scarf became entangled in the wheel of a sports car in Nice in 1927.

The desire for one to one relationships between ordinary Russians and Americans, writes Victor Ripp, an American journalist of Russian background, are wistfully

comparable to the dramatic logic of the Duncan-Esenin legend: if we could only meet on a truly personal basis, free of the burdens of nationality, we could understand each other perfectly. We are all alike under our cultural skin, men and women driven by the same human needs, like Esenin and Duncan, though on not so grand a scale.[4]

Sovietologists, journalists, writers and tourists have frequently asserted that the two nations are either highly similar or that they are polar opposites. The critic Edmund Wilson, who knew Russia very well, was close to the truth when he wrote, "Americans who have decided . . . that Americans and Russians are much alike, discover that in the ordinary technique of life, their habits are antipodally different."[5] Some have held that the "universal human element" and the similarities between the two peoples were bound to bring them together. Ripp notes with irony how, despite the Soviet barrage of anti-American propaganda, many Americans kept marveling at these similarities:

> Isn't it true that of all peoples Russians and Americans go over on a first-name basis most quickly? Aren't we by national temperament equally eager to escape the suffocating politesse and social conventions that constrain sincerity? Isn't it true that there have been moments of affection so elemental that even language was unnecessary—for example, all those intermarriages, with American soldiers stationed in Moscow during World War II, with academics on exchange programs in the years after, where simple, intense feelings overcame all obstacles? Following the curve of the heart, we could be friends.[6]

To answer "yes" to these questions, the individuals who fell in love and married had to overcome images of a vicious enemy that for decades had been stamped into the minds of Russians and Americans. Official propaganda, fervid imaginations, and the two societies' lack of knowledge about each other created grotesque caricatures which differed radically from flesh and blood Russians and Americans.

Those images were fostered by the closed Soviet system. From the 1920s on, America was portrayed in Russia as a country teeming with criminals, drug addicts, the homeless and unemployed. Downtrodden workers struggled to pay for the housing, education, and medical care which were all available free in the Soviet Union. The government-controlled Soviet press spewed out a relentless flow of grinning potbellied capitalists gleefully squeezing their moneybags while emaciated workers collapsed at their lathes. Both countries viewed ordinary citizens as potential intelligence agents, and in the postwar period raging spy mania and mutual suspicion reached their apogee. As late as the 1980s, wrote an American observer of the Soviet scene,

> Ronald Reagan was constantly portrayed as a trigger-happy, missile-flinging cowboy, impetuous, unpredictable, and highly dangerous. The United States is shown to be antagonistic, belligerent, and untrustworthy internationally; ruthless, heartless, and without conscience domestically.[7]

Yet the powerful Soviet propaganda machine did not succeed in producing a totally black image of America. The inferiority-superiority complex which has dominated Russia for decades created a seesaw attitude, which balanced disdain for America with admiration. Though officially America was decadent and rotten, Russians were intensely jealous of anything and everything made in the U.S., and imagined America as heaven on earth. The contradiction in this love-hate attitude is evident in the old Russian joke about a schoolboy who is asked what problems exist in the U.S. He replies that America suffers from unemployment, discrimination, and crime. Very good, says the teacher. And what is our goal in the socialist motherland? To catch up with and surpass America, comrade teacher, the boy answers.

Lack of first-hand knowledge of America made the country even more attractive to Russians. "American dreams are strongest in the hearts of those who have seen America only in their dreams," writes Pico Iyer.[8] It is no wonder that Russians, unable to travel and living in a country with muzzled media, eagerly pounced on any stray American from whom they might learn the truth about life abroad.

The American image of Russians was not much more flattering or objective than the Russian stereotype of Americans. Gallup polls showed that in 1953 only 1% of Americans had a positive attitude towards the USSR, and thirty years later 56% believed it was the evil empire.[9] As Susan Eisenhower recalled, "anti-Communism came naturally to us."[10] Against great odds, the best of American journalism managed to produce a steady flow of objective and often perceptive reporting on the Soviet Union, and American students of that country contributed some excellent popular and scholarly books about the Soviet decades. But all too often the opposite was true. In his book *Faces of the Enemy*, the American psychologist Sam Keen wrote that in coverage of the Soviet Union by *Time, Newsweek*, and *U.S. News and World Report*, "the words most often used to characterize the Russians are savages, dupes, adventurers, despots and barbarians, and their methods of behavior as brutal, treacherous, conniving, unmanly, aggressive and animalistic."[11] Russian men were seen as ruthless Communist agents or crude bears devoid of any social graces, and the women as gorgeous KGB spies or dumpy middle-aged females à la Nina Khrushchev. As Keen noted, "The enemy is seldom pictured as female. At the very least, enemy women remain desirable as sexual objects."[12] James Bond lusted after the beautiful women of *From Russia with Love*. Many Americans saw post-revolutionary Russia as a land of free love and sex, and during the Red scares in America rumors were rife about Russian free love bureaus where any unmarried adult woman could be had by any man, even without her consent.[13]

There was one period, however, when this negative image changed. During World War II when the two countries were allied against Nazi Germany, American screen images of Russians—and in particular of attractive Russian women—were part of a campaign to show the former enemy in a positive light. Even before the war, in 1939, Greta Garbo starred in *Ninotchka* as the hard-boiled Communist commissar who could not resist the appeal of the decadent Melvyn Douglas. The former enemy could be a potential lover or even spouse. In *Comrade X* (1940), the charm of Clark Gable as a journalist stationed in Moscow breaks down the steely will of Hedy Lamarr's Russian heroine, who drives a tank to freedom to save herself and her American lover. *Song of Russia* had Robert Taylor playing an American conductor who marries a Russian farm girl when he realizes that "she's just like an American girl."[14] An occasional Soviet film also allowed for the possibility of romance between a "good" American and a Russian. The American circus performer who is the heroine of *The Circus*, a Russian film of the 1930s, flees to the Soviet Union to escape persecution, falls in love with a Russian worker and lives happily ever after in the land of socialist bliss.[15]

Even during periods of strained postwar Soviet-American relations such as the McCarthy era, the American media allowed for the possibility of love between East and West. In virulently anti-communist comic books such as "Communist Kisses" and "Behind the Romantic Curtain," the American hero vainly swore, "I'm not going to fall in love with a rotten Communist!"—only later to sob, "I realized how much I really cared for Tanya, how much I would lose if she died . . . I know she could never be mine as long as she's a Communist—but I love her and can't let her die!"[16]

In the 1920s and 1930s hundreds of American socialists, blacks seeking a society free from racism, Jews who had fled the tsarist pogroms, Russian immigrants and their children, ordinary workers and recent college graduates were fascinated by the Soviet experiment. Between 1920 and 1925 nearly 22,000 American and Canadian men, women, and families moved to Russia intending to remain there.[17] These idealistic Americans who went off to the USSR to build the world of the future were quickly introduced to Russian reality—and to Russian romance. John Scott, a young worker from Philadelphia, went to Magnitogorsk in Siberia in 1932 because he had

come to the conclusion that the Bolsheviks had found answers to at least some of the questions Americans were asking. They had got away from the fetishization of personal

possessions, . . . one of the basic ills of American civilization . . .
I was going to be one of many who cared not to own a second
pair of shoes, but who built blast furnaces.[18]

Scott immediately fell in love both with the blast furnace and
with Masha Dikareva, a peasant girl who had become an English
teacher.[19] He was bowled over by Masha's beauty, but she was puzzled rather than dazzled by her first American. She had imagined
that all American men were tall, handsome and rich. Instead, as
she recounted to the American writer Pearl Buck, she saw a

> stringy, intense-looking young fellow, absolutely grimy with
> blast-furnace dust . . . I became sorry for him. The first
> American I had ever seen, he looked like a homeless boy. I
> saw in him the product of capitalist oppression. I imagined
> the sad childhood . . . the long hours of inhuman labor which
> he had been forced to perform in some capitalist factory when
> still a boy . . . [20]

He definitely did not fit her stereotype of Americans. "I expected he
would be dressed very chic . . . I thought all Americans must be chic.
But he was dressed in the same kind of clothes the Russians have!"[21]
For Scott her background was as strange as his origins were to her.

The two immediately took to each other. "I became so friendly
with John," Masha said. "At the beginning I was just interested
because he was American. Then I found out he was exactly like a
Russian and many things we found we had in common. Even
sometimes I forget he is American." She was well aware, however,
of the American stereotype of "Bolshevik" women who were ready
for "free love":

> He told me after a while that we could not go on as brother
> and sister. He said we must come nearer or we must separate.
> He told me he likes me and I told him I like him too. But I
> said I would not like, just simply speaking, to sleep with

him. Perhaps I felt he is American and perhaps he might look at me as a Soviet girl who believes in free love or something like that. I felt we should live together with formalities, as husband and wife. I told him I was not a girl if you like to come and sleep with her, you can—I felt I do not like these things. . . . He said to me he would like to get married.[22]

The next day she moved in with the single suitcase containing everything she owned, and they made a marriage license out of a piece of wrapping paper which they bought for three rubles. Married life, Scott wrote in his memoir, was definitely secondary to their work and studies. The couple was so busy that it took them nearly a year to get used to the idea that they were in fact married.[23] Problems at the factory, freezing weather, scrambling to obtain a minimum of furniture and household goods and coping with all the cares of Soviet daily life quickly dissolved cultural stereotypes.

A group of American workers, determined to help the USSR through the introduction of American industrial and management methods, founded Project Kuzbas, a Siberian economic colony administered entirely by Americans. From 1921 to 1926 the group lived in the town of Kemerovo, and by August, 1922 twelve of the American men had married Siberian girls.[24] Most of the marriages proved stable and the families stayed on in Russia, but the regime did not spare these idealists. Though Anna Preikshas, who was twelve years old when she came with her family from the United States to Kemerovo in 1922, lost her father, brother and Russian husband during the purges, she remained convinced that the Soviet system had given her a better education and professional career than she would have had in America. Until her retirement in 1965 she taught English at Dnepropetrovsk University, and was never interested in regaining her American citizenship or in returning to the United States.[25]

Margaret Wettlin, who left Philadelphia for Moscow in 1932 when she was fresh out of college, began teaching at an American school for the children of Ford engineers at a Soviet auto plant in Gorky, and later found work as a translator. She fell in love with the country and with a charismatic Russian theater director, and had no regrets about the fifty years she spent in Russia:

> I have been fortunate on two counts. First, because I went to the Soviet Union in the early thirties and therefore witnessed the end of an extraordinary period of creative activity animated by revolutionary fervor . . . [that] conferred a sense of participation in history-making. My second piece of good fortune was that I met Andrei Efremoff and joined my life to his.[26]

She saw Efremoff as "an impassioned artist . . . a dreamer who believed in the future, as could only be expected of one with his buoyant disposition and infrangible optimism."[27] Though he spoke no English and Wettlin knew barely two hundred words of Russian, the electricity between them flowed at their first meeting. She was instantly smitten by his handsome looks and strength of character.

> But—he could not even speak my language, and our backgrounds could hardly have been more different. Why, then, was I so sure that he was the man who most answered my needs? I could not ignore the physical attraction we felt for each other. But that could not have held us together for thirty-six years of extraordinary vicissitudes . . . He was a dweller of the upper air. His spirit never descended—no, not even when life itself pressed our noses to the ground. It was my early, almost immediate perception of this, that made me so sure.[28]

Through the hardships of war and emotional and physical tribulations Efremoff remained her ideal and a tower of strength. His eyes, she wrote, were "exerting a force I could not define but one that had been guiding me all the days of my life with him . . .

Never . . . had I read anything but goodness in them." Life with such a man was continually exciting. "It was a compulsion with him, a desire to punctuate life's prose with exclamation marks."[29] Efremoff died in 1968, and in 1979, more than four decades after she had left the United States, Margaret returned and settled in Seattle. "I was Mrs. Rip Van Winkle," she wrote, "coming home to the old New World from the new Old World. Rip was away twenty years. I was away forty-two. Rip slept the time away. I lived it eventfully."[30]

A whole book could be written about the American blacks who went off to Russia to seek a better future, and found Russian spouses. Jimmy Winkfield, a jockey who rode for Russian noblemen before the Revolution, married a Russian aristocrat, and became fabulously wealthy before he was forced to flee in 1919 during the Civil War. A black singer from a poor farm family, Coretta Arli-Titz arrived in 1913 at the age of eighteen. She acquired a duke as a patron, studied at the Moscow Conservatory, sang for Red Army troops at the front during the Civil War and World War II, married a Russian musician, and until her death in 1951 was a highly successful Moscow performer of both Russian and Negro songs.[31]

In the 1920s a considerable number of young American blacks set off for the USSR, which was proclaiming itself a mecca for the oppressed and exploited. Lured by the promise of an education, Henry Scott went to Russia as a student in 1928. He made a career as a famous and wealthy tap dancer, and married a Russian girl. Their daughter Margie became a ballerina and choreographer with the Bolshoi Ballet, married a Russian dancer, and decided to make her life in Moscow. Scott, however, returned to the U.S. in 1939 with his Russian second wife, Olga, by whom he had three more daughters. In America he had no professional success. He died in 1945, and forty years later his Russian daughter Margie met her three American half-sisters for the first time at a tearful reunion in California.[32]

Harry Haywood, a black American Communist, went to Russia in 1926 and studied at the Far East University, which was training students to become revolutionaries who would overthrow colonialism and racism in their countries. He soon met and married Ekaterina, a shy Russian nineteen-year-old ballet and English student. Hayward was infuriated by an issue of the school newspaper which caricatured him as an inveterate womanizer in an unsigned cartoon entitled, "Comrade Haywood Doing Practical Work in a Crimean Rest Home," showing him surrounded by a dozen pretty Russian girls. Some forty years later the famous Mexican Communist painter David Siquieros confessed that he was responsible for this art work. Haywood was unable to bring Ekaterina with him to America because his former wife refused to grant him a divorce and the American immigration authorities refused to admit a "Communist" wife. He left Russia; Ekaterina finally gave up waiting for him to come back and remarried.[33]

In the twenties and thirties American blacks were very popular with Russian girls, who saw them as exotic foreigners and victims of a racist American society. The situation changed radically in the postwar era, and in the 1970s black American and African students studying at Soviet universities were targets of ugly incidents when they tried to date Russian girls.

In the late 1930s the harassment and arrests of foreigners led to a slowing down of American immigration to Russia. By 1935 the special shops for foreigners were closed and aliens were being dismissed from jobs, expelled, and arrested. When John Scott went to the United States on vacation, Masha was refused a passport to go with him. She didn't want to leave the USSR for good, and yet when John was told he would no longer be permitted to work at the plant she decided to apply for a visa. "He still wanted to live in America and so I left Russia," she said.[34] During the four years before the family's visas were granted their friends avoided them out of fear of associating with a foreigner. If it had not been for his wife and their children, Scott wrote, he would have been ready to leave the country for good.[35]

Though many disillusioned American expatriates went back to the United States, some of their children decided not to return, married Russians and remained in the Soviet Union, where they and their families are still living today. Those who later changed their minds and wanted to go back to America often had to struggle for decades to obtain exit documents.

Most of the Americans who heard wedding bells in Russia had no idea of the problems they could encounter as foreigners, and as foreigners with Russian spouses. Daunting legal and bureaucratic obstacles often kept mixed couples apart, for until 1946 only one or two exit visas a year were issued to Russians married to Americans. These romances were particularly intense because of the constant awareness that separation could be imminent and permanent. Once a partner returned home, days and nights of passionate encounters could be followed by weeks of total silence. Visas might not be issued, letters not delivered, phone calls interrupted.

Aside from the generally tense state of U.S.-USSR relations, there were several reasons for the Soviet intransigence on marriages to foreigners. A Russian man's marriage and subsequent departure deprived the army of a recruit, and the labor force of a worker. It also meant that in a country where so many men had been killed in the war one less man was available for Russian women. Official explanations of the negative attitude to such marriages alleged that these would-be emigrants knew state secrets, or had access to classified information. What the government really feared was that the Russians who left would reveal to the West the dissatisfaction of their fellow-citizens, while foreigners living in the USSR with a Russian spouse would infect the closed Soviet world with democratic liberal ideas.

In February 1947 an edict of the Supreme Soviet forbade marriages between Soviet citizens and foreigners. Though in general the ban was strictly enforced, a few marriages were permitted. Unlike the unions of the 1920s and 1930s, the mixed marriages of the early 1940s and 1950s were primarily between American men and Russian women, since relatively few American women were then working or living in Russia. By making the law retroactive, the Soviet government exerted pressure both on planned future marriages and on Russians already married to Americans, urging them to divorce their spouses and threatening sanctions if they did not. Measures aimed at preventing and breaking up these marriages included bugging telephones, tailing individuals on the street, threats of job loss and arrest and jail sentences on trumped-up charges. A Russian wife could be forced to write a letter to *Pravda* repudiating her husband, denouncing the U.S., and stating her wish to remain in the motherland. Some women who refused to sign statements renouncing their husbands were sent to labor camps. The wife of an American Foreign Service officer who had been forced to leave when his term was up went out for a walk one day, and was never heard from again.[36]

Following Stalin's death, and in response to international and United Nations pressure, the law was rescinded on November 26, 1953. In 1975 the USSR signed the Final Act of the Conference on Security and Cooperation in Europe, in which the signatories agreed to enable married couples from different states to live permanently in the state in which either resided.[37] Until the introduction of *glasnost*, however, the Soviet authorities continued to create obstacles to mixed marriages by refusing permission to marry in the USSR, denying the couples entry and exit visas, or expelling the foreign spouse. Acquiring foreign relatives through marriage was dangerous for the Russian's family because of an edict of the USSR Council of Ministers barring people with relatives abroad from holding jobs involving access to classified information.[38]

Immigration to Russia resumed in the late 1940s and early 1950s, when American leftists and their families began fleeing the McCarthy witch hunt. The 1960s and 1970s saw a sharp increase in exchange programs, and in the number of American male and female tourists, academics, exchange students, journalists, businessmen and performers who spent extended periods of time in the USSR and were more likely to meet and marry Russians.

Long-term residence in Russia also became more attractive to Americans when the requirement that foreigners living in Russia take Soviet citizenship was lifted. Soviet authorities continued to create difficulties, however, for Russian men involved with the foreign women who began coming to Russia on study and exchange programs. "They are utter male chauvinists," said a West European diplomat in the 1970s. "If a woman wants to marry a foreigner, it can sometimes be worked out. But if a Russian man wants to, it usually leads to trouble."[39]

Nevertheless, once U.S. academic exchanges with Russia took off in the 1960s, and male and female students were able to spend a whole year in each other's countries, Russian-American marriages started blossoming. Faced with the real-life people who filled the libraries, dormitories, and campuses of Soviet and American universities, the image of the dangerous enemy began to fade.

Dateline Moscow

Many of the American correspondents posted to Moscow became deeply involved in the Soviet Union. "Everybody, when they left, took a piece of Russia with them and left a piece of themselves behind,"[1] said an Associated Press journalist. Several took a piece of the country with them in the form of a Russian wife.[2] Edmund Stevens, Henry Shapiro, Raymond Anderson and Eddy Gilmore all acquired Russian spouses during their assignments in the USSR, and Walter Duranty and other correspondents fathered children by their Russian mistresses. Some journalists were highly enthusiastic about the new Soviet system and openly sympathized with the Bolsheviks' goals. Three years after her arrival in 1921, the well-known American Communist journalist Anna Louise Strong, who married a Soviet official, was still enthusiastic: "The heroism, the sacrifice, the comradeship, and the joy that went with it. The joy of pioneers who, in the midst of hardship, exult to believe that they are creating something new."[3]

Louis Fischer, the Brooklyn-born correspondent for *The Nation* who came to Russia in 1922, had socialist ideals and a Russian wife. The son of impoverished immigrant workers, he had great hopes for Russia. "In Lenin's Russia of 1922 I looked not for a better present but for a brighter future," he wrote, adding somewhat naively, "I suspected that Moscow would be fun." By 1938 and the coming of the purges, enthusiasm had waned, resulting in a painful break with the utopian dreams of his youth. "It is not so easy to throw away the vision to which one has been attached for fifteen years. My divorce from Russia was gradual. It has caused me many a heartache nevertheless," he wrote.[4] Permission for his family to leave was denied for over a year, and only the personal intervention of Eleanor Roosevelt finally produced exit visas in January 1939. Fischer subsequently became well known for his biography of Lenin and other works on the Soviet Union.

It is not surprising that energetic and Russian-speaking American journalists intent on familiarizing themselves with Soviet society started by getting to know some of its young and pretty female representatives. The restricted world in which the Moscow correspondents worked was tense, and with the onset of the purges they were subjected to increasing harassment by Soviet authorities. The pressure on the journalists was particularly strong because their job was to report on precisely those things which the regime did not want known. The American correspondents with Russian wives were especially vulnerable, living in fear that they or their spouses might be arrested or expelled, or that the spouse would never receive an exit visa.

Tamara Kolb-Chernesheva and her husband, the Associated Press correspondent Eddy Gilmore, both wrote detailed memoirs of their experiences, he in *Me and My Russian Wife*, and she in *Me and My American Husband*.[5] Gilmore was swept off his feet by Tamara. "I knew I had never met anyone and would never meet anyone quite like Tamara Kolb-Chernesheva," he wrote.[6] The couple met in 1942 when he was working in Moscow and a friend of Tamara's who was dating an American set up a double date. "You mean you are asking me to have a date with a capitalist?" Tamara inquired of her friend Tanya. "He's a capitalist . . . but not a real one," said Tanya. "You see, this one's a capitalist without capital." Gilmore definitely did not fit Tamara's stereotype of an American:

> He looked so funny. His face was big, round, and very red and he did not have too much hair. Also, he was box-shaped, one of the squarest-looking men I have ever seen. He was wrapped in what looked like an extremely warm overcoat, and like the cartoons in *Krokodil* and other Soviet publications of capitalist fascist beasts, the overcoat had a fur collar. Beneath that splendid coat I was certain that

Mr. Gilmore had a large round stomach across which must hang a watch chain of pure gold.[7]

If all foreigners were like these two, the girls thought, they must be very bizarre. Tanya's date, John, "was short and pale, with so much hair that his hands reminded me of my favorite ape at the Moscow zoo."[8] Nor was Gilmore strikingly handsome. "I have never won any beauty contest," he wrote.[9] As Tamara described him, "My husband resembled a Russian general. He was big, bald, and barrel-chested, with a seventeen-and-a-half inch collar." The Russian girls were much taken, however, with the Americans' manners. "They were so polite compared with young Russian boys my age," noted Tamara. Gilmore's behavior particularly impressed her. "There was something about him which I liked. I think it was his manners. He removed his hat when he was introduced. He held my arm when we crossed Gorky Street, at that time of year caked with ice and slippery." During their first date in the Georgian Aragvi restaurant, Tamara recalled, "I was swept up in a sort of euphoria."[10] In wartime Moscow, this first trip to a luxury restaurant in the company of foreigners babbling in a strange language left the hungry girl too frightened to touch any of the elegant dishes.

> I do not know what they must have thought of me, for I tried and tried but I could eat nothing. I suppose I was affected by a combination of teenage shyness, gnawing hunger, the glittering (for me) surroundings, meeting foreigners, and just plain Russianness. Dostoyevsky, I am sure, could have explained it. I cannot.[11]

Tamara was touched and dumbfounded when the Americans handed her a "doggy bag" with the leftovers for her family. She was surprised by how fast and decisively the foreigners behaved:

> As frequently has been my experience with Americans, I could not at first understand what was going on. Americans

are so unpredictable. They act and move so quickly, often from a motivation that I neither realize nor understand.[12]

Gilmore was entranced by Tamara:

> . . . an average-sized girl with the biggest, brownest eyes I'd ever seen. Her hair was brown too, and it hung long and thick over her thin shoulders . . . Her nose was turned up, her lips were full and her figure would make you throw rocks at the rest of the girls . . . She had very long eyelashes over those wondrous eyes, and if you'll pardon me for being a bit sloppy, she was about the cutest thing I'd ever seen. And that still goes . . . It was an unbelievable evening in my life and, of course, I fell in love with Tamara.[13]

After she started dating Gilmore, Tamara was picked up in the street by the secret police and taken to Lubyanka prison. "You are here because you have been degrading yourself and betraying your country and our wise and fatherly government by your persistent association with foreigners, and in particular with one foreigner," an NKVD general informed her.[14] When she remonstrated that the Americans were Russia's allies, he replied that the fact that they were on the same side against Hitler was merely an accident of history. As she related in her memoirs,

> "I have a daughter your age," he said. "I would prefer to see her dead than to have put herself in your position. This man, this American, is playing with you. You are his toy." "He has told me he wants to marry me," I managed to spurt out. "Marry you?" He laughed a very loud laugh. "He will never marry you. Never." I remained silent. Perhaps the general was right.[15]

After a five-hour interrogation Tamara was handed papers banishing her within forty-eight hours to Siberia. Gilmore could scarcely believe that Tamara had been arrested because of her contacts with him:

> We knew that before the war Soviet citizens did not frequently make friends with foreigners. But a war was on now and Russia was receiving aid, and much aid, from the United States and we were allies. It was inconceivable that the Soviet authorities would object to their citizens associating with the few Americans stationed in Moscow . . . If she were in trouble with the secret police it meant that I was the cause of the trouble . . . I don't believe I ever felt more helpless.[16]

Appeals to the authorities succeeded in having the exile changed from Siberia to a village south of Ryazan where she had relatives. Gilmore managed to get food, clothes, and a letter to her in exile, saying that while he was in Russia he could do nothing to help her, but he was sure he could act effectively from America.

Back in the U.S., Gilmore asked his friend Wendell Willkie to intervene with Stalin. In a cable to the Kremlin, Willkie argued that Gilmore needed to return to Moscow to continue his coverage of the Red Army's struggle against the Fascists, and that the Soviet leader's assistance in letting Gilmore marry Tamara would be deeply appreciated. Once the story was splashed over the pages of the *New York Times*, Gilmore returned to Moscow. A few days later the couple was married in a ceremony featuring a speech on Russian-American peaceful coexistence.

Tamara was still not fully aware of all the latent problems in her Russian-American marriage:

> In marrying an American I realized that I was doing something very different, that I was setting myself apart from friends and perhaps family. If I realized all this I am afraid I gave no serious thought to what could be the inherent dangers in an American-Soviet alliance such as my husband's and mine. When one is in love one does not become

preoccupied with such things. If I ever thought of them they gave me no worry.[17]

From 1943 to 1953 the Gilmores lived in Moscow, where two of their children were born. As the cold war intensified and Tamara's Russian friends stopped seeing her, she was followed in the street, and told to divorce her husband. Like the other foreign journalists with Russian wives, Gilmore obtained permission for his family to leave only after Stalin's death. The family lived in the U.S. and England until 1967, when Gilmore died of a heart attack in London, where he was working for the Associated Press.

Despite the couple's happy life together, Tamara was acutely aware of both her stereotype of the enemy, and of the real cultural and personal differences existing between her and her American spouse:

> All my conscious life teachers and instructors had slammed into my brain that capitalist America was my homeland's implacable foe, that ideologically and politically they were as incompatible as vinegar and milk, or honey and bath water, yet here I was wed to one of these Americans, and a rather conservative one at that . . . Honey and bathwater?
>
> If America and Russia are unable to exist without conflict of interest and ideologies, bickering and hints at war, how is it that an American and a Russian were able to live happily together for a quarter of a century?
>
> My husband and I were so different that I was constantly amazed we got along at all.
>
> He liked jazz. My preference is for classical and semi-classical music. I am always late. He was punctual. He was unable or unwilling to bargain over everything, while I believe I could hold my own at an Arab bazaar . . . He rose with the sun. I can lie in bed all day . . . Claret was his favorite wine. Champagne is mine . . . In the theater I am carried away by ballet. Eddy Gilmore would rather have watched acrobats . . . At a baseball game he was in seventh

heaven. I have yet to discover what goes on. In his whole life he never smoked as many as a dozen cigarettes while I am an addict. He never once raised a hand to our children. I slap and spank my daughters when they are naughty. My husband scoffed at the suggestion that ghosts exist. I not only believe in them, I have seen them . . . He doted on fried oysters. I had just as soon eat fried snakes. He called corn-on-the-cob a delicacy. I think it is hog food. How did two persons of such enormously dissimilar tastes, beliefs, backgrounds, likes, dislikes, fetishes, customs and characteristics manage to live together, much less remain happy?

I would be lacking in frankness if I did not confess that during our ten years together in Russia my husband and I had our share of domestic crises.[18]

Tamara's list of differences should have been required reading for all the mixed couples who believed that obtaining a visa was the sole requirement for perfect marital bliss. Though the Gilmores' different attitudes towards time, food, money, the arts and child rearing were fraught with potential conflict, the couple, like their two countries, managed to find a *modus vivendi* for coexistence.

Tom Whitney, who was an Associated Press correspondent, also fell madly in love with a Russian girl. At a reception shortly after he was sent to the American Embassy in Moscow in 1944 to assist Ambassador Harriman, Whitney met Julie Zapolskaya, a beautiful singer and musician:

In a corner in an armchair sat a small girl with dark brown hair and green-gray eyes and a small nose which seemed to have about it an air of healthy contempt for the goings-on. She was dressed in a black silk print dress decorated with bright orange, pink and yellow flowers. Her features were delicate and sensitive and her eyes were bright. She was interesting in an aristocratic way, and impressed me as a very unusual person.[19]

Harrison Salisbury, who began working in Moscow as a United Press International (UPI) Moscow correspondent in 1944 and went to the *New York Times* in 1949, was also immediately struck by Julie. He recalled her as "a slender girl with narrow shoulders, gray-green eyes, high cheekbones, thin face . . . temperamental, brilliant, a musical genius, unpredictable, dangerous, an *enfant térrible* who might pounce at any moment."[20] "I was smitten with interest in this cool girl and determined to get to know her," Whitney wrote in his memoirs, *Russia in My Life.*[21] Her stubborn refusal to meet him during a week of phone conversations left him even more intrigued. When she finally agreed to go with him to Gorky Park, the pretty singer and musician immediately let him know her credo. "'Only one thing in the world is important. And that's love. All the rest is nonsense.' This was her religion. By the time I dropped her off near her home she had made a long start on converting me to it," Whitney wrote.[22] The two spent long hours wandering around Moscow, holding hands, sitting on park benches and in movie theaters, and gazing at each other over a single candle in a tiny room of a friend of hers.

The couple endured all the hardships the Soviet system imposed on Russian-American romances:

> There was this conspiratorial ring to our affair—for [a] reason. The Soviet government has never approved of romances between its citizens and foreign representatives in the Soviet Union . . . Julie had accepted the risk because she was a daredevil, because she refused to be told by anyone what she couldn't do, and because she had a deep liking for me. The conspiratorial atmosphere only heightened the feeling of romance. If we had tremors of fear, we had other tremors, which affected us more vitally. The fact was that we were in love.[23]

Like Gilmore, Whitney was faced with the problems and consequences of marrying a Russian in those grim years:

Some foreigners may have married Russian girls in ignorance of the risks, but not I.

I knew all about this—I knew the dangers. But I also knew there was a chance things would work out. I knew of several Russian wives who had been exchanged for tankers of American aviation gasoline at the beginning of the war. And there were others permitted to leave the Soviet Union in less sensational fashion. But one could never know.

One was dependent on the political situation. One had to hope—and fear. And this was the most terrible thing, this uncertainty. So marriage to a Russian was not something to be undertaken lightly. At the same time the thought of leaving Julie became steadily more unthinkable. I found myself faced with a horrible dilemma.[24]

Once the couple got married, Whitney's life was split between the American Embassy where he became head of the Economic Section, and time spent at home with Julie. With the intensification of the cold war the two worlds grew further and further apart. Julie could not get work, her friends were afraid to see her, and she was cut off from everyone except Whitney and her mother.

As I look back now I can't think of that period in late 1946 and 1947, when Julie got cut off from her work as a composer, without a shudder. It was as if an icy hand had suddenly emerged from nowhere and began touching things all around—turning everything it touched also to ice. The cold war was well named. We in Moscow felt its coming directly in our own personal lives.[25]

In 1947 Whitney became a correspondent for the Associated Press. He had several good offers from American universities, but as long as Julie was not given an exit visa he refused to leave Moscow.

I knew that the only way I could protect her was with my own person. The Russians had never molested the wife of a foreigner whose husband stayed with her so long as he was there with her . . . She was stuck in Russia—and I was going to stay with her.[26]

The couple survived their isolation by going to theaters, movies, and picnics, and by leading an intense social life within the diplomatic colony. There was also company from another quarter. The pair became a virtual threesome, since Harrison Salisbury barely bothered to hide his attraction to his friend and colleague's wife, and Julie did not seem averse to the *Times* reporter's attentions. Salisbury was fascinated by the Russian blend of pure femininity and passionate emotions which proves so attractive to American men. Night after night she and Salisbury stayed up until three in the morning in the Whitneys' kitchen,

> talking, talking, talking, 'clarifying our relations,' as she said, her words for that most Russian of conventions, talk *po dusham*—talk from the soul—laying bare the deepest of feelings, beliefs, the roots of behavior. Never before nor afterward did I have such talks, talks that sometimes left my spirit raw or reeling, but in the end, I know, ripped from my consciousness layer after layer of hypocrisy.
>
> Juli *(Salisbury's spelling: LV)* was an outrageous experience for a Midwesterner like myself, as she had been for Tom. She was the essence of the feminine, in part intelligent, in the Russian sense of that word—educated, sophisticated, socially conscious—in part earthy Russian woman, and in part Juli . . . Russia is female and the female principle is dominant over the male. I do not believe this is true in the United States.[27]

She thoroughly enjoyed flirting and playing the coquette, a role to this day assumed and played with virtuosity by Russian women. Juli was a master of the art; the long, lingering look, the cast-down eyes, the over-the-shoulder glance, the enticing gait, the lowering of eyes and sweep of long lashes, the whirl of a skirt, even the drop of a handkerchief — every nuance of the coquette, played as an art, a sport, an amusement, and sometimes as a very serious thing.[28]

This kind of ultra-feminine woman, who is becoming an endangered species in the United States, is a magnet for American men, and Salisbury was duly grateful to Whitney for showing enormous patience in putting up with his colleague's constant soul-searching sessions with his wife.

The virulent anti-foreigners campaign of 1953 intensified the pressure on Whitney, whose prior work for the OSS and the U.S. Embassy made him a prime target for Russian suspicions that he was involved in espionage. Julie's visa was finally granted in June, 1953. Happy as he was to be going home, Whitney had mixed feelings. As was the case for so many of his journalist colleagues, Russia had acquired a strong hold over him:

> I had left Russia, maybe for good. But I had left some of myself behind. I had eaten Russian bread. I had experienced Russian hospitality. I had loved and been loved in Russia . . . And I had taken some of Russia with me—in my heart. Some of the passion, some of the suffering, and some of the sweeping scope of that broad country and that generous people, even some of its vitality and creativity, had gotten into me and become part of me. Russia was in my life and I wouldn't, of course, ever be the same again. Nor did I want to be. I was glad this was the way things were. And I was also glad to be going home.[29]

Whitney continued to work for the Associated Press in London and New York, and in 1959 retired to a Connecticut town where he worked on translating Solzhenitsyn's *Gulag Archipelago*. Julie recorded several record albums of Russian songs, but her successful singing career was brief, for she died of cancer in 1965 at the age of forty-six.

Raymond Anderson of the *New York Times* met his wife Tina in Red Square in the summer of 1958, when the handsome young journalist was taking photos while on assignment for the *Richmond Times Dispatch*. A commotion began when a group of French tourists, surrounded by Russians staring and asking questions, tried to explain that they had to get back to the hotel for lunch and pushed their way back to their bus. Tina, a petite Russian girl in a red polka-dotted dress who had been shopping nearby and knew French, had stopped to help translate for the tourists. The girl caught Anderson's eye, and he asked her if he could take her picture. Tina agreed, but she was rushing to catch a train to Leningrad, where she was going on vacation, and was scared when she discovered that her new acquaintance was an American. Attracted and intrigued, Anderson made a date to meet her at noon three days later in Leningrad at the statue of Peter the Great. She was frightened, but taken with her attractive new acquaintance, and thinking he would probably not show up, she went to the rendezvous. The couple spent the next few days touring Leningrad, getting to know each other, and falling in love.

Tina, who was a student of French from Kuibyshev, was twenty, and Raymond was thirty-two. Her parents were economic planners, for whom America was as far away as the moon. Anderson had studied Russian on the GI Bill and gotten an M.A. in Russian at the University of Wisconsin. He was separated from his wife, and this was his first trip to Russia.

For more than a year the couple corresponded. Tina was impressed by the young American's sense of humor and ability to express himself in Russian. She wrote him of her dreams: to see the world and join the Communist Party. "I can promise you'll see the world with me," he answered. He could not promise Party membership, but Tina quickly discarded this idea. In 1960, now a reporter for the *New York Times*, Anderson came back to Russia intending to marry Tina. After the American pilot Gary Powers' U-2 plane was downed by the Soviets on May 1, however, the journalist's visa was not extended and he was forced to leave the country. At the end of March, 1963 Anderson finally made it back to Moscow, and the couple received permission to marry two days before his departure for the U.S. at the end of April. Tina remained in Kuibyshev, a pariah at the institute where she now taught French, since her friends and colleagues were deathly afraid of contacts with the wife of an American.

At first reluctant to give Tina permission to leave, her parents relented when they realized that otherwise they would lose their daughter. She was in love, and sure that with enough patience she would get out. In December, 1963 she got her exit visa and joined Raymond in New York. He was assigned back to Moscow; she managed to rejoin him there, but the next few years were filled with battles over her American passport and over Soviet entry and exit visas for her and the couple's two sons.

In August 1968, while the Andersons were on vacation in Greece, Raymond filed a major story on the dissident physicist Andrei Sakharov. His Soviet visa was canceled, and he was given seven days to return to Moscow to get his children and leave the country.[30] Expulsion was the price of honest journalism. For years Tina was not able to return to see her relatives and friends. In America she became an outstanding professional simultaneous interpreter, and, ironically, sometimes found herself working for the high-placed Soviet officials whose bosses and policies had separated her from her native country. Despite all the difficulties, Tina felt that life had dealt her an extraordinarily lucky card, "one in a million," as she put it.[31]

The American correspondents who entered into these mixed marriages in the 1940s and 1950s were embarking on a risky voyage which permanently changed their lives and careers. Russian fear of Western journalists who could reveal the truth about the "Soviet paradise" was intensely strong, and harassment of American correspondents, including constant surveillance, bugging of cars and apartments, blowing out of car tires and even incidents of physical violence continued until the 1980s. Only after the Soviet press achieved real freedom with the advent of *glasnost* and *perestroika*, were the journalists able to meet and marry Russians without fear of personal or professional reprisals.

Divided Houses, Divided Spouses

Though the war years provided American military and embassy personnel as well as journalists opportunities for meeting Russians, marriages were often thwarted by both American and Russian officialdom. One of the most tragic wartime romances took place between the well-known Russian actress Zoya Fyodorova and Jackson Roger Tate, an American naval attaché who was setting up an airfield for American pilots to bomb Japan from Siberia. The beautiful actress and the tall and handsome attaché met at a reception in Moscow, and immediately fell in love.[1] She was 32 and he was 46. Though Zoya spoke very little English and Tate almost no Russian, they began seeing each other, communicating with the help of a dictionary. After a few evenings of going out to dinner Tate began staying overnight at Zoya's apartment. She was convinced that her involvement with a foreigner was not dangerous because she was so well known. "I'm so famous they won't touch me," she said. Since Zoya did not want to leave Russia, and Tate could not imagine living there, they dreamed of spending six months in Moscow and six months in the United States. At the end of the war Tate planned to return to America, complete his divorce proceedings, and come back to marry Zoya.

The couple was so sure of their future that they celebrated V-E day in May 1945 by conceiving a child, whom they decided to name Viktor or Viktoria in honor of the victory. Two weeks later Zoya was sent to perform for Russian soldiers at Black Sea hospitals, and the next morning Tate was declared *persona non grata* and given 48 hours to leave the country. When he tried to get assistance from the State Department he was told that there were plenty of beautiful women in the United States, and that he should not cause trouble in the Soviet-American relationship. Once he left Russia, Tate had no further news of Zoya, and he had not seen their daughter Viktoria, who was born after his departure. His numerous letters remained unanswered—until he received a letter, signed by a stranger, informing him that Zoya was happily married, with two children, was upset by his efforts to contact her, and begged him to leave her alone.

The letter, of course, was a piece of KGB "disinformation." Since the end of 1946 Zoya had been an inmate in the Lubyanka prison, sentenced to twenty-five years as an enemy of the people, an American spy who had plotted to kill Stalin and planned to build an underground tunnel to bomb the Kremlin. But Tate didn't know that, and his ardor was considerably dampened by this seemingly radical change in her life and feelings. Viktoria was then eleven months old.

Zoya angrily asked her interrogator if he called love a crime. If that were so, she had committed a crime. "I met an American and I fell in love with him," she said. And she did not regret it. The colonel replied that to fall in love stupidly was a crime. And so was having given birth to a potential enemy of the country instead of having had an abortion. Tate, she was told, was a spy. During all her time in prison, including one year in solitary confinement, Zoya refused to confess her "crimes."[2] Zoya's sister Alexandra was exiled to Kazakhstan with her two children and with Viktoria, who grew up thinking that Alexandra was her mother. Eight years after her arrest Zoya was amnestied. "A mistake," she was informed.

After Zoya's release Viktoria joined her in Moscow and learned that "Aunt Zoya" was really her mother. She was fifteen years old when Tate learned from an American who had seen Zoya in Moscow that mother and daughter were alive and well. Viktoria had been raised believing that her father was a Russian pilot who had been killed during the war; Zoya told her the truth about that, too. Viktoria desperately wanted to contact her father. Zoya tried to dissuade her, saying that he was the reason she had been imprisoned. When Viktoria asked her mother if she had a photograph, Zoya replied that when she was arrested everything had been confiscated. She told her daughter to stand in front of a mirror and look at herself. Then, said the actress, she would see her father.[3]

Like her mother, Viktoria became an actress. She hoped that one day her father in America would see one of her films and come to Moscow to meet her. In 1973 Tate managed to get a letter and photos of himself to Zoya. He could not imagine, he wrote,

> that a great nation could feel any danger from us after so long a time or cause sorrow to a child who was the only result of a great love . . . I am now 75 years old and my life is far behind me. I loved you then, Zoya, and I love you still . . . [4]

When Tate sent Viktoria an invitation to come and visit him in America in 1974, he was a retired admiral, remarried and ailing. Viktoria could not get a character reference from the film studio, and her request for a visa was turned down. The official reply was that a bout of alcoholism, two marriages and a succession of lovers showed she was immoral and "completely ill-informed and unsympathetic to the Communist cause." After calling a press conference of Western correspondents, and making the whole story public, Viktoria was allowed to leave, and in April of 1975 she arrived in Florida to meet her father. She described how he had

> the same eyes I have . . . He felt so guilty for what had happened to my mother and to me . . . He only said, "I didn't imagine that someone could be so punished for love."[5]

When Viktoria came to see him when he was dying of cancer in a hospital in 1978 he repeatedly told her that Zoya was the only woman he had always loved.[6]

In the meantime Frederick Pouy, a Pan American pilot, had read in *People* magazine of Viktoria's desire to meet her American father, and wrote Tate saying that since he often flew to Russia, he would be glad to take anything the admiral wished to send his daughter. Viktoria repeated family history by falling in love with an American. "It was love at first sight," she recalled. "He said, 'My name is Fred,' and I fell in love even before he finished his sentence."[7] Viktoria had not planned to stay in America, and as she and Fred had both been married twice, they wanted more time to get to know each other. But the memory of what had happened to Zoya after she parted from Jackson Tate was still vivid for her daughter, and a week before Viktoria was to return to Moscow in June, 1975 the two got married. A year later Zoya Fyodorova arrived in Florida to meet her new grandson, Christopher, and to see Tate. They had not met for twenty-nine years, and never saw each other again before Tate's death in 1978 at the age of 79. In 1981 Zoya was murdered in her Moscow apartment in mysterious circumstances, allegedly during a burglary.[8]

The American military produced quite a few other Russian-American wartime romances. Fearful of security leaks and blackmail, the Military Mission and the American Embassy tried vigorously to discourage staff and enlisted men from marrying Russians. The State Department was also well aware that each marriage turned into a headache for the Embassy once an American began requesting support for a Russian spouse who had been refused a visa. But romance did not listen to rules. Thomas Watson, later Ambassador to Moscow, was with one of the American air crews in Russia in 1942. He recalled how the ardent desire for female company won out over the fear that the girls were working for the KGB:

> Women constantly introduced themselves to us. We figured they were informers, but we'd have gone stir-crazy not talking to anybody but each other for three months. Most of the married men stayed straight but things got pretty complicated for some of the crew. At one point three of them were seeing the same girl, whose name was Ludmilla and who claimed to be a ballerina.[9]

Despite the rule that any Army or Navy men who married a Russian would immediately be transferred, there were two such cases during the first two months of Averell Harriman's wartime tenure as Ambassador. Though the husbands were not transferred immediately, they were eventually required to leave. This was a rather heartless ruling, since it was obvious that the Russian wives would not get exit visas. One enterprising Embassy staff member, Ellsworth Raymond, managed to get his Russian ballet dancer wife and infant son back to the United States in 1943 on a Navy ship traveling through submarine infested waters. Though he had won his battle with the Russian authorities, Raymond ran into trouble with American officialdom, for his marriage to a Soviet cost him his new job in military intelligence in the Army General Staff in Washington, and he was forced to quit government service and make a career in academics.[10]

In the 1940s and 1950s American military personnel, embassy employees and correspondents seeking exit visas for their Russian spouses found that the American Embassy was not very helpful; fear of aggravating already strained U.S.-Soviet relations made the State Department extremely cautious.[11] Harriman refused to put pressure on the Soviets for visas for wives of members of the Embassy staff or the Military Mission, declaring that he had "too many requests of major military and political importance to make to use up his influence on trivial personal cases."[12] For the separated couples, however, the lengthy and indefinite separations were certainly not trivial. While the Soviet authorities were far more inhumane in their attitudes, the Americans bore their share of the blame for the undermining of some marriages. All the same, between 1941 and 1950 nearly 350 Russian wives of American citizens applied for exit visas, including 97 wives of U.S. army veterans.[13] Only after Stalin's death in April, 1953 was the U.S. ambassador Charles Bohlen authorized by Secretary of State John Foster Dulles to request visas for American spouses from Foreign Minister Molotov. (Ironically, Bohlen's own daughter, Celestine, later married a Russian whom she met while reporting from

Moscow for the *New York Times*). As the new Russian government tried to improve relations with the West, attacks on American journalists as spies and warmongers ceased, and soon the Russian wives and children of American correspondents and Embassy employees were granted permission to leave.[14]

Until the arrival of *glasnost*, the atmosphere of sickly paranoia and secret police harassment continued to dog Russian-American romances. And even in later years, fear inhibited the development of these ties. In the 1980s Elena Khanga, granddaughter of Oliver Golden, an American black who had moved to Russia in the 1920s, met an American in Moscow. His spoken Russian was so good, however, that she was afraid he was an intelligence agent. Fear won out over attraction, and when he said he wanted to continue seeing her Elena gave him a false address and telephone number. Years later, when a chance encounter brought them together, she was haunted by what might have been had she given the man—who turned out not to have been an agent— her real number. "Even today," Elena wrote in 1992, "I think of the love that might have flowered between the two of us if we had not been trapped in the dying days of the Cold War. I see the whole episode . . . as a metaphor for mistrust . . . and suspicion."[15]

The climate of the totalitarian state often made Russians and Americans suspect each other and their fellow-countrymen of working for the other side. In some cases their suspicions were justified; in others they were not, and the good names of innocent people were smirched. Romantic involvements were particularly vulnerable to blackmail and mutual suspicion. As Tamara Gilmore noted,

> During the long years when Joseph Stalin dominated over two hundred million Soviet citizens, every Russian girl who kept company with a foreigner came under a sort of double suspicion. The foreigners usually regarded her as an espionage agent, or at least as an informer of the secret police,

and the Soviet authorities considered her a spy working for foreign powers, or if not that, a poor security risk.[16]

It was extremely difficult for the Americans to tell which girls were informers and which were not. Many women who hung around hotels for foreigners, or were assigned to them as interpreters and secretaries, had instructions to cultivate their clients. Tamara Gilmore gave an example of a girl whose specialty was American or British air force officers; when a man completed his Russian tour she was automatically assigned to his successor.

While Russian girls who fell in love with the foreigners to whom they were assigned by the KGB have been the material of a slew of spy novels, there was no dearth of real-life KGB efforts to use beautiful Russian women to seduce Americans. Whitman Bassow, a Moscow UPI and *Newsweek* correspondent who has chronicled the adventures of American journalists in Russia, described an incident in 1958. In Russia, men and women traditionally share railroad sleeping accommodations, and on a trip from Moscow to Leningrad Bassow found himself assigned to a compartment with a very attractive blonde, who treated him to champagne and donned a filmy nightgown. Her attempts to seduce him were not exactly subtle: "I like you," she purred. "You are an intelligent, handsome man. I have always wanted to make love to an American. I hope you will not deny me the opportunity." Bassow declined. The next morning he saw the girl being met on the train platform by two stocky men eager to hear her report.[17]

The Moscow Embassy was for a long time a target for such incidents, and when Ambassador Bohlen discovered that a CIA officer was sleeping with a KGB maid he issued orders against any involvements between Embassy personnel and Soviet citizens. Nevertheless, at least twelve Embassy employees fell into Soviet love traps during his tenure, and in 1981 a Marine stationed in Leningrad married a Soviet girl.[18]

Some Russian-American romances did involve informers and espionage. Such was the case of Clayton Lonetree, an Embassy

Marine guard accused of passing documents to the Russians as a result of his affair with one Violetta Seina. This Russian beauty, employed as an embassy receptionist, had a so-called uncle, in fact a KGB officer, who tried to shake the young Marine down for Embassy documents. Violetta had so entranced Lonetree that even while in jail back in the United States awaiting trial he pined for her, convinced that she really loved him.[19]

There were dozens of cases of blackmail. An American translator was warned by the KGB that she would never see her Russian boyfriend again unless she agreed, while working with a Russian ballet troupe performing in the United States, to report to the KGB on which dancers were likely to defect. For decades any American diplomat, student or journalist who spent a night in the Soviet Union with an attractive and unknown Russian took the risk of possible blackmail.

Rightly or wrongly, Americans married to Russians and living in Russia sometimes suspected each other of collaborating with the KGB. Margaret Wettlin, the wife of the theater director Andrei Efremoff, admitted that during her nearly fifty years in Russia she and some of her American acquaintances had at various times passed information to the KGB, in order, as they saw it, to protect their Russian families and friends from arrest.[20]

Even in the U.S., Russian-American marriages were not safe from the long reach of the KGB. In the 1930s, while in the United States, Leon Teremin, a Russian musical inventor, married Lavinia Williams, a ballerina with the First American Negro Ballet. Teremin had invented an electronic instrument operated by sound waves, played by waving the hands over the instrument, and the device, which was named the teremin in his honor, caused a sensation in the music world. In 1938 Teremin's American career and marriage were abruptly terminated when he was kidnapped from his New York home by Soviet agents, who felt that his talents in the field of electronics could be better used to help the Soviets develop telephone bugging devices. Though he was considered as politically suspect because of his years in America, and spent time in prison, he was later given a teaching post and became quite well known in Russia, where he died in 1993 at the age of 97.[21]

Despite such cases of blackmail and harassment, the growing number of Americans touring, studying and doing business in Russia in the 1960s, followed by détente, the Nixon-Brezhnev visits and the expansion of academic exchanges in the 1970s, led to a dramatic increase in mixed marriages. Most of the early unions had been between American men and Russian women, but as more American women went to Russia to study and work the balance was redressed.

"If there are going to be more exchanges of people between the Soviet Union and the United States, as President Reagan has suggested, there will be more marriages such as mine," said Sergei Petrov, a Russian married to an American who waited for eight years for his exit visa.[22] Along with more marriages came more Soviet exit visa refusals. For the State Department the divided spouses represented a sticky human rights issue which would not go away, regardless of the motivations for these marriages and the individuals involved. Each Soviet-American summit dealt with a list of these couples, and the hopes raised when one or two individuals were released were dashed as other cases remained unresolved. Eighty per cent of the mixed couples' requests for Soviet exit visas were granted, but others were kept apart for years. Susan Finkel met her husband Matvei, an electrical engineer, while she was studying Russian in Moscow in 1977, and they married in 1979. Matvei's application for an exit visa was refused 15 times, and he was fired from his job and forced to work at a subway ticket window. Even when their daughter was born in the U.S. in 1986, Susan could not get permission to visit him.

Sometimes the Soviet authorities deliberately set the couple's wedding date after the expiration of the American spouse's Russian entry visa, and then refused to grant him or her a new entry visa. In the 1970s, phone calls to Russia from the U.S. had to be ordered several hours or a day in advance, and the caller was frequently told by the Russian operator that no one was home, though the spouse had been sitting all day by the phone. Mail was read by the censors and was often undelivered. The Soviet spouse could be followed, summoned by the KGB, or beaten up. In the short time they had together in Russia, couples were forced to behave as though they were engaging in espionage. There were calls from phone booths to avoid bugged hotel telephones, letters with code words, and bribes for the "floor ladies" who monitored the comings and goings of hotel guests.

In 1985, when the Divided Spouses Coalition was founded, there were still about thirty Russians married to Americans who had not been allowed to leave.[23] Many of the spouses resorted to writing letters to U.S. Congressmen and Senators, and making appearances on TV spacebridges, where Russian and American audiences could hear their stories. Sandra Gubin-Lodisev, the Divided Spouses Coalition spokeswoman, waited from 1981 to 1985 to be reunited with her husband. A year after his arrival to the United States from Kiev, however, she filed for divorce, suing for more than $100,000, including the $20,000 she had spent on trying to obtain his exit documents.[24] She was not the only "divided spouse" whose marriage failed. The overwhelming problems of fighting the authorities could blind both spouses to the real personality and character of their mates, and created the illusion that once they were reunited all the couple's problems would be solved.

The November 1985 release of a third of the still divided couples was timed to the Geneva summit, and in the summer of 1989 the last of the high-profile long-term cases, Sergei Petrov, received his exit visa. That summit also pried loose a Soviet exit visa for Irina McClellan, who had been separated for eleven years from her husband, Woodford McClellan, since their marriage in 1974. Their story was one of the most publicized of the lot. During a visit to the USSR in August 1972, McClellan, a 38-year-old University of Virginia history professor, met Irina Shvetsova, an interpreter and employee of the protocol division of the Institute of World Economy and International Relations. Both were divorced; their passionate romance came as a surprise to both. "Entering into a genuinely personal relationship with a foreigner was the last thing I could imagine for myself," Irina wrote in her memoir, "yet I was drawn to this man with a suddenness that bewildered me. How to explain it? I'm not sure anyone can explain falling in love, this sudden, unexpected attraction."[25] She wondered whether part of the attraction was the knowledge that since the American professor would soon be leaving, the romance was condemned to be brief:

> His lack of reserve—common among Russians but rare among Americans I had met—puzzled me; we had known each other only five days. Why was he unburdening himself? Or was that the key, the fact that he barely knew me and would soon say good-bye? Unable to answer both those questions, I was struck at the similarity of our lives. We were both reasonably successful at our careers but failures at marriage.[26]

Her friends thought that her romance with a foreigner would wreck her life and that of her daughter, Lena. McClellan returned to see her, briefly, in December 1972, and of that time Irina wrote:

> The four days Woody was in Moscow are fixed in my memory as a time of almost dreamlike perfection. Nothing special happened. A man came across the ocean to love me. We talked about our lives during the four months we had been apart, touched only lightly on troubles . . . The strength we drew from each other as our love reduced outside difficulties made them seem manageable, their solution certain. There were days, nights, only four of them . . . but full of wild ecstatic sharing of all we possessed. Never had I felt so comfortable with a man, so complete, so whole. Our parting was sad, but not desperate. I knew he would come back, and soon . . . How to describe that love? What made it so grand?

Neither of us sought to attract the other; attraction existed. We accepted each other as we were the day we met, sensed a freedom to speak honestly without pretense or reservation.[27]

Irina's mother snarled at her daughter that she had sold out to the imperialists for panty hose. Irina protested that her only goal was to be with McClellan, and that marriage was the only way for them to be together. "Marriage was not my goal, nor was living in the West; being with Woody was,"[28] she wrote. If it had been possible for such couples simply to live together in Russia or the U.S., a great many disastrous marriages might have been avoided.

Years of visa refusals and KGB harassment made the couple fear they would never be reunited. In her memoir Irina confessed that loneliness and despair led her into other relationships. McClellan joined the Divided Spouses coalition. "It's obvious that the protracted separation has changed our relationship," he wrote after she was arrested by the KGB at a demonstration in 1977. He urged her to try and piece together a normal life by denouncing him to the authorities and telling them she had made a mistake in marrying him. McClellan's appeals for help to the State Department met with little success. His problems, he felt, were seen as "minor irritants" in the broader context of Soviet-American relations, and his case, he concluded, was an ominous signal to Americans planning to marry Russians.[29] By November of 1985 Irina's endurance was nearly exhausted, and the call informing her she was getting an exit visa reached her at her lover's house.

The departure to join a husband she had not seen for eleven years, and from whom she had grown apart emotionally, was extremely difficult, for her feelings were very mixed:

I was about to leave everything summed up in the concept of homeland: my native city, which I loved deeply and in which I had spent all forty-seven years of my life; my street;

my mother; the many friends who had helped me survive through the long, difficult years . . . I was about to bid farewell to all that I loved, and after eleven and a half years of struggling to leave, the thought that I might never see it again brought inexpressible pain. I was flying to a freedom I knew only in theory and a husband whom, after eleven and a half years, I did not know at all.[30]

In the second half of the 1980s the American Embassy in Moscow was flooded with applications from Americans who wanted to marry Russians and needed the so-called "marriage letter," a document certifying that the bearer was indeed a single American citizen. "There were dozens of them," a former consular official related. Most of the American girls who came through his office were very young women who had come to Russia on tours or summer study programs and had met their intendeds in Red Square, outside hotels, and on beaches. The young men generally began by inquiring whether the American would like to sell her jeans or change dollars for rubles. The approach was so brazenly black market, and the young men were so obviously interested solely in getting to the West, that the diplomat was dumbfounded. What did these apparently sophisticated women see in these self-serving young men? The girls' answer was usually that the Russians treated them like ladies, lit their cigarettes, held their coats and poured their wine, everything young men in the U.S. no longer did.

As for the American men who showed up in the Embassy wanting to marry Russian women, they tended to be middle-aged. Their fiancées were usually pretty and well-groomed tour guides, translators or secretaries who showered them with attention and flattered their egos.

Aware of the formidable difficulties involved in obtaining exit visas, particularly for Russians holding any form of security clearance, and of the Russian partner's possible materialistic rather than romantic motives, the Embassy quietly tried to dissuade the

Americans, pointing to possible denials of visas and the subsequent cost of lawyers, travel and transatlantic telephone bills. Couples who were engaged but not legally married often failed to realize that their relationship carried no weight with the Soviet authorities, and that chances of an exit visa were remote. But if the Americans kept hearing wedding bells, the Embassy had no choice but to type out the letter. It could give advice, but it could not control the behavior of its citizens. Once a spouse's visa was refused and some Congressman or Senator began lobbying for his constituent, the Embassy and State Department had no choice but to go to bat for their citizen.

Perestroika and *glasnost* brought new relaxation. In 1991, five of the American inspectors assigned in Votkinsk to monitor Russian compliance with the 1987 intermediate-range nuclear missile treaty married Russian women from the escort unit assigned to them.[31] In May, 1995, the Embassy lifted, for its personnel, the ban against "intimate or romantic relations" with Russian citizens, and the Russian Ministry of Foreign Affairs quietly repealed its own similar ban. In June, 1996, concerned over security leaks, the State Department issued new instructions—that any such liaison on the part of Embassy personnel be reported immediately to the appropriate Embassy officials.[32] But being required to report a romantic involvement is not the same as being forbidden to engage in one, and the practical effect of this edict remains to be seen. In fact, these bans on "unsanctioned contacts" between the Embassy staff and Russians had long been ignored by both Russian and American diplomats.[33] As the late Edmund Stevens, a longtime Moscow correspondent, himself married to a Russian, noted, authorities on both sides were obliged to face the fact that "love often refuses to be governed by citizenship, passport, and visa formalities. Again and again the all-powerful agencies of sovereignty have been forced to yield to the human heart, whose ingenuity succeeds in overcoming all the obstacles devised by artful bureaucrats."[34]

FINDING A SPOUSE

Why Do I Love You?

*Every foreigner is a messenger
from the world of dreams.*[1]

"I felt like something between Santa Claus and God," said John of the way Russians reacted to him during his stay in St. Petersburg on a faculty exchange in 1969. "I thought Fred was a millionaire," Irina said of her first meeting with her future husband in Moscow in the 1980s. In the 1960s and 1970s Americans were treated as millionaires and sugar daddies by their Russian acquaintances— providers of food from the hard-currency shops open only to foreigners, jazz records, Western books, panty hose, lipstick, sports equipment, short-wave radios, tape recorders: the list was endless. The goods and privileges which even young Americans possessed lent them an aura of wealth and mystery, making them seem like all-powerful beings from another planet. "We were often made to feel we were the sole fragile link with the outside world," a New York journalist commented ruefully.[2] A young Russian woman who has been wed to an American for over two years is still hiding her marriage from her cousins, fearing that they would be jealous or would make their own demands on him.

For Russians, a relationship with an American has always meant access to privileges as well as to a passport. As early as the 1930s, according to the journalist Eugene Lyons, special stores with hard-to-get food products and luxury goods were reserved for foreigners and members of the Soviet elite. A foreigner was much in demand, "sought after by practical ladies of easy virtue for his food supply, much as a wealthy man under capitalism might be sought after for his bank account. Many a citizen of the U.S.A. wondered in the wee hours of the night whether the Tanya or Olya or Irina by his side loved him or loved his food card more."[3]

The British journalist Jo Durden-Smith, who arrived in Moscow in 1989, accurately described the fascination and attraction Russians and Westerners held for each other, and how Westerners often seemed to Soviets like extra-terrestrials.

> We were colorful; we wore clothing the Soviets could only dream of; and everywhere . . . we were followed by eyes that seemed to be sizing us up and egging us on, demanding that we play the part of foreigners—like ourselves, only more so. It was like being permanently on stage; half zoo animal, half star.[4]

The double role of millionaire and outer space alien assigned to them by Russian acquaintances gave some young Americans an exaggerated view of their own self-importance and attractiveness.

When Russia began opening up in the 1960s the women tended to be more aggressive than the men in seeking foreign spouses. This was because, in the wake of World War II, women outnumbered men, and because—with compulsory military service and jobs involving classified information—Russian men had a harder time obtaining permission to leave the country. As Durden-Smith recounted:

> I remember on that first trip meeting a young actress . . . in a Leningrad hotel, and feeling no surprise at all that she should be sitting, flushed, on a plastic banquette, virtually proposing marriage to me over our first hard-currency beer . . . I didn't take it personally; I simply thought of it as

a generalized tribute to the mythical place I came from. It wasn't until later that I began guiltily to realize just how desperately she must have wanted to escape her *own* place.[5]

Though he rejected this lady's advances, Durden-Smith later wed another young Russian. Elena and Russia, he admitted, provided him with a newfound sense of excitement and self-importance and a pitch of emotional intensity rare in Western relationships. Many American spouses say that they are fascinated by their Russian partners' emotional depth. Describing his feelings for Elena, Durden-Smith wrote:

> . . . though she spoke wonderful English, she was herself so utterly, almost incomprehensibly, foreign. She was irrational and superstitious and mercurial in her moods; she could go from laughter to tears to laughter again in the time it would take me to consider a sentence. There seemed to be no gap in her—no intervening, filtering gauze of (what we call) civilization between emotion and expression, private and public, inside and outside. She was instinctive, primitive, and cunning. And though this often made for a rough ride over the obstacle course of our developing relationship, it also opened up to me a world in which I became less self-important and less prejudiced—and a lot more aware that I was visiting somewhere alien, a place that lived by different rules from mine, and by a different code of conscience.[6]

The strangeness of Russia, and the passionate intensity of Russians helped lower visiting foreigners' inhibitions, and made them act differently from the way they behaved at home. Elena's intensity and the alien surroundings let Durden-Smith's emotions rise to the surface. "She has begun to tear away the carapace of private restraint and reticence that passes for good manners and self-restraint in the West, and I am secretly glad . . . I'll never be able to predict her or fully to understand her."[7]

People who choose a spouse from a different culture often do so because they are unable to find a place in their own society, reject its values, or seek a niche elsewhere and would prefer a mate unaware of their alienation.[8] A case in point was a young Texan who felt himself more of an outsider in New Jersey than in Russia, and said he was more comfortable married to a girl from St. Petersburg than to someone from Trenton.[9]

Foreign spouses also act as magnets for social misfits, very shy or unattractive people, and products of unhappy families. A relatively homely U.S. citizen soon finds that an American passport makes him or her much more popular in Russia than in his own country. Intercultural couples often feel that they are unique and somewhat different from their compatriots. Hooking up with a foreign partner—and particularly with the "enemy"—is a clear way of rejecting the values of parents, peers and one's own society. As an American married to a Russian and living in Moscow remarked of his friends in similar marriages, "In one way or another, we are all misfits."

Some individuals seeking their roots feel they have found them in another society. A young American commented that his wife's values—and the scent of her Moscow apartment—reminded him of his grandparents' home. "I knew I wouldn't find this in America," he said.[10] Americans whose Russian roots go back several generations, as well as children of Russian immigrants who never truly adapted to American society, have chosen to marry Russians. "It was just like my grandmother's kitchen," Laura Mason said of the home of Alexander Khutorsky, her Russian émigré fiancé. She was surprised to see his mother preparing jellied cow's hooves just the way her grandmother used to. "The people who immigrated two generations ago were doing everything they could to assimilate, and now my generation wants more ethnicity," she said.[11] Even if they do not have roots there, people may fall in love with a country and its culture. That was what Jo Durden-Smith's wife Elena meant when she screamed at him, "You didn't want to marry *me*, Jo! You wanted to marry *Russia*!"[12]

The desire to "marry America"—and go there—is not the only reason why Russian women are attracted to American men. Julie Whitney rightly commented that "a woman in Russia has a chance to be almost everything except a woman."[13] Though the Soviet regime originally backed equality between the sexes, Russian women have suffered terribly from the ravages of history. They fought in the revolution, the Civil War, and World War II. The deaths of over 40 million Russian men during these upheavals, the collectivization of agriculture, the purges and the camps for decades forced women to run both the home and the workplace. Fifty years after the end of World War II, there are still ten women for every nine men.[14] The wear and tear of daily life, crowded apartments and long lines in stores have taken their toll. The writer Aksyonov commented that by the age of thirty the average Russian working woman had forgotten the art of love and had neither the time nor the energy for sex.[15] Competing forces of femininity and fatigue have created two images of Russian women, the slim, elegant blue-eyed blonde of the spy novels, sporting bright red lips and three-inch spike heels, and the stout, gray-haired woman in baggy jerseys, her gray hair pulled into a tight bun, drooping from exhaustion, a perpetual scowl engraved on her wrinkled face.

Russian tradition always emphasized femininity and concern for personal appearance. "If someone says I'm feminine I take it as a compliment," said one young girl. "To me, femininity encompasses a lot of things—delicacy, a little mystery, an ability to bring out the attractive qualities in oneself and hide the bad ones." Another young woman declared that "a girl should always be charming and sweet . . . she must be beautiful—well, not necessarily beautiful, but well-groomed."[16] Since competition for available men is fierce, the tactics for attracting one, such as good grooming and taste in clothes, are extremely important. A Russian woman journalist was surprised at how American feminists disdained Russian women who enjoyed dressing up for men.[17]

Despite the changes wrought by *glasnost*, Russian women do not accept the feminist notion of total equality between the sexes or the need for women to do everything men do. "In Russian, the word *feministka* is a pejorative, meaning a bossy man-hater," commented Elena Khanga.[18] Though the younger generation is starting to think in terms of real career opportunities, making big money and working abroad, many Russian women still dream of staying home and being cared for by a strong and competent man. The writer Tatyana Tolstaya commented that while the American feminists were fighting for the right to work in coal mines, Russian women were fighting *not* to do so.[19]

Though he may pay lip service to the equality of the sexes, the Russian male, as Chekhov wrote in one of his stories, basically believes that women are an "inferior race." "You're behaving like a woman" is the ultimate insult. The Russian Orthodox church has always encouraged obedience of the wife to her husband, and the sixteenth-century Code of Laws for the Household carefully codified the manner in which husbands may beat their wives.

Despite the restrictions on women's rights, legions of strong Russian women played a major role in Russian society and culture. The heroes of folk epics take orders from their wives and mothers, who "come to their rescue in dangerous situations, and save them from inevitable doom," explained Tatyana Tolstaya. "Strong women run family life through control over everything, power at times extending to tyranny—all this is the Russian woman, who both frightens and attracts, enchants and oppresses."[20] As the heroine of Ludmilla Petrushevskaya's novel *The Time: Night* sadly recalled,

My dear mother, before complete disaster set in, succeeded brilliantly in driving my poor husband out of the house and always got her words in on cue: Who's the head of the family, she'd ask (so sly), I ask you now, who's the head of the household around here (meaning, of course, herself).[21]

Russian women have been obliged for so long to cope on all fronts that they have become rather cynical about Russian men, who, in turn, resent these domineering but capable females. Nearly an entire postwar generation was raised without a man in the house. The hardships of these years created, as the British commentator Ronald Hingley observed, "a corps of formidable, energetic and sometimes lamentably strong matrons," women who can tolerate extremely difficult conditions, and empathize with and understand suffering.[22] Russian women simply assume that men are generally incompetent, and that when the chips are down they can only rely on other women. As two Swedish women journalists who interviewed a wide range of Russian women concluded, they "yearn for men who are strong, protective, and good fathers, and find instead men who drink heavily, refuse to share housework, and have limited interest in children."[23]

The entire Soviet system worked against the fulfillment of the dream of a strong and protective man. To be successful, wrote the sociologist Igor Kon, a Russian man "had to be devious rather than bold, servile rather than proud, conformist rather than independent . . . At every moment of his life, the Soviet boy, adolescent and adult was likely to feel socially and sexually dependent and frustrated."[24] A young Moscow single mother bitterly remarked that "seventy years of Soviet rule taught men to be selfish and passive. The biggest problem I see is the total lack of responsibility of our men."[25]

Here's how Polina, a young woman from Smolensk, described herself in 1995 in a letter to a young American with whom she corresponded through a dating service:

> I've got a gentle character. I never was able to be active in a relationship. But over the last 70 years Russian men have stopped feeling that they are the head of the family and a pillar of support for women. From childhood on we were told that men and women are equal in everything. Many of our men are infantile, and women have to decide everything for

them. A new type of woman has been formed in the Soviet Union. Deep down, a woman has become more of a man than a woman. Our poet Evtushenko was right in saying that "the best men are women." In my character there are no such male traits, although, like all women in our country, I have to hustle—rush to work, study, stand on line, do housework. Gradually, all of this leads to a loss of one's feminine core, to a roughness of which I'm very frightened.[26]

Russian women complain that their husbands are little boys, whom they can console or with whom they can sympathize, but not men on whom they can lean. "If I got used to rearing a twelve or fifteen-year-old boy, why shouldn't I rear a forty-year-old man?" one woman wondered. "The difference between them isn't all that great."[27] Once her man is hooked, a sweet young thing begins to show her claws, and an American husband may only then realize what a strong woman he has acquired. The stereotype of the feminine, romantic Russian girl makes the strong, dominant nature of so many of these women come as a shock to a foreign husband. Jo Durden-Smith had clearly understood the feminine steel hand in the velvet glove when he remarked of Elena that "I sometimes think she's like some prefeminist Western woman of the fifties. But that conjures up something passive and fluffy . . . she seems . . . at the same time often hard and deliberate."[28] The Russian femininity which so captivates American men is coupled with a toughness American feminists could envy. And while Russian women may look down at males, a scarce man is still the most highly valued commodity. Most Russian girls, even those aware of the great difficulty in finding a strong, loving and sober husband, sincerely want to get married.

In looking for a mate, Russians and Americans tend to see each other as endowed with precisely those qualities which are lacking at home. As opposed to passive, boorish and intoxicated Soviet males, Americans have the reputation of being clean, polite, considerate, and hard workers.[29]

Russian women are impressed by the way Americans are always saying please, thank you, and excuse me. "He's always so polite," Svetlana said of her American husband Mark. "He treats me with real respect." She was impressed by the way Mark came straight home from work every night. "He never goes out drinking all night with his friends," she said. "He takes a drink before dinner, but I've never seen him drunk. Can you *imagine* that?" The head of a matrimonial agency for Russians seeking American husbands remarked that her American clients had a wonderful reputation with Moscow single mothers who despaired of ever getting married. Since a child means the need for a bigger apartment and more money for food and child care, Russian men do not consider single mothers as desirable wives. The young Russian wife of one American was somewhat cynical about her compatriots' interest in American men. "These days, what kind of a Russian can you marry?" asked Lida. "With a factory worker, you'll starve. And he'll bore you to death. A 'New Russian' businessman is dangerous. His money is here today, gone tomorrow, and he could easily be knocked off by the Mafia. With an American you know you're taken care of for life. Besides, more girls here speak English than any other foreign language, so you can communicate. Who wants to go to a dump in Germany or Scandinavia when you can live in America?"

Some of the Russian women who sign up with the marriage agencies feel that, in addition to the foreign passport, they are getting qualities which men in their own country do not provide. Olga, a 29-year old music teacher, wrote:

> Everyone knows that life in America is much better than here in Russia. Even poor people there have cars, houses and color TVs. And there's always plenty of food to eat. But the most wonderful thing about America is the men. They're much more handsome than Russian men. They don't have gold fillings in their mouth or rotted teeth like all my old boyfriends. And they don't boss you around and treat you

like you're their slave. I dream every night of going to
the United States, marrying a handsome man and having
children. I can't wait to go. As soon as I find the right man,
I'm going to apply for an exit visa.[30]

Russian women who are eager to be housewives and mothers,
and who are free from the desire for total equality with men which
characterizes so many American feminists, are extremely attractive
to American men. Russian girls offer something American women
do not: pure femininity and the willingness to play a wife's traditional role. Compared to American women, Russian girls seem old-
fashioned and feminine rather than feminist. A young American
man who had spent time in Moscow commented, "They'll do
anything to make their husbands happy. They're very sexy, they're
great cooks and they're not spoiled like American women."[31]

These differences in the attitudes of Russian and American
women were evident in an incident which took place during a
joint mountain-climbing expedition in the U.S. A Russian man,
who went back down a slope to help an American girl who was
moving slowly because she was tired, was deeply insulted because
she greeted him with annoyance rather than gratitude. One of
the American counselors explained to the group that "although in
our country he was acting like a male chauvinist, in his country he
was acting like a gentleman."[32] Another Russian was similarly
startled when in response to his offer to help with her heavy suitcase, an American girl retorted, "Why are you so sure I'm weaker
than you?"[33]

The negative reactions of Americans and Russians to certain
types of behavior in their own cultures attract them to each other.
A young American who married a Russian commented, "I'm tired
of American women who gallop about the streets in tailored business
suits and running shoes . . . They're all hung up on careers, on
financial security . . . They don't look at a man, they look at his
car and his address. I dreamed of meeting a woman who would
look me in the eyes."[34] Harvey Balzer, the director of Georgetown

University's Russian Area Program, commented that "American men are somewhat sick of emancipated women, and Russian women are somewhat sick of domestic dictators. Even men I know who write about women's rights wouldn't get up from the dinner table to help clear the dishes. You've got this funny situation where the American man is looking for an unliberated woman, and the Russian woman is looking for a slightly more liberated man."[35]

It is clear why Russian women are attracted to American men, but what do Russian men see in American women? Aside from the promise of a comfortable life in the U.S., they look for women who do not treat them as children and who are not in a perpetual state of exhaustion. The openness and independence of American women are also very attractive. "She knows how to amuse herself in her spare time," said Carol's husband, Fyodor. "She isn't always yelling at me to do this or that around the house." Another Muscovite liked the way his American wife handled her job and housework. "My Russian ex-wife was always complaining she was tired," he said. "Of course she had to stand in line in the stores, but it's not just the supermarkets and appliances that make life here easier. Laura is so much more efficient, and she's not always complaining about how tired she is." "Muriel is much more direct and honest than most Russian girls," said Sergei. "She says what she thinks, and she doesn't play coy all the time. Even though we have a lot of arguments, I feel that she's a real friend."

American women see Russian men as handsome, romantic, strong and, despite a good dose of male chauvinism, extremely charming. Unscathed by American feminism, they still open doors, hold coats, pay a woman compliments, pick up her check in a restaurant, and feel it is their role to take care of a member of the weaker sex. They tend to be more sexually, intellectually, and emotionally self-confident. "He knows he's a man," said Leslie, a thirty-year old American teacher, about her Muscovite husband. "He doesn't spend his time worrying about who he is." Jane, a young journalist who met her artist husband while she was posted to Moscow, had previously had several affairs in Russia. "You don't have to worry about AIDS the way you do in the States," she said. "Dmitri doesn't analyze our relationship all the time. My American boyfriend had been to so many shrinks he treated me as if I were one, too." Anne was impressed by her husband's love of literature and poetry. "In California the only men I knew who recited poetry were gay."

Some American women are pleasantly surprised by the Russian penchant for heavier females. Russian peasant culture has always equated health with weight: plumpness pointed to a woman who could bear children and do her share of the work. *"Popravit'sia,"* the Russian word for "to put on weight," also means to be looking better. Anorexic models and skeletal females surviving on aragula and bean sprouts are not attractive to Russians, who prefer some "meat" on the bones. Tamara Gilmore recalled that one reason she did not have many Russian boyfriends was because

> I am not the type Russian men like. In those early war years I was far too thin for them. Their ideal is shorter and a good deal broader. They like them squat, curvy, and apple-cheeked, not tallish, bony, angular, and with the exaggerated muscles that consistent training for dancing brings about.[36]

That Russian preference is most welcome to plus size American girls, who find far more admirers in Russia than in the U.S.

Not all Americans and Russians, however, are enthusiastic about marrying a foreigner. Since it is hard enough to have a successful marriage with someone of the same race, religion, ethnic and national background, is it not enormously risky to opt for a person with radically different traditions and expectations of marriage? "I've always discouraged Russian-American romantic relationships because the differences between American women and Russian men are so vast that it's hard to have a cup of coffee, much less date someone," a young American woman working in Moscow told an interviewer. A male expatriate agreed. "At the end of a hard day, you want to speak your own language," he said. "You feel better dealing with people of your own background." A support group has formed in Moscow to help American women cope with their Russian boyfriends.[37] One Russian writer is convinced that Russians can only be themselves with another Russian. "I believe that when you're sprawling on the couch you can't be cosmopolitan," he said. "Here, over a borshch in all its beauty, but with all its flaws, our ethnic essence is revealed, which we want to share only with those who are like us."[38] And Natalia Vetlitskaia, a popular young Russian singer who had no interest in romance with a Westerner, said she believed that Russian men were more sincere and less money-minded. "Probably only Russian men can understand a Russian woman," she commented.[39]

For the ordinary American, however, reading the Russian soul is even more difficult. Mistaking the desire to escape to America for real love was the fateful mistake of Bob Reilley, a young New Jersey factory worker who fell for Aina Robertovna, a beautiful dark-haired girl from Leningrad who broke his heart along with his bank account. Her goal was crystal clear. "I wanted to live in America more than anything else. Nothing else was so important to me." Marrying a Russian boyfriend would have meant that "I would commit suicide in five years."[40] While studying English she supported herself by selling American books and clothes on the black market and working part time in a library. In 1984 the 22-year-old Aina met Bob Reilley in a Leningrad park while he was on a tourist trip. A colleague recalled how right after that encounter Aina rushed into the library, asking her girlfriends for help in wiping off her pancake-thick makeup. She borrowed a pair of slacks and tights to replace her miniskirt and fishnet stockings, since the young American did not like what Aina thought was the latest fashion. She did not find him attractive. "I can certainly see why he says he doesn't have a girlfriend," she joked.

The new image worked. "When I first saw her I thought she was really pretty. Really nice," Reilley said. "We spent a couple of dates together, and I felt she really liked me, and I was crazy about her. So by the third day I felt like I was in love with her, so I asked her to marry me, and she said yes. It was really romantic." Four-teen months later, after he had spent more then $15,000 on four trips to see her, after the wedding in Leningrad in September, 1985, and after the intervention of two U.S. senators who thought they were helping the cause of true love, Aina arrived in New York to face red roses and cameras. But it was America she wanted, not Reilley. Aina described herself as a sophisticated city girl and Reilley as a small-town boor. She liked classical ballet and he liked rap music. He wanted a home and family. She wanted money, and a glamorous career, not the life of a New Jersey factory worker's wife. After six months she left him, hoping for a career as a Manhattan model and actress. In the end Reilley seemed to understand that this Russian steamroller did not need him or anyone else. "She's not looking for a man. She's looking out for herself."[41]

In the 1980s girls like Aina were strolling around the parks pre-tending to be interested in practicing English. In the 1990s they were signing up with international dating services and advertising in the newspapers for American husbands. The boom in dating services, lonely-hearts ads and mail-order bride and groom cata-logues was a result both of post-*perestroika* freedom and the acute financial difficulties caused by the economic crisis. While the mass media deluge the Russian public with ads for Japanese video equipment and vacations in Cyprus, the average family has trouble affording decent meat, fresh fruit or winter boots. In these circum-stances the attraction of the West is particularly strong, and Bob Reilley's experience by no means unique.

In the last few years Russian and American dating services designed to find American husbands for Russian women have mushroomed, matching up partners through video cassettes, computer questionnaires and electronic mail. While the older generation of Russians finds these ways of meeting a life partner cold, calculating and rather bizarre, young people see nothing tawdry in seeking an American spouse through personal ads or by using marriage agencies. There are more than 40 such agencies in

Moscow and hundreds in the U.S., running the gamut from highly professional firms to fly by night scams. The "Moscow Connection" agency claimed to have signed up more than 200,000 Russian professional women hoping to meet and marry an American. A Russian television program, "The Lonely Hearts Club," broadcasts five-minute interviews with American bachelors. American firms such as "Foreign Relations," "Anastasia," and "World Class, Inc." deluge their clients with glossy magazines packed with photos of gorgeous Russian women, descriptions of exciting tour packages, and hopes of marital bliss. "It doesn't matter if he's old, fat, or ugly—what matters is that he can get her out of Russia," one Muscovite girl said cynically. "Love has become a luxury," said Svetlana, a 28-year-old Russian language teacher. "I'll be old and gray before we can afford love."[43]

One of the largest American mail-order marriage services is Scanna International, which claims to have signed up 6,000 male subscribers to catalogues featuring photos of 30,000 mostly Russian women. Scanna provides its clients with travel arrangements to Russia, and even a helpful "Survival Guide" providing arrangements on bringing flowers (only in odd numbers, because even numbers are associated with funerals), opening doors, helping with coats, and other gallantries. Though glowing testimonials to Scanna's success assert that Russian women "are the best in the world," not all the matchmaking has fairy-tale endings.[44] Seeking the girl of their dreams, American men with no knowledge of the Russian language or culture often fail to realize that the girl behind the photo is likely to be a tough and determined young woman out to better her bank account, housing and wardrobe by marrying any eligible male possessing an American passport and a decent income.

Sob stories told by stunning Russian girls of drunken husbands who mistreated their children, fears of the return of Soviet totalitarianism, and assurances of a great interest in America, the outdoors, family barbecues and family values are highly successful with balding, middle-aged farmers and timid insurance agents who have never in their wildest fantasies been the subject of so much adoring female attention. The American's magic words "I have my own business" conjure up images of sprawling estates and luxury yachts; once in America, the girls are distressed to discover that the "business" is a tiny shop or deserted warehouse.[45]

The marriage between Natalia Sadchikova and Scanna client Donald Davis is a sad example. At the age of 42, Natalia came from Vladivostok with her 3-year old daughter Alina to marry the 54-year-old truck driver from New Jersey. Davis had found her letters romantic and lyrical, and was touched by her unhappy life in Russia. The role of savior rescuing a Russian woman from a miserable life has long had an appeal for American men, though today the misery is more often a question of making ends meet or breaking free from a disastrous marriage than escaping the perils of a totalitarian society.

Unlike many of Scanna's other clients, Davis did not go to Russia to meet his future wife before deciding to bring her to the U.S. "It was a complete disaster, not a minor but a major disaster," he said. That, the *New York Times* reported, was "one of the few points on which he and Ms. Sadchikova are in agreement."[46] Natalia complained about American food. Davis complained that Alina's crying kept him up at night. He was impatient with Natalia's poor English and with having to explain everything to her. "I think we are like a little puppy you see on the street," she said. "You say, 'Oh, poor little puppy, no one loves him. I take him home.' Then in home he makes wet on the floor, he wants food and play, and you put the puppy back in the street."

Another Scanna couple managed to turn the business of mail-order marriage into a mail-order business. In 1992, inspired by newspaper articles on Russian women interested in bettering their lives through marriages to American men, Weston Rogers, a thirty-five-year-old divorced Dallas computer programmer and self-described "nice guy," decided that by the end of the year he was going to marry a Russian girl.[47] The materialistic motivations of many of these women did not faze Rogers: What was so bad about that when so many marriages based on "superficial love and passion" fell apart?[48] Rogers drew up a plan of action that would have done credit to a Fortune 500 strategic planner, setting up a computer base for his correspondence with Russian women and drawing up a questionnaire which, aside from an inquiry about the ladies' measurements, sounded remarkably like a job application. His letters to the women selected from the Scanna catalogues (including one who turned out to be pregnant) were filled with loving sentiments. He was delighted that in their replies to his missives the ladies claimed to be madly in love with him. The girls chorused complaints about the rudeness of Russian men and stressed their sincere desire to marry a kind, considerate American. It was Natasha Savkina, a 19-year-old beauty from the small town of Azov, who knew not a word of English, who appealed to Rogers most. (Scanna provided translation of the letters). After a brief and unhappy marriage to a man who abused her, Natasha was living with her parents and going to trade school.

In June 1992, determined to fulfill his one-year plan, Rogers borrowed $6,000 dollars and set off for Moscow, where a car, interpreter and apartment awaited him. His schedule was a model of efficiency: two days for each of four girls, plus a week with the one he selected. Surrounded by attractive women, Weston spent a week in Moscow. Lunches and dinners well fueled by vodka, wine and cognac alternated with visits to the Kremlin, the subway, and museums. Rogers was immediately taken with Natasha's striking beauty and lively personality, but decided to send her back to Azov to think things over. He barely had time to see her off before the plane bearing his next candidate arrived.

Though all of his conversations with Natasha had taken place through an interpreter, Rogers remained convinced that she was the one he wanted to marry. Following a few more days with her upon her return to Moscow, he was also convinced that she was genuinely in love with him. His proposal was accepted, and at the end of November Natasha arrived in Texas on a fiancée visa, meaning that for the Russian spouse to stay in the country the couple had to marry within three months.

To Weston's surprise, after a few euphoric days spent exploring shopping malls and health clubs, Natasha became depressed and irritable, and cried a great deal. She thought she would go crazy, she wrote in her diary. Finally, to his horror, Natasha declared in a television interview that she did not love him. "All Russian women want to marry American men for better life only," she announced.[49]

Yet Rogers stubbornly held fast, and three years later the couple was still together. Natasha learned English. "I am much happier today but not as [happy] as I want to be," she said in another interview.[50] While the "dream marriage" Rogers wanted had not come about, the couple made the most of their union. Weston began promoting his self-published book, *Love Letters From Russia*, a combination of true confessions, correspondence with Russian women, a detailed account of his week in Moscow, his marriage to Natasha, and practical advice for would-be American grooms, including taking Kool-Aid and chocolate chip cookies to Russia and having your intended's handwriting analyzed. Meanwhile Natasha offered a "support hot line" to American men interested in marrying a Russian.[51] There was, however, no happy ending to the story, for the couple eventually split. Undaunted, Weston Rogers set off to find another Russian bride.

Today, publications ranging from the Moscow newspaper *Private Life* to *New York* magazine are filled with ads from matchmaking agencies and Americans eager to risk long-distance marriage. "I have a herd of horses and a cattle farm, my friends are immigrants from the USSR and help me translate letters, I need a 25 to 35-year-old woman, nondrinker who would like to be a wife and mother," runs an ad in *Moscow News*. The Russian magazine *Amour* calls itself the "Courier of Lonely Hearts." "Men From the West are Looking in Russia for the Women Chosen for Them by Fate," trumpets the cover of one issue. Through full-page color photos and glowing descriptions of themselves, the hopeful candidates try to attract a Russian mate. Thoughtfully included in the magazine are bits of advice on how to apply lipstick, an 18-day "Hollywood diet" heavy on boiled eggs and black coffee, and a virgin's prayer for marriage.[52] The American men who use these ads and dating services don't seem to be bothered overmuch by the thought that their sole attraction may lie in their passports: "I think love is a little hard to fake," "She's not like that. She wouldn't do it."[53]

"If every trip worth taking is both a tragedy and a comedy, rich with melodrama and farce, it is also, at its heart, a love story," says the writer Pico Iyer.[54] This is particularly true for those who return enamored from a journey across the sea. A foreign spouse is the ultimate souvenir from a trip abroad. But it cannot be easily returned, exchanged, stuffed into a closet, or consigned to the wastebasket. The souring of sentiment has legal as well as psychological consequences. Generally speaking, the couples who embark on these marriages are persuaded that mutual attraction and love will conquer all obstacles. In the last few years more and more Russians and Americans have decided to take that risk.

COUPLES

Everyone falls in love with what
he cannot begin to understand.[1]

Zara Witkin, the model socialist convert of the American 1920s,* was the son of Russian-Jewish immigrants, a child prodigy who entered the University of California at sixteen and graduated as the class valedictorian. The great Depression convinced the young engineer that capitalism was doomed. When the Soviet-American Trading Company (Amtorg) offered him a job in the construction of the Moscow subway, he jumped at the chance and left for Russia in 1932.[2]

With him he took the image of his ideal bride, the Russian movie actress Emma Tsesarskaya.[3] He saw her first in 1919 in *Village of Sin* and then saw her eight times in *Her Way of Love*, in which she starred as a peasant woman who gives her all to the Revolution; he was obsessed, and, as he recorded in his memoirs, dreamed of love with her in a glorious new society.

> The heroic beauty of a Russian woman came to symbolize that dream for me. She seemed to me the incarnation of the splendor and creative life of the revolution . . . In that dark,

---

*See Introduction, p. vii

beautiful face on the screen, I had read some deep, instinctive riddle of my own destiny . . . What was the strange power of this unknown woman in a faraway land? Here was the perfect symbol of the new heroic woman of revolutionary Russia. In some strange manner, I suddenly felt my destiny bound up with her. She seemed the bridge between the social order in which I had been born and reared and another in travail in a distant land, her country. Between the actual woman and her role there could be no differentiation. In my mind they were one. I must cross continents and oceans to find this woman even at the ends of the earth . . . [4]

One day, soon after his arrival in Moscow, Witkin saw his "Dark Goddess" on the street. "Her radiant countenance was vibrant with the electric force which I had sensed in her image years ago." More in love than ever, he managed to persuade Eugene Lyons, the well-known American Moscow correspondent, to introduce him to Emma. He was enraptured:

A broad forehead with powerful natural eyebrows, slightly unsymmetrical. Large, brilliant eyes, dark hazel in color. A straight, short nose, typical of the Ukraine, exquisitely molded, the nostrils quivering with nervous energy like those of a race horse. Delicately chiseled lips, a strong chin. Round, full, glowing cheeks which dimpled when she smiled. Glistening, perfect teeth. Free from all cosmetics, her face aglow with vivid health. Parted in the middle, her great wealth of dark brown hair was heightened by the control over her features which made their expression majestic . . . Broad-shouldered, deep-breasted, she stirred recollections of the great Venus, which Rodin, in his ecstasy, named the Venus Genatrix.[5]

Witkin got her to take English lessons from him. Though she spoke no English and his Russian was shaky, the lessons quickly turned into something more:

Our lessons increased in length, from one to five hours. They expanded into golden periods of the richest communion. This love, which had been a vision of unattainable joy and was now a living reality, had become the vital element in my life . . . From it I drew the strength and joy to sustain me in the difficult life I had chosen . . . My quarters seemed cramped and unpleasant until the advent of the noble beauty who has become my constant friend.[6]

He admired the way Emma coped with the difficulties of daily life, her independent spirit, the way she never let him help her take off her boots or accompany her home at night. At times she was affectionate, "enfolding me in her hair, a living garment;" at times she was more distant and had a nickname for him, "Heavy Industry." Zara, nonetheless, felt that he and Emma were two souls in perfect harmony, that "our lives, which had flowed so remotely apart from each other, were blended into a single, indivisible stream." He proposed: "'Will you come with me to my country?' Looking me full in the face, her eyes shining with divine tenderness and strength she answered, 'I know all! I will be with you!'"[7]

But her glow faded. Giving up a lucrative career for a very uncertain venture into Hollywood was not all that attractive for a highly popular and patriotic Soviet movie star. Nor was his promise to build a magnificent home in California much of a lure for a woman showered with gifts by her Russian admirers.

In May 1933, the Dark Goddess began avoiding seeing him, saying that her father opposed her leaving Russia, that she would never be allowed to return and that her departure would be the ruin of her career and family. Witkin was sure there were political reasons behind her sudden change of attitude, and that "Father" was Emma's euphemism for the secret police. He was devastated. "My soul seems sliding towards a terrible abyss," he wrote in his diary. "Without the Dark Goddess, life seemed a frightening desert."[8] Poor Zara: what he wouldn't, couldn't see was that she had fallen in love with another man—whom she eventually married—and was using her father's alleged objections as a polite way of breaking with her American suitor.

For a while, "I remained in Russia, despite the wrecking of my private dream," Witkin mourned.[9] While still grieving over his Dark Goddess, Witkin took up with another Russian woman. "You Russian women are heroines. What joy and strength your companionship brings! It cannot be found anywhere else in the world,"[10] he said to his new friend. In 1934, however, his romance with Russia ended; he left the Soviet Union for good.

Armand Hammer, the American businessman who also played a role in Russian-American relations, was similarly lovestruck the moment he met his future wife. In 1925, while on vacation in Yalta, Hammer was taken by friends to a gypsy concert. He glanced at the singer, Olga Vadina, and felt

> as if I'd been struck by a bolt of lightning; she knocked me out. She had an extraordinary combination of dark skin and light blue eyes, with honey-blond hair and a glorious figure. Was I smitten! All through her performance I sat with my mouth opening and closing like a fish out of water. While she sang romantic gypsy ballads in a low, sexy voice, she stared straight back into my eyes and her smile was like fire. I just had to meet her.[11]

That Olga was married to her manager did not deter Hammer in the least, and a divorce was quickly arranged. "She sang with a throaty, smoky voice like Dietrich," Hammer recalled, "and she looked quite like Garbo, though she radiated a lot more passion and vivacity than either of them. Like many Russian women, she was as temperamentally volatile as a racehorse, a real prima donna; but I wasn't complaining. I knew that I had taken on a very exceptional woman." On an evening in March 1927, three hundred wedding guests partied until five in the morning with vodka flowing non-stop. The couple began traveling to the West, and a son Julian was born in 1929. Hammer's brother Victor followed his example and married Varvara, a divorced Russian gypsy singer. "Such women seemed to have a fatal attraction for us," Hammer observed.[12]

Armand's young wife fell in love with the glitter of the West. When he took her to Paris, he wrote, "Olga was almost beside herself with happiness . . . [She] couldn't wait to plunge into this society. She was like an exotic tropical bird who had been confined for years in a cage, muted and clipped, and was now suddenly released, soaring and singing."[13] Olga mostly remained in Moscow, however, while Hammer commuted to Paris and New York, and the separations took their toll on the marriage. She refused to move to New York to join him unless the Russian peasant nanny who had been her nurse could leave Russia to join them and help look after their son. Hammer managed to get the nurse out—no mean feat in 1932—but even this could not save the day.

Olga's vision of life in the West did not correspond to Hammer's. He was interested in the world of commerce; she was in love with high society.

> Her difficulties made things worse between us and seemed to bring into focus the fact that we had very little in common. She wasn't interested in business; I didn't care much for the kind of light entertainment that was her passion—big band music, for instance . . . Olga and Palm Beach were made for each other . . . She loved the parties and her name appeared regularly in the society columns of the local papers, especially after she was named as the best-dressed woman in Palm Beach. But the gulf between us was widening. . . . And my attentions were wandering. On my many evenings alone in New York and around the country, I began to date other women and I suppose that, from about 1934, I was really looking for another wife.[14]

As Hammer's infatuation cooled the couple began drifting apart, and eventually they were divorced.

Homer Smith was a black American journalist who went to the Soviet Union in 1932 to "walk in dignity," as he put it in his memoir, *Black Man in Red Russia*. For thirteen years he was a Moscow correspondent for the American Negro press. At a New Year's ball in 1935 he fell in love with a stunning brunette. "My eyes followed her like a theater spotlight focusing on a stage star. I thought she was the most beautiful girl I had ever seen and thought idly of Natasha Goncharova, the Moscow beauty that Pushkin had married."[15] Unable even to find out her name, he returned to the same ball for three years in a row, but had no luck. Just when he was starting to despair of ever seeing her again, he found himself sitting next to her at a film showing at the Journalists' Club and immediately asked her for a date. Her name was Marie. An affair developed—though, as he wrote,

> there were 'operational problems' that do not exist in America. There were no family cars to park in romantic spots, since Russian families just didn't have cars. And private love-making at home was all but impossible as almost all Russian families lived in one or at most two rooms. Actually, Marie Pyotrovna's family had two.[16]

In summer he wooed her in the parks and on the Moscow river excursion boats, and in winter they held hands in the theater and went skating. Smith was delighted with how simple it was, in the Soviet Union, to get married:

> Russian girls are so independent that they do not have to ask parental consent to marry; it would have been considered puritanically bourgeois for a young man, sheepishly and hesitantly, to ask a father for the hand of his daughter. Parents were merely informed of a *fait accompli*. And that's just what

Marie Pyotrovna did after we went to the Marriage Bureau and signed our names in the Registry in January of 1938.[17]

During World War II Marie lost her job, and harassment became so intense that in 1945 Smith decided to leave. It took more than a year to obtain exit visas for his family. The couple and their two children lived in Ethiopia, where he felt the family could live free from the pressures of racism, and then in 1962 made their way to America.

Lee Harvey Oswald and Marina Prusakova met in Minsk, a provincial Belorussian city, in March 1961. Marina had long had a liking for foreigners, whom she found more polite and better brought up than Russians. The story she recounted over and over to the Warren Commission investigating the assassination of President Kennedy was of a poor orphaned girl with no interest in politics, who had fallen in love with an American defector. [18]

At the age of 18 Marina had moved from Leningrad to Minsk, leaving her maternal grandmother and stepfather to move in with her uncle, Colonel Ilya Prusakov, an engineer working in the Ministry of Internal Affairs, and his wife Valya. More or less penniless, Marina lived off chance acquaintances before landing a job in the pharmaceutical section of a city hospital; this gave her some spending money and a social life. At a dance she met a man she thought was from the Baltic Republics because of his accent. He turned out to be an American. Oswald was 21, Marina 18.

> I liked Lee immediately. He was very polite and attentive, and I felt that he liked me, too . . . I remember having on my favorite dress made of red Chinese brocade . . . and my hair was done à la Brigitte Bardot. That evening I even liked myself . . . [19]

Oswald was equally attracted. He recalled that at the very end of a boring trade union dance he had met a girl with a French hairdo and who was wearing a red dress with white slippers. "I dance with her . . . We like each other right away," he wrote in his diary.[20]

Marina was taken with Oswald's attitude to the United States: although critical of its unemployment, racial discrimination and expensive medical care, he warmly defended its democracy and freedom of the press. He had decided to live in Russia, he said, because he thought the Soviet system was better.

A few days later, they met again, and went for a walk.[21] After another meeting at a dance Marina invited Oswald to her uncle's home; her aunt seemed impressed with his manners and neat appearance. The romance advanced quickly. "I decide I must have her," Oswald wrote. "She puts me off and so on April 15 I propose. She accepts."[22] Marina admitted later that she was more attracted to his large apartment than to him: the studio was in a building with a river view. A friend recalled her saying that one reason she was so eager to go to the United States was that she had always wanted to have a room of her own.[23] In later years she gave other reasons as well. "I was interested in him because he was different, he would broaden my horizon, and all the other men I wanted had been taken or didn't want me."[24] An illegitimate child raised by a grandmother and stepfather, Marina was as much of a misfit as Oswald, whose father had died while his mother was pregnant and who was also raised by a stepfather.[25]

In May, 1961, only a few weeks after their marriage, Oswald told Marina he had changed his mind about living in Russia. He wanted to go home, and so she applied to leave the Soviet Union with him.

The marriage was in trouble from the start. Oswald's Russian was shaky and Marina knew no English. He accused her of being a poor housewife and a bad cook. She criticized him for his sloppiness and refusal to help. She no longer found him neat and clean, and complained about his wanting to make love without brushing his teeth.[26] The birth of their daughter June in 1962, and of her sister Rachel a year later when they had settled in America, strained the relationship even further.

Marina found Dallas and Fort Worth ugly and disorganized. Lee discouraged her from learning English, so as to keep her dependent on him, and she soon gave up her language lessons.[27] She had not wanted to marry a Russian, being afraid that he might beat her; she ended up with an American who beat her, even when she was pregnant. Eventually she began to stand up to him, and left him. But she came tearfully back. And though Lee kept abusing and insulting her, she turned down offers of help from Russian émigré friends to move in with them.[28] In January 1963 she wrote to an old flame in Russia that her husband did not love her, and that their relationship had changed in America. "I kiss you as we kissed before," she wrote.[29] Oswald intercepted the letter and made her to tear it up, threatening to send her back to Russia.

The couple kept separating and reuniting. With no money and no English, Marina's alternatives were sparse. Like so many Russian wives, she thought she could bear the burdens imposed by a weak but brutal mate.

> I felt that this man is very unhappy, and that he cannot love in any other way. I was sorry for him, and frightened . . . he needed me. What can you do when a person has been this way all his life? You can't reform him at once. But I decided that if I had enough patience, everything would be better and that this would help him . . . [30]

Marina's daughter June, now a young woman in her thirties, has paid tribute to her mother's determination and strength during the difficult marriage and the terrible years which followed:

> Lee wasn't much of a husband, he wasn't much of a father . . . He beat my mother. There were times when we lived in poor housing, or were taken in by others . . . Mom kept us together. She was pretty strong. She kept herself together for us.[31]

After the assassination of President Kennedy, Marina was shaken and furious. "If . . . I could talk to him," she said of Oswald, "I would give him such a scolding that he would die all over again."[32] Thirty years later she was still bitter. "I don't like him. I'm mad at him. Very mad at him," she said to Norman Mailer in an interview in 1995. "How dare you abandon me? In circumstances like that? I mean, *you* die but I'm still here licking my wounds."[33]

In 1972, shortly after Joseph Stalin's daughter, Svetlana, defected to the United States, she married William Wesley Peters, an architect, a disciple of Frank Lloyd Wright. Quarrels ensued. After years of enduring the forced communal atmosphere in the Soviet Union, the last thing Svetlana needed was collective living in Peters' communal housing project of Taliesin. Nor did her unbalanced emotional state bode well. The marriage lasted only twenty months and produced a daughter, Olga, who returned to Russia with her mother in 1984 and then left with her again for the West in 1986.

Svetlana accused Peters of marrying her for her money; she complained that she had not been really free in the West for a single day.[34] By 1992 she was destitute, having spent her funds on various charities and failed projects, and was living in a British charity hostel for people with severe emotional problems. Seeking a retreat from the world, she converted from Russian Orthodoxy to Catholicism, and took monastic vows. In 1996 she was, for a short while, a nun in an Italian convent.[35]

By the end of the cold war Russian-American marriages were taking place at all levels of the two societies. The most well-known—called the "apotheosis of Soviet-American relations"—was the marriage of Susan Eisenhower, granddaughter of the American President, to the Soviet space scientist Roald Sagdeev.[36] No previous marriage across the great divide had involved people of such prominence on both sides.

Sagdeev had been the Director of the Soviet Institute of Space Research and a member of the Congress of People's Deputies. Susan Eisenhower had managed a consulting firm advising American companies doing business in Russia, and was a director of the Eisenhower World Affairs Institute. They met at the 1987 Chatauqua conference on Soviet-American relations. As she first saw him, he was "a rumpled, professorial-looking man" with unruly reddish-brown hair, thick glasses and bright blue eyes, so short that the tall, large-boned American woman in chic tailored suits towered over him.[37] They began seeing each other when she took on the job of helping with the English version of his memoirs. A 38-year-old American Episcopalian and a 57-year-old Soviet Tatar, a non-practicing Muslim, they made an unlikely couple.

After two unsuccessful marriages, with three daughters, Susan Eisenhower was not eager for another plunge. Sagdeev was separated from his wife and had two adult children and several grandchildren. Both felt a great sense of responsibility to their governments as well as to their families, and were fully aware of the shock that a marriage between two such public figures would create in both their camps. In her account of their romance, *Breaking Free: A Memoir of Love and Revolution*, Susan wrote, "We were two highly visible people from two countries that had spent trillions of dollars defending themselves against each other. And in Sagdeev's case, he was an important official in a sensitive government sector."[38]

Sagdeev was still legally married. Susan Eisenhower did not envision living in Moscow as the wife of a Soviet official. As she noted ironically, she had worked as a tour guide at Freedom's Foundation in Valley Forge, edifying the tourists on the subject of "America's valued institutions that were imperiled by Soviet Communism all over the world."[39] There was no assurance that Soviet officialdom would bestow its blessing on such an unusual union or that Sagdeev, given his access to classified information, would be able to travel freely between the two countries. While disagreeing with many Soviet policies, he was deeply patriotic and would never agree to defect. As the romance blossomed Susan was torn between her emotions and her fear that the relationship was doomed. "My dilemma was that my heart carried Sagdeev with me, but my head was demanding his immediate eviction."[40]

From the outset she was attracted by his intensity. After their first serious talk at the Chatauqua conference, "I could not shake the spell of our intense conversation. My head was swimming. While American relations with the Soviet Union had improved a great deal over the previous year, conversations were usually quite stiff, and still within a mutually recognized safety zone. There was something about Sagdeev's demeanor and the way he talked that deeply unsettled me. His openness and humor belied everything I knew about Soviet social behavior."[41] Like other Americans in love with Russians, she was caught up in feelings which were so strong precisely because the relationship seemed fated to end. "The mounting intensity of his confidences gave me the impression that he was conscious of the passing nature of our friendship and was trying to absorb as much of it as he could—before it vanished."[42] Yet as they continued to see each other at conferences around the world she was increasingly attracted by "his gentleness, his intelligence, his kindness and most of all our mutual trust. If life can be unpredictably short, isn't the loss implied in not doing something—not risking oneself—the thing one regrets?"[43]

Long separations, bugged phones and censored letters heightened the tensions. "We are again cut off from one another with no communication," Susan wrote in 1988, when she was in the United States and Sagdeev was in Moscow. "It feels like a death—the total and complete severance from a loved one."[44] She kept rereading affectionate notes Sagdeev had passed to her at meetings in Moscow—"to reassure myself that our relationship, so intense and fulfilling when we were together, still existed when our absence made it seem to evaporate."[45]

"I am so spoiled by you now—cannot stay, cannot live without you even a day, no a minute, a second," Sagdeev wrote her while on an official trip to Lausanne.[46] "From the moment I met you," Susan replied, "I was drawn to you by your tenderness and your sweetness and all the lovable qualities I can't find words for."[47] One of her letters to him beautifully expressed the intensity of her feelings. "Remember," she wrote, "it was you who captured my heart some time ago. Whatever happens, you should know that you will always have it."[48] She was deeply touched by a note from Sagdeev saying he was putting his driver and car at her disposal while she was in Moscow, because he would feel better knowing that she was being "taken care of." "I don't know if he could have possibly guessed," she wrote, "that no man I had been close to had said he would feel better if I were 'taken care of.' All my previous experience had told me that men knew how to exploit my strength with little or no regard to the age-old notion of 'taking care.' His obvious desire to win my heart was also in stark contrast to the ambitious but afraid-to-commit men of Washington."[49]

The romance survived close-range surveillance by KGB long black cars, strange breakdowns of Sagdeev's car, and a break-in at his apartment. "Think about it carefully before you marry," an official pretending to be a friend advised him. "The cultural differences are too great."[50] Susan's family, however, was highly supportive of her plans. And in the end their feelings for each other won out over any differences in their background and over the attempts at harassment. Once they decided to go ahead and Roald obtained a divorce, they felt it was their duty to inform their governments. Roald broke the news to Soviet officialdom, and Susan informed the State Department. President Bush responded by calling to congratulate her, and arranged a prewedding dinner.[51]

Planning the wedding reminded her of the bilateral disarmament negotiations which she and Roald knew so well.[52] For each concession on one side there was one on the other. The wedding took place in Moscow, emphasizing the fact that Sagdeev was not defecting to America, and the American Ambassador to

Russia, Jack Matlock, whose son had a Russian wife, offered the premises of the ambassadorial residence Spaso House—technically American soil—thus providing Russian-American symmetry for the venue of the wedding. On February 9, 1990 Susan and Roald were married in a five-minute civil ceremony at Moscow "Marriage Palace Number 1" followed by a Protestant service at Spaso House—featuring, ecumenically enough, a Russian Orthodox choir, and with the Mufti of Moscow, the spiritual leader of the Tatar Muslims, in attendance. Roald said his vows in Russian and Susan said hers in English. "We thought," she explained, "it was important for both of us to fully understand what we were committing ourselves to."[53]

And today the commitment has held firm. Husband and wife still work together on many projects and serve, Susan wrote, "as a bridge between both societies."[54] To resolve differences of opinion they like to use disarmament language and tactics such as, "Let's put a moratorium on this," or "Let's act with parity."[55] Unlike many Russian-American couples, they do not have a communication problem, since Roald speaks good English and Susan has been studying Russian. The couple decided to live in the United States during the school year, because of the schedules of Susan's daughters, and to spend their summers in Russia; they travel frequently between the two countries. Sagdeev was appointed Distinguished Professor of Physics at the University of Maryland, and Susan is Chairman of the Center for Political and Strategic Studies. The two are active in helping Western public and private organizations understand the rapid changes taking place in Russia.

During the last few years many less famous Russian-American marriages have made it into the society pages of U.S. newspapers, and many, many more never achieve print. One reason has been the growth of American businesses in Russia. American law firms in Moscow employ young American attorneys; several have mastered Russian and acquired Russian spouses. Robert Scudder, the chairman of Brightstar, an international business research company, married Marina Zaikovskaya, former managing director of a Moscow company which offered civilians rides on Russian fighter aircraft.[56] Stanley Judd, adviser to the government of Kirgyzstan, a senior manager at Price Waterhouse and a former special counsel to the Securities and Exchange Commission, met Tatiana Pyotrenko, a 26-year-old high-school teacher of Russian literature, at a performance of a British play in the Kirgyz city of Bishkek. During the intermission he leaned over to ask her about the mysterious husband in the play. She misunderstood his question and answered that she had no husband. Judd was 63 and Tatiana 26 but that didn't stop him. He arranged to meet her the next day, and they were married at Judd's Washington home in October, 1995.[57]

The steady proliferation of Russian-American marriages has run the full gamut of American society. An actress from Florida married a rabbi from Kishinev. A Harvard graduate working in the Moscow office of the International Foundation for the Development of Humanity married a Moscow travel agent. A businessman working on a privatization team auctioning off Russian farms married an eye surgeon from Nizhny Nivgorod. [58]

Carol, the daughter of a wealthy Ohio businessman, met Fyodor in the summer of 1975 in Leningrad while on a student trip. Petite, slim and vivacious, she was the first American girl he had ever known. A heavy-set young chemist with dark eyes and a quick smile, he was fascinated by her easy-going manner, her openness, and her curiosity about the Soviet Union. Carol was a student of comparative literature, in love with Russian nineteenth-century novels. She and Fyodor had a passionate romance walking along the banks of the Neva, drinking wine in cafés and holding trysts in her hotel room, after bribing the floor lady with two pairs of panty hose and a bottle of French perfume. Carol thought Fyodor was the most intelligent and fascinating man she had ever met. He took her to the theater and the Hermitage Museum, lectured her on art, brought her flowers every day, and was quietly self-confident without being arrogant. Never had she met an American male so free of doubts about himself, his masculinity, or his chosen career.

The three weeks of Carol's stay was time enough for Fyodor to propose and for the couple to consider themselves engaged. There was no time to get married before her visa expired, and since Carol had to return to college for the autumn semester she planned to send Fyodor an invitation to come to America where they would marry. Her parents were horrified, sure that Fyodor was using their daughter to get to America, but Carol was adamant that he was the love of her life.

Immediately after applying to leave the country Fyodor was drafted into the army. For two years they communicated by phone calls and notes smuggled in by friends; after he was discharged Carol was repeatedly refused a Russian entry visa. But she got her story into the newspapers and made distraught appearances on TV talk shows, and four years later Fyodor was finally allowed to leave. Her parents, reconciled, gave a big, glittering wedding. Then reality set in.

After three weeks together and more than four years apart, the couple had to get to know each other all over again, and Fyodor had to adapt to the United States. He could not get a position as a research chemist and had to settle for part-time work as a hospital lab technician. Carol taught comparative literature at a small Ohio community college. Once the thrill of being reunited with Carol wore off, Fyodor was miserable. He had trouble communicating in English, missed his friends and parents and, gorging on cheeseburgers and French fries, became seriously overweight. He began blaming Carol for bringing him to this country where he could not even get a "normal job." Increasingly, he would go out in the evenings to drink with his Russian émigré friends.

Carol understood how deeply he was hurt by his failure to find work in his field, and how difficult he was finding life in America. Still, she couldn't help wondering if she'd made a mistake. She didn't want to ask her parents for financial help, but when she and

Fyodor began fighting over money she asked them for a loan. After the years of waiting, the publicity campaign and the enormous emotional investment they had made in each other, they were both reluctant to concede failure, and decided on a six-month trial separation. Carol's parents were now supportive of Fyodor, for they had grown to like this earnest young man and felt that he really loved their daughter. And the separation turned out to be a good idea. Carol and Fyodor missed each other, and got back together after three months. A year later Fyodor landed a job as a research chemist with a large industrial firm. His English had improved considerably. And Carol had an offer from a large university for a teaching post with tenure and more pay. Fyodor joined a health club and shed the extra weight. The couple bought a house and went on a trip to Paris and London, fulfilling Fyodor's lifetime dream of seeing Europe. Some twenty years after they first met, Fyodor and Carol are still together. Fyodor now prefers to speak English to Carol, and they have gone on several visits to his parents in Leningrad, now St. Petersburg. "When he stopped saying that it was my fault that his Chevrolet wouldn't start I knew we would make it," Carol said with a laugh. "And I don't tell him it's his fault when we have to wait for our luggage for two hours at the St. Petersburg airport."

Mark and Svetlana are a very different kind of couple. Mark, a historian, graduated from Yale in full-scale rebellion against his strict Orthodox Jewish background. Tall, with gray eyes, he was balding by the time he was 20, and his shoulders were so stooped he seemed to be perpetually looking for something he had dropped. In 1982, when he was 25, he went on a research trip to Kiev and there met the 21-year-old Svetlana, a music student, a pretty blue-eyed blonde, but shy, with a slight stutter. Mark knew his parents would disapprove, as she wasn't Jewish, but he was smitten, and that was that. As for Svetlana, the daughter of an automobile factory worker and a cafeteria cook, she had never imagined she would wind up in America with a Jewish intellectual husband. At the civil ceremony her parents dabbed their eyes and offered toasts, but Mark's parents refused to fly over from Chicago to attend. Once he brought her home, however, they were won over by her affection for Mark and her promise to raise their children as Jews.

But that was not to be. She decided after three months of marriage that her health would not allow her to have children. She suffered from a variety of allergies and phobias, and was deathly afraid of pesticides, food additives, rock music, barking dogs and dishwashers. Mark was content to humor her idiosyncrasies and devote himself to his research. The couple lived on a diet of whole-wheat bread, oranges, bananas and huge pots of Russian borshch, which she made from organic vegetables. She introduced Mark to folk remedies, treating bronchitis with mustard plasters, and sore throats by gargling with raw egg yolk and sugar. Though they did not travel much, since she was afraid of the microbes in airplane cabins and food poisoning from airline meals, she managed to overcome her fears sufficiently for an annual visit to her parents in Kiev. The rest of the time she stayed home playing her collection of classical music.

Aside from some phrases needed for shopping, Svetlana did not make much progress in English. The couple spoke only Russian to each other, and Mark took great pride in the fact that his knowledge of the language had improved so much that he was often mistaken for a native speaker. Once he decided that he could easily commute to the city university where he taught, they moved to the suburbs, paneled their house with cork to shut out noise, and proceeded to grow their own tomatoes, acquire three cats, and adopt a happy Chekhovian existence removed from the bustle of urban American life.

Muriel was a green-eyed freckle-faced redhead, an only child. In the small Vermont town where she grew up her father ran a prosperous real estate company, and her mother did volunteer work and belonged to a bridge club. She majored in English and drama and studied Russian. When in 1980 she married an architecture student her parents gave a wedding party for 400 guests on the spacious lawn of the family house. The couple moved to New York; she worked as a free-lance magazine writer while he finished his graduate studies. A cozy studio apartment on Riverside Drive was their happy home.

But four years later, when she was 27 and on a magazine assignment in Russia, she met Sergei, a tall, blond, strikingly handsome sculptor with dark brown almond-shaped eyes and high Slavic cheekbones. His Western designer clothes emphasized his broad shoulders and muscular physique, and their encounter at a raucous Moscow party ended with them rolling on the floor in a passionate embrace.

Sergei told her she was beautiful and brilliant. She found him fabulously attractive. He gave her beautiful amber jewelry, took her to concerts and expensive nightclubs and introduced her to his friends—painters and sculptors who gathered in their studios to drink vodka and listen to American jazz. He said he couldn't live without her. She was utterly entranced. Once she was home she promptly divorced her husband, returned to Moscow and married Sergei. Three months later he arrived in New York.

For all his speeches in Moscow about about the meaning of creative work, Sergei now lost all interest in sculpting or any other occupation, preferring to stay up every night with fellow Russians downing endless bottles of Stolichnaya vodka and French champagne. After a few drinks, tender words would give way to muttered insults. "You stupid bitch," he would mumble, "what am I doing with you in this lousy dark apartment?" This plain little girl from the sticks, he felt, should be eternally grateful to have such a handsome man for her husband. Their tiny studio could barely contain his tirades and his friends. He kept Muriel up late every night and she failed to meet several magazine deadlines. After sleeping until noon, he needed a good deal of tea and several hours of weight lifting, showering and primping in front of the mirror to get into shape for the next night's round.

When her own friends came over, evenings that began with candlelight, baroque music and Chablis often ended with him raging at Muriel and at America, bringing her to tears and embarrassing her friends. When the guests had left he would apologize abjectly, assuring her that he adored her. And she, for all her tears, was still in love with him and afraid of losing him. His stunning good looks, his elegance and his knowledge of the arts still charmed her and her friends. Some ordinary American now seemed, to her, a boring alternative.

Though their cash was running low, Sergei spent freely, exceeding the limit of the credit card she gave him, stocking up on caviar and smoked salmon, filling out his wardrobe with $600 cashmere sweaters, and insisting that they go out to dinner several nights a week to expensive French restaurants. As the bills piled up he got her to borrow from her parents. His phone calls to his parents and friends in Moscow averaged five hundred dollars a month. In two years' time they were $70,000 in debt.

And Sergei was getting bored. While she was out on magazine assignments and interviews he browsed around the stores and drank wine in West Side cafés. Muriel, he complained, was always tired after work. He started calling up young women, and occasionally he stayed out all night, leaving her to phone friends in desperation to see if he had dropped by someone's house for a late-night drink.

Underneath it all, Sergei appeared to appreciate Muriel's love and devotion, but, as he saw it, he had not come to America to be cooped up in a cramped studio or to eat at McDonald's, and her wealthy parents would always be there to assure him the kind of life he had come for. He was confident that no matter what he did she was so much in love with him that she would never leave him. So, as Muriel struggled with their debts, he played on a seesaw balance of affection and insults to keep her emotionally his slave. Four-letter words and vodka bottles hurled about the room alternated with passionate nights and whispered endearments. Caught up in their mutual dependence, they are still together, their quarrels somewhat less stormy, their emotions still running high.

Joyce was 26 when she met Pyotr, a recent immigrant from Odessa, at a friend's house in 1986. A bubbly, brown-eyed girl from New York, she was immediately attracted to him. Though not strikingly handsome, the dark-haired and athletic young man was sincere and gentle. Her parents were of Russian-Jewish stock, and Pyotr's jokes and love for cabbage soup and potato pancakes reminded her of her grandparents. She had studied Russian in college, and spoke it fairly well. Recovering as she was from a breakup with a depressed and neurotic American boyfriend, this cheerful Russian who played the accordion and loved to laugh seemed the perfect antidote. They were married, and a year later Joyce gave birth to a girl, Maria.

After the child's birth Pyotr's attitude began to change. He became jealous and possessive, expecting Joyce to be at home all the time, causing scenes when she had to travel for her job with an international advertising agency, and resenting it when she wanted to spend an evening with a girlfriend. A dentist in Odessa, he had a hard time mastering English well enough to pass his exams to practice dentistry in the United States, and as his enthusiasm about his new country turned to anger, his past life in Odessa began to take on a rosy hue. He had dreamed of a huge house and a sports car, not of a dark two-room apartment in Queens and filthy subway cars. Joyce became for Pyotr the incarnation of an America that had let him down. He found her housekeeping sloppy and when, after a hard day in the office, she phoned a Chinese restaurant for some take-out he accused her of feeding her family on "slimy Asian garbage." "You're an American child with a Russian father!" he would yell at their daughter. "You shouldn't be eating this poisoned Chinese junk!" He wanted Joyce to dress in conservative tweeds, white blouses and black skirts; she liked bright colors, miniskirts and plunging necklines. He berated her for gaining weight and for never doing her hair the way he liked it.

When Pyotr finally passed his exams and opened a practice, his hopes of getting rich foundered in a sea of mortgages and loans for his office and car. All his bitterness he vented on Joyce. Though he barely made enough money to support his family, he screamed at her that she should quit her job and stay home to take care of the house and the child. "I thought he wanted a wife— and discovered he wanted a maid," she said to a friend.

His diatribes in front of her friends made them virtual social outcasts. Joyce's girlfriends would come over only when Pyotr was away. When he yelled at Maria for refusing to speak Russian the child burst into tears and made fun of his accent in English. He ranted that only in Russia was it possible to get a decent education, and spent hours on the phone every day with his domineering mother, Lidia, who had emigrated with him, expatiating on the evils of American life. Following these conversations he would threaten to leave Joyce, go live with Lidia, and find a Russian girl who would stay home and devote herself solely to her family.

Joyce was persuaded that most of Pyotr's problems were caused by cultural differences rather than by his stubborn personality, and she kept on trying to help him adapt.[59] But that proved hopeless, for Pyotr blamed her for all his problems, from his troubles with getting patients to his difficulty in understanding a bank teller. "I thought a man who was so kind to his dog would be nice to me, too," she said. "I guess he can only relate to dogs. Russian dogs."

One day she discovered a listening device in a closet: Pyotr was bugging their phone, suspecting her of having an affair. She seriously thought of leaving him, and decided to stay only because of Maria. After seven years, however, she could no longer stand Pyotr's jealous rages and unrelenting criticism. She moved out with Maria and demanded a separation.

Irina was a strikingly beautiful student of English and linguistics from St. Petersburg, with a whispery voice, glossy black eyelashes and the figure of a model, as well as a fiery temper and steel will. She married her university boyfriend to escape the young men who buzzed around her like flies, but she soon tired of her husband and began making the rounds of American graduate students and professors studying in Leningrad in the 1980s. Irina was always ready to help with their language projects, enhancing her linguistic advice with dinner and wine in her kitchen whenever her husband, a geologist, was away on one of his frequent field trips. Marrying him, she realized, had been a mistake. Though he was eager to have a child, she had seven abortions by the time she was 34. No tying herself down with a baby and missing her chance at something better!

That chance made its appearance in the form of Fred. He was a lanky 42-year-old American divorced publisher from the South who specialized in books about Russia. Irina embarked on a campaign to seduce him over candlelight dinners while her husband was away. Fred was enchanted. Here was the Russia he had always dreamed of—pretty, feminine, and his. Once Irina was sure of her conquest she told him, sweetly, that she was pregnant and would divorce her husband to have this love child. Fred, leaving on a six-week trip home, promptly proposed marriage. When he returned she was divorced, and they were wed, though immediately afterward she informed him that unfortunately she'd had a miscarriage.

Knoxville was, for Irina, a disappointment. The publishing house turned out to be a room in Fred's basement, and Fred was by no means the rich businessman she had imagined. She did produce a boy and a girl, and imported her mother and retarded sister from Leningrad to baby-sit and help with housekeeping while she taught Russian at a local junior college. Irina proved an excellent teacher, popular with the students, and was equally strict with them and Fred, who was not quite sure how his dewy-eyed pussy-cat had turned into such a sharp-clawed tiger. He, however, was too busy worrying about how to feed his large household and get a larger mortgage to have much time for serious thoughts. He still adored her, and Irina was deeply touched by his devotion to her and her family. "I never expected such honesty and fidelity," she confided to her mother. "That really makes me love him more than I ever thought I would." They are still together, one case where a calculated seduction led to a marriage likely to last.

The experiences of the couples living in Russia are as varied as those of the ones in America. The question of whether the Russian husband or wife married the American to go abroad may continue to haunt many of the couples living in America, but this is not a factor for those who choose to remain in Russia. Some Russian spouses decide to stay for family reasons, or out of patriotism, or because of poor English, professional commitments, fear of not finding a job, or dislike of the American way of life, or simply because they enjoy living in Russia. American spouses who have opted for life in Russia also give varied reasons—that they are complying with their mate's wishes, dislike American values, find Russians and Russian culture congenial, or feel that today it is more interesting, exciting and profitable to live in Russia than in the United States.

Annabella Bucar was a white-haired octogenarian who walked with a shuffling gait, but her sparkling blue eyes flashed in excitement when she recounted the story of her life. The daughter of Yugoslav immigrants to the United States, she was the oldest of eleven children and barely 30 when she arrived in Moscow in 1946 to work for the American Embassy. An attractive blonde who wore her long hair in a braid wound around her head, Annabella was excited about her new job, and had started studying Russian. Though Embassy personnel had few opportunities to meet ordinary Russians in those days, and such contacts were discouraged by the Americans and the Soviets alike, the Russians occasionally organized outings to the theater followed by receptions where the Americans could mingle with the Russian performers. At a party after a performance at the Nemirovich-Danchenko operetta theater Annabella met a handsome and talented young singer, Nikolai Lapshin. They fell in love. As marriage to a Russian was unthinkable for an Embassy employee, Annabella walked out of the Embassy and defected to the Russian authorities.

For the first years of their marriage the couple lived in near total isolation. Annabella was ostracized by the American community, and Nikolai's friends were afraid to associate with him because of his American wife.

Annabella got a job with the Moscow Radio English-language service. For the first few years she was accompanied daily by four secret-police escorts, two of whom remained outside the radio building while one stayed in the corridor and the other sat outside the studio where she worked. The rationale was that the Central Intelligence Agency might try to kidnap her. She and Nikolai had a son, and when the boy was four years old she was forced to take Soviet citizenship, thus losing her American passport. As she was made to work night shifts and slept during the day, she saw little of him when he was small.

In 1949 a book entitled *The Truth About American Diplomats* was published in Moscow under Annabella's name. The strident style of this attack on American embassy personnel, vilifying them as vicious spies engaged in slandering the Soviet Union, did not sound like the work of an American. Today it seems evident that the book was written by the Soviet authorities, a standard practice of the time, and that she had to accept authorship under the threat of reprisals against her and her family. The book was widely read in Russia, however, and was reprinted in several popular magazines.

It was not until 1991, after 45 years in Russia, that Annabella received permission from the Russian and American governments for a visit home to the United States. At a family reunion she met dozens of nieces and nephews and had a chance to catch up with her friends. Today, back in Moscow, she says she misses her American family. "You get used to doing without all kinds of things. It's the people I miss. I want to go home!"[60] At age 85, however, Nikolai did not want to move to America. Their son has a family of his own and is hesitant about emigrating. More trips to the States were the most Anabella could hope for. But that was not to be, for she died in the spring of 1998.

Sara Harris visited Russia as a young girl in 1963 and returned to live there in 1967, after marrying Alexander Kamenshchikov, a Moscow journalist. Her mother cried but her father was delighted. He had lived for two years in Russia in the twenties, working for Harvester Corn, and retained his enthusiasm for the Soviet experiment. "You'll be a pioneer just like the pioneers in America," he told his daughter.[61] From a three-story, eleven-room house in Westchester, Sara moved to a small Moscow log cabin without running water. There she lived for six years with her husband and his grandmother, and eventually with her three children.

Though Sara shared her father's enthusiasm for socialism, the challenge was daunting. "I kept asking myself, can I do it? Can I survive?" she said. While she could make a life in Russia, her husband had no desire to live in America. Alexander was a model of responsibility. "He felt he had taken me away from everything— my home, family, and friends, and that he had to make up for it by doing everything and being everything for me," Sara recalled.[62] For eleven years he supported the household while she raised the children and studied at Moscow State University, earning a degree in economics. She then went to Radio Moscow's English-language section. "There were times I'd wake up in the middle of the night and ask [myself] what the hell am I doing," she said in an interview, "but I've been happy here for many years. My demands are low."[63] Then Sara became the primary breadwinner as a producer at Moscow's ABC television studio, while Alexander worked part-time as a literary editor of a magazine for Russian and American teenagers. "He's not a typical Russian," she said of her husband; most Russian men, she felt, would be resentful if their wives earned more than they.

Russian-American relations had changed radically by 1977, when Joanne Turnbull was a student on a language-study program in Moscow. A friend asked her to take a letter to a young zoologist, Nikolai Formosov. In some ways the two are opposites; she is a tall, bubbly and enthusiastic blonde, who is interested in languages and literature, and he is a short, stocky man who talks and moves slowly and deliberately. Yet she fell in love with him and his country. On her return to the United States Joanne continued studying Russian and dreaming of ways to get back to Moscow. Several years elapsed. Nikolai got married; Joanne took up with with someone else. Yet they continued to correspond. Nikolai's marriage fell apart, Joanne's involvement soured, and when she returned to Moscow in 1983 to work for *Newsweek* they were reunited, married and have lived in Moscow ever since.

Joanne has wholeheartedly embraced Russian culture, and is intensely interested in the country's literature, art, and history. She speaks Russian with near-native fluency, and she and Nikolai, whose English is not fully fluent, speak Russian to each other. The daughter of New England academics, she had always been repulsed by the American pursuit of material welfare and by keeping up with the Joneses, preferring a modest apartment with lots of books and the company of interesting people. She loves Moscow, the markets, museums, and antique bookstores, the snowfalls of winter and the flowers of summer at their country house.

"Joanne has dropped American values but not fully accepted Russian ones," Nikolai commented. "And that makes me feel very free," she added.[64] Though she loves Russia, she has retained her own identity. As for Nikolai, his curiosity about the West is satisfied by their brief trips to the United States to see Joanne's family, who also visits them. Despite the hardships of Moscow life, he is too deeply Russian to want to live elsewhere.

The couple seems ideally happy. Words and ideas tumble out as they interrupt each other in conversation and finish each other's sentences. They live with their five-year-old daughter in a large and sunny apartment near Moscow University where Nikolai works.

Joanne has been active with a journal of literary translation, *Glas*. "In Russia I can do free-lance work, take on interesting translations, and have plenty of time for myself and my family," she said. "If we were living in the U.S. I'd have to work full-time to have an apartment like this and to pay for child care for Anna." Aside from American visitors, the couple's friends are mostly Russians. They avoid "the bubble," the world of Americans who live in segregated apartment complexes and socialize only with each other, and Joanne clearly enjoys the intellectual and emotional intensity that life in Moscow can bestow.

Two years ago Mary C. met Boris, a St. Petersburg television journalist fluent in English, while he was posted to the U.S.[65] To marry him she gave up her lucrative job as a paralegal with a large law firm, dropped her plans to go to law school, sold her cooperative apartment, packed up all her belongings, and moved to Russia. The man she did this for has much to recommend him. Boris is a charming, dynamic man with a shock of blond hair, his blue eyes radiating energy as he dashes about St. Petersburg in his red Porsche. Boris admires America and loves his American wife. But he fears that she will never be happy living in Russia.

Mary hates Russia. She finds St. Petersburg dirty and provincial, full of people who stare at her foreign designer clothes. As she finds Russian impossibly difficult, she has made little effort to master the language, and still has difficulty getting around by bus or subway. She meets her American friends in the Western-style bar of the Evropeiskaya Hotel and waits for her husband to pick her up. And she intensely dislikes the frequent socializing with Russians that is part of her husband's work, and which Americans such as Joanne find the highlight of their lives in Russia. "I never want to eat another herring salad or drown in more of those endless Russian toasts," Mary C. said.[66] "I find the whole culture totally alien. It's not even European—it's an absolutely different world from France or Italy!"

Mary complains that their guests treat her more like a waitress than a hostess. "It's because Russian men are all so blindly sexist." Boris is the most "liberated" Russian man she knows, and "he's probably only that way because he's spent so much time in America." Not all her American friends agree. "Mary expects everybody to behave like an American," one of them commented. "The Russian men feel they're paying her a compliment by treating her like a pretty woman—which she is!"

All Mary has in St. Petersburg is Boris, and she wishes he could spend more time with her, vacationing in the United States or traveling in Europe, but his professional job ties him to St. Petersburg. They both say they want children, but "I couldn't *imagine* raising a child in this country," Mary adds. "That really scares me. I just hope it somehow all works out."

When he was twenty and his father went to Moscow on business, Dick G. came along for the ride. That was in 1990. Today he's back in Moscow selling imported videos and video technology, and operating a thriving English-language video rental service out of his apartment. Hundreds of tapes line the walls of his living room from floor to ceiling. One day while on his way to the police station to extend his visa, he introduced himself to a very pretty blonde girl who caught his eye. Sofya was a bookkeeper two years older than he, with a three-year-old son, Oleg. They started dating, and she moved in.

Dick has no background in Russian culture. He speaks Russian just well enough to do business. Though Sofya's English has made great strides and little Oleg, who has been watching American videos, has started to speak English, Dick admits that he and Sofya often have linguistic misunderstandings. But few Americans in Russia have adapted to the country as well as he. He knows how Russian women expect to be treated: as soon as Sofya comes home he jumps up to take her coat. He treats little Oleg like his own son, and he loves the way Russians drop by at all hours for tea, vodka, and endless conversation. Dick found that his visits to

America with Sofya proved far more expensive than life in Moscow. "It was terribly difficult to teach her to shop when we visited my family," he commented. "She didn't quite understand the value of the dollar."[67]

Though Dick was a Trotskyite in college, it is not ideology which makes him want to live in Moscow. "This place is so exciting!" he exclaimed. "You wake up in the morning and never know what will happen in the afternoon. In New Jersey you know exactly what will happen. But here in Moscow, in August 1991, when I was driving my ex-girlfriend to work I looked out the window and there were these four tanks coming down the road! And then I looked into the rear-view mirror, and there were some eighty tanks behind me! I was practically laughing from excitement—it was so great. Then I saw she was crying. I guess she was scared." Though Dick may find such abortive political coups exciting, most Russians would be delighted with a little less excitement and a little more stability. He stays in contact with his family by phone calls. "My parents don't mind that we're here. My mother feels that if I'm happy, it's O.K. And if I need help—well, then, come home. But I'm not going anywhere for a while. This is too exciting."

Svetlana Kozlova and Bob Coalson admit to more material reasons for staying on in Moscow: the lack of job prospects and the difficulty they would have in affording an apartment comparable to their spacious quarters in a high-rise on Kutuzovsky Prospekt.[68] Svetlana, who works as manager of *Newsweek's* Moscow office, and Bob, who writes for the English-language *Moscow Times*, met at Cornell University where she was an undergraduate on an exchange program student and he was a doctoral candidate in Russian nineteenth-century literature. Svetlana felt lonely in the small university department where all the students had known each other for years, and spent two hours on their first date telling Bob how intensely she disliked America. Until he met Svetlana, Bob had no interest in going to the Soviet Union, for he was interested in Russian nineteenth-century literature, not in the turmoils of present-day Russia. But Svetlana made a difference.

The couple are a study in contrasts. She is from St. Petersburg; he comes from a small town in Iowa. He, in his mid-thirties, is very quiet, while Svetlana, a few years younger, is outgoing and voluble. He is conservatively dressed and has short hair and glasses, while her long dark hair and long skirts make her look like a sixties flower child. He speaks good Russian, but they tend to communicate in English, in which Svetlana is fluent.

In Moscow the couple have good jobs, but the American market for teaching Russian literature is saturated. Since their apartment is part of the *Newsweek* complex, as long as Svetlana works for the magazine they can live and work in the buildings in which the offices are located. Eventually they may move to the United States, but—for economic reasons—not yet.

On the whole, Russian-American marriages lived in Russia have been more successful than those lived in the United States. Many of the Americans who agree to settle down in Russia have been there previously, speak the language, and have a reasonably sound knowledge of Russian life. Unlike many of the Russians who move to America, they do not expect to live in luxury, and have low material expectations. Nor are American expatriates thrown up against a confusing welter of banks, supermarkets, taxes and conspicuous consumption. The Russian spouse's family and friends also usually provide much stronger emotional support than is true of American families in the United States.

In some cases—fortunately for both parties—Russian-American involvements stopped short of marriage. The American Ballet Theater dancer Gelsey Kirkland came to idolize Mikhail Baryshnikov, the Russian ballet star. As she wrote in her autobiography, *Dancing on My Grave,*

> Misha was a miracle. Bursting upon the scene . . . he offered
> the opportunity to share . . . his genius . . . I never doubted

that the partnership would prevail as the ultimate expression of our love . . . We just needed time . . . as dancers and as lovers.[69]

The glamorous defector from the Kirov Ballet was charming and a brilliant dancer. While the two were superb together on the stage, offstage, as Gelsey let slip to the press, it was something else.

He comes from a wholly different background. He has a Russian temperament, and all Russians I have known are moody.[70]

And extremely difficult. If he loved her, why was he denigrating her work and hurting her? For the American ballerina's vulnerable ego he was too much to handle. She was also upset by his stubborn refusal to believe that Americans were capable of understanding Russia and Russians. "We hurt each other in so many ways . . . I felt like I had to disguise my own inner identity." She became an emotional dishrag. "I allowed myself to be turned into a servant, as devoted in the bedroom as . . . in the ballet studio."[71]

The two were on different wavelengths. "What was perhaps for him a casual affair was for me a prolonged catastrophe of heart and mind." Her Christmas gift to him, a carefully chosen antique ring, was reciprocated by a box of candy. For her he was the universe; for him she was an excellent dance partner and a pretty girlfriend. The end of the affair is all too well known. After their breakup Gelsey was involved in a series of destructive relationships and became addicted to cocaine, and Baryshnikov, by then the director of the American Ballet, had to fire her.

Then there was the case of the Soviet defector Arkady Shevchenko, who had been a high-ranking United Nations official, and Judy Chavez, the prostitute provided him by the Federal Bureau of Investigation. The FBI and CIA needed to keep their prize informant satisfied while they debriefed him on his inside knowledge of Soviet politics and politicians, and when Shevchenko announced that he needed a woman, Judy Chavez was chosen to fill the need. In her book *Defector's Mistress* Judy wrote that the pudgy, middle-aged, heavy-drinking Russian didn't want the bondage, vibrators, "talking dirty" or kinky sex which were her specialties. He wanted to make her into a lady, and bought her expensive chocolates, French perfume and conservative tailored suits.[72] She had a wardrobe of leather outfits and miniskirts. A dress Shevchenko bought her, she wrote, "was dark blue and it was too mature for me. God, I felt like I was thirty years old when I put it on. But it was just the kind he thought was nice."[73]

Problems began when he grew jealous. "If I catch you with other men I'll kill you," he threatened. He even thought of marrying her. The FBI agents who accompanied all their outings sympathized with Chavez' problems in dealing with this troublesome client who splattered egg on his shirt and began downing vodka early in the morning. "As far as I'm concerned you've earned every penny you've ever made," one agent said to her. The tough American call girl was quite overcome: "Andy drained me emotionally in a way that a series of tricks wouldn't have. And he took up so much of my time."[74] His Russian love of incessant talking was too much for her. In the end she prevailed on the FBI to free her from her patriotic task. Shevchenko eventually married an American court reporter and settled down as a government and private consultant. He was widowed soon, remarried, and died in 1998.

ADAPTING

"I love my wife . . . but she will always be an intimate stranger to me," a Frenchman said of his American spouse.[1] The Polish-born writer Eva Hoffman has analyzed beautifully the problem that arises when the person you are closest to is also maddeningly incomprehensible.

> Perhaps you cannot love one person when you don't love the world surrounding him and the common sensibility that somehow expresses itself in each one of us . . . After the immigrant's dendrites stop standing on end from the vividness of first impressions, comes this other, more elusive strangeness—the strangeness of glimpsing internal landscapes that are arranged in different formations as well.[2]

The foreign spouse must adapt to both a new partner and a new culture. For Russians, the first jolt of leaving the motherland is followed by the shock of American reality, and for Americans living in Russia—even after the collapse of the USSR—day to day married life is quite different from the sheltered existence of an exchange student or employee of an American firm. "Someone has said that Russians make the world's worst émigrés," wrote Tamara Gilmore, "that no matter how lush their lives in a foreign land they still like to sit around the samovar and talk and dream about mother Russia."[3]

Few Russians are immune to spasms of homesickness and intense patriotism. Masha Scott, the teacher who married the American idealist John Scott in the thirties, wrote that "I was surprised, perhaps, that he wanted to go back to America—I felt that my country was so good and so unusual. At that time I never thought to go with him. I never thought to leave Russia."[4] Masha's adaptation to America proved more difficult than John's adjustment to Russia. He came to the USSR out of idealism; she went to America because she was following him. Marina Oswald was also highly ambivalent about leaving Russia and was afraid of a new and unknown country.

Even those who hated the Soviet system are deeply attached to their country and highly apprehensive of the outside world. Irina McClellan, who spent eleven years fighting to join her husband in America, was overcome with anxiety when the way was clear.

> I was preparing myself emotionally for life in a new country. For a Russian born and raised in one place, educated in a closed society, unaccustomed to change, the prospect of being uprooted is terrifying; my eyes often filled with tears as fear of the unknown rushed through my mind.[5]

A young Russian woman was amazed at the behavior of her girlfriend, who had just left Moscow with her American husband. "You'd think she had everything," she commented. "He's handsome, rich, kind, and he's adopting her little girl. But she was crying all the time. It was so hard for her to leave Russia."[6] Homesickness was the main reason why Marina Oswald wanted to return to Russia. It was something, she wrote, that could only be understood in a foreign country.[7] Viktoria Fyodorova, though happy with her husband and baby, could not rid herself of homesickness.

"Nostalgia even now sometimes comes up, especially when I fight with my husband and think, well, now I'll pack up—and go there."[8]

While Americans expect that everyone will like the United States, the initial reactions of Russian spouses run the gamut from intense admiration to intense dislike. The poet Sergei Esenin was not favorably impressed. "I'm going back to Russia," he said to a group of American journalists. "I'd rather live on black bread and vodka there than have the best you've got in the United States . . . I found America a country which did not appreciate art and is filled with crass materialism."[9]

Isadora Duncan was pained by Esenin's reaction, and the poet himself was ambivalent. After returning to Russia he said to a friend, "I shan't become part of the West, and yet I have drifted away from Moscow . . . I want America, but I do not accept the America that I saw."[10]

Tatiana Leshchenko-Sukhomilina, a young Russian actress who married an American lawyer, Ben Pepper, in the 1920s, also had trouble with American materialism. "I detested everything in New York with its petty-bourgeois style, its race after dollars, its lack of culture, I hated it, it bored me. I couldn't stand it and ran away from the U.S., despite Ben's and my love, despite all the comfort and good things available to me." She found Americans as unpalatable as their country: "We Russians are broader, more cheerful, internally freer. They say that they have freedom, that they can say anything, write anything, but for some reason they are all so uptight, so slow, so biased."[11]

As Vassily Aksyonov has noted, the Soviet press accounts of American slums, racial discrimination, drug abuse, crime and unemployment often had the opposite of the intended effect. Anti-American propaganda created for Soviets a romantic picture of America as an ideal and prosperous country, and hundreds of Russian émigrés were bitterly disappointed with the nation they found.[12] The Russian image of America was also that of colorful large cities such as New York or San Francisco, and spouses who ended up in the backwoods were in for a shock. Though today the uncensored Russian press and the hundreds of people traveling back and forth are changing the Russian picture of America, deeply ingrained biases still persist.

And many Russians still suffer from that famous superiority-inferiority complex. For years they were told that everything Russian was superior to everything Western, and yet the explicit goal of the USSR was to catch up with and surpass America. Muriel was furious when Sergei spent forty dollars on a bottle of French champagne and then insisted—as he savored every sip— that Russian champagne was incomparably better. A Russian who is torn between fascination and frustration with the United States frequently reacts with an aggressive assertion of Russian superiority. "In our country" was the favorite opening of almost every sentence Pyotr and Irina uttered after their arrival in the United States. This was inevitably followed by an assertion that in Russia "It was much easier to find your way around the subway," or "You didn't have to fill out pages and pages of income tax forms." Irina McClellan recalled her first reaction on seeing Woody's house: "It was a cheerful little place, yet my heart sank; it was not mine, everything was strange."[13] The foreign surroundings deepened her alienation and nostalgia. "I thought about Moscow, where every-thing was familiar, even the misery."[14]

The pain of leaving family and friends is compounded by the loss of a government that took care of everything—housing, edu-cation, health, and jobs. While coping with these losses, language problems and culture shock, the newcomer must learn how to use the phone, mail, bank, stores and dozens of other services.

And the abundance of individual choices both intrigues and confuses. From canned soup to a condominium, everything seems available, but how does one choose? Irina McClellan wrote that

> America stunned and blinded me with its brilliant and rich variety. In years of dreaming, I had not given a thought to strangeness. Was I not, after all, a teacher of English? And

did I not have many American friends to tell me about this country? It is, however, one thing to read and hear, another to encounter reality: gaudily dressed, dauntingly self-confident women; hordes of carefree children of all hues; everyone speaking English, which even dogs seem to understand; comfortable private homes; brightly colored, flashy automobiles; on all sides everything new, new, new.[15]

Today Russia has supermarkets, but in decades past American stores were an overwhelming experience. And even though the super-stores are dazzling, shopping can still be fraught with problems. What does the label promising a new, super-improved, preservative-free brand X mean? The overwhelming abundance of products and gadgets . . . Irina McClellan says of her new American house:

When I tried to conquer the kitchen, it puzzled me with its appliances, its cabinets and refrigerator full of boxes and packages and fresh food I couldn't understand. I had never seen breakfast cereal or biscuit dough in cans, never encountered artichokes or broccoli or zucchini. I needed a special dictionary for the food and an instruction manual for the stove—everything I touched seemed to burn or boil over.[16]

Roles are reversed; the person who at home was a confident, sophisticated host is now a helpless dependent.

As the Moscow fear slowly evaporated, a new, American one came into being, one that sprang from my near-complete lack of understanding of American culture, life, and language. It also weighed on my poor husband, who remembered the competent, educated, worldly-wise woman he had known in Moscow. That was the woman he wanted, the one he had waited for. What he got was a child in a woman's body: questions, questions, questions . . . "If you'll be a patient teacher," I told Woody, "I'll learn more quickly, and life will be easier for you. Remember how patient I was in Moscow? Now it is your turn."[17]

Traditionally, it was the wife who said, "whither thou goest I shall go," but today it may well be the man who moves to his spouse's country. In a delicate role reversal, she must be his guide, mentor, and teacher. "I screamed at Muriel every time I bought the wrong thing in the store," Sergei admitted. "I knew I'd misread the labels, but I said she hadn't explained to me clearly what to buy. It all seemed so easy for her—it made me furious. In Russia I could get to see the vice-minister of culture in two minutes. Here I can't find my way to a men's room."

After three years in America, Fyodor was still hoarding empty aspirin bottles and jam jars because containers had always been in short supply in Russia. Each small mistake was an embarrassment—like buying sanitary napkins instead of table napkins because he thought "sanitary" meant they were cleaner.

Behavior appropriate at home can look strange in a new country. It can be extremely difficult to distinguish between traits and reactions which are specific to an individual's psyche and those which are culturally determined.[18] Muriel doesn't know if Sergei is always late because he is Russian or because he is Sergei. Pyotr can't tell whether Joyce keeps burning the hamburgers because she doesn't know how to cook or because she is making an American feminist statement about sharing housekeeping duties. In the heat of a marital spat it is much easier to yell "You lazy Russian!" or "You stingy American!" than to think about cultural norms.

As the husbands and wives in a new country go through the process of adapting, their mates often acquired a new awareness of their own culture. The American partners tended to see themselves as individuals, and their spouses as products of a "foreign" culture. "Until Sergei got here, I never thought of myself as part of a culture, as an 'American,'" Muriel said. "For Sergei, my doing things one way or another is not just a result of my being Muriel—it's because I'm Muriel the American."

Western status symbols highly valued in Russia can lose their meaning in the United States. Tamara Gilmore tells of a young Russian woman whose Western clothes were the envy of her Moscow friends. After her first outing in Baltimore, her new husband's home, she burst into tears: "It's so awful here. Here in America everyone has pretty clothes. I can't stand it. I look like everyone else."[19] In the early sixties, an American journalist had difficulty persuading his Russian wife that a huge red sedan would be a garish *faux pas*. "I felt starved for color, for things that were expensive—and looked it," she said. He liked small and intimate restaurants; she wanted large and flashy ones. She adored large five-star hotels; he preferred country inns. "He had to remodel me completely," she recalled, "and make me understand what was in good taste, and what was vulgar and *nouveau riche*."

In pre-*glasnost* Russia, the precarious conditions in which Russian-American romances developed gave Russians a distorted picture of how Americans behaved at home. After the years of separation Irina McClellan had to adjust to a husband she had never seen in his own environment.

> The Vadim of Moscow no longer existed. Not only had he aged during the long separation, he was now an American Vadim, or rather, Woody, a man I had never known.[20]

As the journalist Eugene Lyons observed, American spouses could seem, to their Russian mates, a good deal less glamorous in the United States than they had been in Russia:

> I was to run into [these Russians] in New York in subsequent years, a little wistful over their lost fatherland and usually disappointed in the bourgeois dreamland; those

American husbands who seemed rich and unique in Moscow proved very small and drab fry in their native setting.[21]

Sometimes the difficulties of adapting may seem just too over-whelming. Here is how Viktoria Fyodorova described her feelings during her first years of marriage:

> I think it's better when people marry those of their own nationality, when there are shared roots. For me the first year, the first two years were horribly difficult, I had not only to learn about the country, the language, etc.—I had to adapt to that kind of life my husband led. Then the child was born, almost right away everything descended on me . . . I had to change 95 per cent of the habits from my past life, adapt to the new society. Yes, I became what is here called a suburban American wife, who, true, has no regrets. And races around all day, and goes to bed at midnight with half of what needs to be done still not done. There's no time to read or draw. I'm painting and redecorating the house. And about family life of a Russian wife and an American husband. It's really rather difficult. Suddenly here I had to accept a lot of things. He'd say "Things aren't done here this way.'[22]

Some Russian spouses react by pouring all their energies into mastering the new culture. "I must have wrecked at least twenty checks while Carol was showing me how to write them," Fyodor said. "But I wasn't going to come running to her every time I had to pay a bill." Others try to soften the jolts of American life by associating primarily with other Russians, and accepting infor-mation about America only from them. "When Muriel tried to explain to me how to use the Yellow Pages it all sounded so con-fusing," Sergei said. "But my Russian friend Dmitri, who's been here for three years, explained it to me in five minutes. When you're surrounded by all these foreigners the only people you can rely on are your own people."[23]

More than that, the American mate is often made the scapegoat. "It's 'Well, you got me into this, so now you can get me out of it,'" Fyodor said, explaining why he kept yelling at Carol during his first year in America. "Sort of, I gave up my country and everything for you, so you'd better make it worth while." "Sergei seemed to be out looking for things to jump on," Muriel said. "He was so frustrated and angry. I—and America—were to blame for the fact that it was raining."

In time, the Russian may become Americanized while the American Russifies, each becoming somewhat different from the person who first attracted the other.[24] Muriel complained that Sergei, who in Russia had never much cared for material possessions, became obsessed with buying clothes and stereo equipment. Tom Whitney wrote that after he and Julie had lived for a while in the United States,

> I looked at that chic, cosmopolitan, sophisticated New York woman there across from me and I asked myself: "Where has that Russian girl gone—that girl I met in Moscow so long ago wearing that black silk dress with the orange, pink and yellow flower pattern, that girl with whom I fell in love in the Gorky Park of Culture and Rest?"[25]

Neither has it been that easy for American spouses to adapt to married life in Russia. In the 1920s through 1940s the idealism of the American socialists, blacks, and children of émigrés helped them cope with difficulties of Soviet daily life which would have proved intolerable for people who did not believe in the system. The Americans who settled in Russia in the 1960s and 1970s were generally better informed about the country, better prepared for Russian reality, and less alienated from American society than the early idealists. Social contacts with Russians were much easier than in earlier decades, and the foreign spouses did not live in fear of arrest. Until *perestroika*, however, they were as subject as their Russian spouses to the whims of the bureaucracy, constant shortages, and cramped living conditions. While in the 1930s Americans were forced to give up their passports and to wait for decades for exit visas, today people like Dick G. can shop in modern Moscow supermarkets, order in pizza, and leave the country at will.

Though this was not their original expectation, some Americans ended up better off economically in Russia than in the U.S. Tom Crane moved to Moscow in 1985 when he married Rita, a Russian tour guide, and worked as an English-language style editor for Novosti Press Agency Publishers. "This taxi driver I was riding with once," he recalled, "just couldn't believe I would come to the Soviet Union, because he figured I could live so much better in the United States, be rich. But in fact, I'm better off here."[26] Until the collapse of the USSR which led to galloping inflation and soaring prices, the low rents and inexpensive food and transportation, job security, free education, medical and child care and good salaries paid to Americans made Russia a real bargain. Tom Crane lived far better in Russia than he could have in the United States. And during the Soviet era Russian cities were among the safest in the world. Even today, young couples such as Svetlana Kozlova and Bob Coalson feel they have better jobs and housing in Moscow than they would in the U.S.

Not all of the American spouses who went to the Soviet Union believing in the Soviet system succeeded in finding their niche. "Westerners have no place in Russia," wrote John Scott shortly after he left Russia in the 1930s.

> Men and women from Western Europe and America may occasionally succeed in understanding it, but it is almost impossible for them to fit into it. I went to Moscow and became an observer, which was, perhaps, all I had ever been really. Had it not been for Masha and the children I should have left Russia entirely. As it was I hung on for three more years, until at long last we were able to go to America all together.[27]

Many Americans of Scott's generation were forced out of Russia by the purges, and those who married Russians in the 1960s and 1970s were subjected to milder forms of Russian xenophobia. To this day, Americans are still not accepted as full-fledged members of Russian society, for, unlike America, Russia has never had a tradition of melting-pot immigration and assimilation.

Paula Garb married the Russian tour guide she met on an excursion to Lenin Hills during a tourist trip to Moscow in 1965, when she was 17. They lived in Moscow and had two sons, but the couple's relationship deteriorated rapidly. In her book, *They Came to Stay*, about Americans who emigrated to the Soviet Union, she describes her own experience:

> The result was a disastrous marriage from the first day I arrived . . . It was one thing to expound upon love, marriage and children theoretically in letters, and quite another to deal with real life situations. The problem was that we were not well matched as individuals, and that was exacerbated by our sharp cultural differences. My whole period of adjustment to life in the Soviet Union was heavily colored by a miserable family life. Almost every day I told myself I would pack up the next day and go home. But a stubborn personality and inability to accept failure kept me in Moscow and with my husband for two and a half years.[28]

Learning how to shop and get medical and child care was like learning how to swim. "My husband and his relatives gave me brief instructions to Soviet procedures in each of these areas, that is, showed me the water, and then threw me in to figure out what to do next. By the end of the first year I felt I could maneuver my way through any situation in any sphere of Soviet life."[29]

The marriage did not last, however, and in 1972 after her divorce Garb returned to America with her children. But she missed her Russian friends and the advantages of Soviet life, and three years later she returned to Moscow. There she worked for a publishing house and Moscow Radio's English-language service, and did undergraduate and graduate work in anthropology. Paula became an internationally recognized expert on Abkhazia, the region of the Caucasus where people are reputed to live to well over a hundred years of age.[30] Though she liked her well-paid job as an English translator, appreciated the free higher education she received and enjoyed the close friendships, she felt that "I would always be an alien in the Soviet Union."[31]

In the late 1980s she returned to live in America, where she is now a university lecturer, and still travels frequently to Russia to work and to see her son and his family in Moscow; her younger son has moved to the United States. After twenty years in Russia, however, she found readapting to American society a "traumatic" experience.

Some Russian-American couples who had lived in Moscow for decades felt that after the collapse of the Soviet Union their lives had become so unstable that they decided to leave. Political uncertainties, financial difficulties, crime, and fewer contacts with family and friends because people were spending more time trying to make money to cope with rising prices, all aggravated marital relations. This was the fate of several couples Paula Garb described in her book.

Patty Montet, a Russian-language student from Louisiana, was introduced to married life in Moscow in 1982. "I was really depressed the first few months because I found out Andrei wasn't a perfect person," she recalled. "I began to realize he was a human being, that he had faults. And the cold Moscow winter added to my depression." Patty was homesick for America—even for the junk food—and felt cramped in the couple's small apartment. "I was crying all the time those first few months," she recalled, until she got a job as a translator with Progress Publishers and a larger two-bedroom apartment with more space for the couple and their three children. Yet when she took her family on a vacation to the United States, to her surprise, she found herself longing to go back to Moscow. "That was the first time I realized—this is where my home is," she said.[32] Nonetheless, the marriage began to crack, and in the 1990s it collapsed along with the Soviet system.

In some ways, life in Moscow and other Russian cities is easier for Americans today than it was under Communism. The orange juice and toilet paper that used to be such luxuries are now readily available. But rudeness, inefficiency and a cumbersome bureaucracy are still there, along with the newer social ills of rampant corruption and crime. The goods filling the stores are often priced beyond the reach of Americans as well as Russians, and the American spouses continue to run up against a host of daily problems. How do you call a plumber? What do you do if the phone doesn't work? Those Americans who speak Russian, appreciate Russian culture, have many Russian friends and are not terribly interested in consumer goods, adapt successfully. The rest are still apt to have a tough time.

A daily irritation can grow into a bane of the Americans' life in Russia. "I can't stand the way everyone makes your business their business," Mary C. exclaimed. "Some old lady is always frowning and pointing disapprovingly at your short skirt, or telling you to wear a hat in winter. It's my business, damn it!" During a visit home in Boston a young woman married to a Russian found herself telling a young mother in a supermarket that her child was not dressed warmly enough for a cold winter day. "At that point," she recounted the incident, "I realized how Russian I'd become. The American woman told me in no uncertain terms where to go!"

For all that, the transplanted Americans attest almost uniformly to the powerful emotional hold that the country and its people—to say nothing of their spouses—acquire over them. "I've never had such warm and intense relationships, with both men and women," said one such husband of his life. "It will be very hard to go back to cocktail party conversation after this." Upon their return to the United States the Americans often trade horror stories about the life they left behind, but they also tell of the magnetic attraction that pulls them back to Russia, hardships be damned.

At the outset of an intercultural romance, body language, gestures, and sexual attraction may serve as primary means of communication; but daily life requires speech. Language determines our reactions to the world around us, and Russian and English are vastly different linguistic systems.[33] As the anthropologist Edward Hall pointed out, "No two languages are alike; some are so dissimilar . . . that they force the speaker into two different images of reality."[34] For an American the word "lunch" may conjure up a ham and cheese sandwich, while for a Russian it points to a vegetable salad followed by soup, meat, potatoes and dessert.

Linguistic misunderstandings make for marital misunderstandings, and even the Russian and English ways of addressing one's spouse are markedly different. Since Russian makes heavy use of the diminutives of a name, Maria can become Masha, Mashenka, Mash, Marusia, or Musia. Attempts at doing something similar with English names produce condescending baby talk—"Marykins," or "baby Mary." An American has one word, "You," for everyone, stranger or intimate, while Russian has two—*ty*, implying intimacy or familiarity (as the French *tu* or German *Du*), and *vy*, which is reserved for the outside world (like the French *vous* and German *Sie*). "How can you make love to a girl and call her 'you'?" Sergei asked an American friend. "That's what you call the man who sells you gasoline." "I had so much trouble saying *ty* to Fyodor," Carol said. "In our textbooks and in Russian language class everyone always used *vy*. He was so upset when we'd been living together for several months and I'd still be saying *vy*."

Compared to the sharp rising and falling tones of Russian, American intonation patterns and gestures are extremely restrained. The rising pitch in a Russian question such as "Is this *your* wallet?" may sound to the American as if the spouse—who is making a perfectly reasonable inquiry—is angrily questioning the truthfulness of a statement. A flat and monotonous intonation in Russian, however, can lead to even greater misunderstandings. Sergei continually accused Muriel of giving him orders, because her American intonation made a question such as "Shall we go to the movies?" sound like "We're going to the movies!"

The spouse with better linguistic skills has more control over the couple's conversations and their relations with the outside world. Because Sergei relied on Muriel's excellent Russian and refused to make the effort to master English, she wound up becoming his interpreter, manager and secretary. Mark found that after Svetlana arrived his Russian improved so greatly that at first he did not pressure her to improve her English. And a spouse who wants to learn English may find that mastery of the language does not always come easily. Tamara Gilmore commented after her arrival in the US that "although I felt I was rapidly learning English, I still had great difficulty speaking and writing it. That continues to be true. Russians are supposed to be outstanding linguists. Not this one."[35]

The foreigner's problem can be compounded by a rejection of the new culture and fear of losing one's identity along with one's language. Even a person who emigrated as an adult can lose his native language after years of being constantly surrounded by foreign speech. After nearly fifty years in Russia, Anna Preikshas speaks better Russian than English.[36] Fyodor was so terrified of losing his Russian that, at first, he refused to speak English to Carol. He insisted on getting the Russian equivalents for such newly coined English terms such as "answering machine" or "food processor," not wishing to speak fractured Russian stuffed with English words. When speaking a foreign language a sophisticated intellectual can sound like a construction worker, and Sergei was hurt when a friend told him he sounded like a poet in Russian and a Mafia boss in English.

Trying to function from day to day in a stubbornly resistant foreign language can be highly frustrating, and listening to a spouse babbling in broken Russian or English can be grating on the nerves. It also can make for serious misunderstandings. Even for those who are fluent in the partner's language, stress can cause linguistic difficulties. Joanne Turnbull speaks excellent Russian, while Nikolai's English is relatively shaky. "At first we had all kinds of misunderstandings," she said. "Once while we were moving heavy pieces of furniture we got so upset we couldn't even get 'to the left' or 'to the right' straight in Russian or in English." Mark described how a rude salesgirl in Kiev who screamed at him while he was trying to buy a lamp reduced his fluent Russian to a first-grade level. A mature adult's reflexes, deepest thoughts and feelings are woven into the vocabulary, structure and syntax of his native language. As Eva Hoffman put it, "For a long time it was difficult to make these most intimate phrases, hard to make English—that language of will and abstraction—shape itself into the tonalities of love."[37]

When Lee Harvey Oswald arrived in Russia his Russian was so ungrammatical and strongly accented that people laughed at him, and when Marina corrected him he would get peeved.[38] When she arrived in America their roles were reversed. In a letter to her former colleagues at the pharmacy in Minsk, Marina wrote that she was mispronouncing American words.[39] Sergei always complimented Muriel on her excellent Russian during their courtship in Russia, but in America he took out his frustrations with English by complaining that her knowledge of his language was dreadful. During her first few years in Moscow, Paula Garb's language problems aggravated her already poor relationship with her Russian husband:

> My husband, who had learned fluent English at college, insisted I speak only Russian to him. I was crying out of frustration when he pretended not to understand my English. To say the least, it was bad for communication between people who understood each other so little as it was, but it certainly helped me learn Russian quickly.[40]

Tom Crane noted that his attitude towards the Russian language changed when he settled down in Moscow. "I feel more responsible for speaking Russian correctly," he said.[41] Identification with his wife and with her country led to identification with the language.

Constant exposure to a foreign language can lead to gaffes in your own. After spending two years in America, Pyotr's Russian was so full of English words that his cousin, who came to visit, kept interrupting him to ask what he meant. When Carol returned from a month-long trip to Russia with Fyodor she caught herself saying to an American friend "Let's sit in a taxi," instead of "Let's take a taxi," because she was translating the Russian expression literally into English. Evidently, in adapting to the spouse's culture, one can sometimes go too far!

FOR BETTER OR FOR WORSE

Passions and Psychobabble:
Roles and Sex

"Husband and wife are one Satan," goes a Russian proverb, meaning that spouses share everything with each other, including their attitudes towards life. This, however, has not been the experience of most Russian-American marriages. Differences in roles and expectations, common enough between spouses of the same culture, can become major sources of conflict when the couple comes from very different backgrounds.

Most wives in Russia wound up doing all the shopping, cooking, and cleaning. Margaret Wettlin resented it when her husband Andrei would not do the smallest things about the house, such as hang a picture or make himself some tea. To avoid constant flare-ups she hired a maid. "I did not want my love to be incinerated on such a paltry pyre," she wrote.[1]

Even if a Russian wife works, the man looks on himself as the breadwinner and on her as responsible for the housework and child care. A Russian journalist invited to an American colleague's home was taken aback, the American recounted, when his host made the drinks and barbecued steaks while the wife rattled on about her children. The Russian had his own report on the evening. "American men are under the thumbs of their wives. It was awful. I hardly had a word with the poor man. If this is women's liberation, I hope we don't get it here."[2]

No wonder so many Russian women see American men as knights in domestic armor. In his letters looking for a Russian bride, Weston Rogers emphasized that he intended to help keep the house clean and did not expect his wife to cook, as he liked eating out, and this must have sounded to the ladies like a promise of paradise.[3] Russian men, on the other hand, are thrown off by the unwillingness of "liberated" American women to take on the role of homemaker. One Russian complained that his American working wife's refusal to do housework made his apartment "empty and soulless." He was ready to take out the garbage, but not to make dinner or sweep the floor. "That's all stuff a woman should do."[4] Yet Russian men can learn to do it, too—especially, apparently, when they're still on Russian soil. Nikolai Formosov helps Joanne with shopping, cooking and caring for their daughter Anna, and Boris often drives by the stores on the way home from work to make shopping easier for Mary C.

Different concepts of intimacy can cause serious misunderstandings. Russians do not like to engage in detailed analysis of their feelings towards each other with their spouse or lover. Pyotr adamantly rejected Joyce's pleas to discuss their deteriorating relationship, or to entertain the notion of marriage counseling, and Gelsey Kirkland was infuriated by Baryshnikov's refusal to talk.

The American infatuation with "professional help" and "mental health" puts most Russians off. One Russian husband I know agreed to see a marriage counselor, but after two sessions he refused to go again, declaring that the psychologist was "on his wife's side." Russians believe that people should solve problems and conflicts on their own, or with help from friends. A Russian journalist was surprised by the widespread role of therapists in the United States:

Sooner or later, in any marriage, even in the most happy marriages, the spouses experience a period of spiritual disharmony.

Here Americans are no different from the rest of mankind. They differ in their approach to the problem. As a rule they do not allow it to be resolved on its own: they go to a psychologist, sexologist, or both at once. And I want to emphasize a specific trait—the aspiration of Americans to total candor. To unveil everything secret, to talk through everything.[5]

For Russians, true intimacy lies in the silence of a couple who understand each other by a look or a gesture. As Victor Ripp wrote, "The American habit of parading personal detail startles Russians. Our fascination with intimacies is more than bad taste; it suggests an utterly alien way of looking at life."[6] "Everyone has to have something that's secret, that's his or her own," Fyodor said to Carol. "If you really love each other you understand everything without words." As a matter of fact, the American penchant for self-analysis and "letting it all hang out" strikes Russians as mostly superficial: when it comes to a real opening up, Russians find Americans quite closed.

A subtler problem is the different attitude towards sex. The ambivalent American approach combines elements of Puritanism and Freudianism, while in the Soviet era the prevailing attitude blended the rigid moralism of the Russian Orthodox Church with the full force of government censorship.[7] After the initial revolutionary fervor, which proclaimed that making love was like drinking a glass of water, sex became a nonsubject. Books and other writings were pruned by the censorship of any references to what went on in the bedroom. Sexually titillating materials were banned as products of the decadent West, sex-related research was forbidden, and sexual permissiveness was seen as a form of political opposition.[8] Bodily functions were a taboo subject.

State control of the individual's behavior was intended to include control of sexual behavior, this "irrational, individualistic, capricious and spontaneous activity," as the sociologist Igor Kon wrote.[9] When things began loosening up, in the early 1960s a book about sex problems began by earnestly informing readers,

"There is a great difference between a man and a woman."[10] The taboo on talking about sex was so strong that in 1986 on a Donahue-Pozner television spacebridge, a middle-aged Russian woman made the sadly famous public announcement "We have no sex here!"[11] It is hardly surprising that when the Soviet system collapsed and censorship was ended a wave of hard-core pornography swept over the Russian popular press and newsstands.

The consequence of all this is a glaring contrast between a kind of puritanism that avoids the slightest mention of sex and a tolerance for obscene jokes and language that shocks even sophisticated Westerners. Ronald Hingley remarked that the other side of the puritan coin is the "Russian equivalent of locker room stories, which may be extremely amusing or which may alternatively descend to a level of obscenity and tastelessness almost passing belief." Igor Kon observed that "there has always been much more vulgarity in Russia than eroticism."[12] Whenever Pyotr announced with a smirk that he was about to tell a great Russian off-color joke Joyce cringed at the thought of how her American friends would react. Verbal reticence, however, does not mean a lack of sexual activity. A recent survey of sexual activity in fifteen countries shows Americans as the most active nationality, engaging in sex 135 times per year, with Russians in second place with 133 acts annually.[13]

The years of official silence on sex left Russian women extremely ignorant on the subject. Many had never tried anything except the missionary position, and found oral and anal sex disgusting. Abortion, coitus interruptus and tea leaves are the extent of many Russian women's knowledge about birth control. After the loss of population in World War II the postwar campaign to raise the birth rate led to a deliberate shortage of contraceptives, and to this day the most common means of birth control is abortion. In this Russia is still the world leader, for a Russian woman has seven to twelve abortions on the average.[14] Nor has there been a widespread campaign promoting condoms as a way of preventing the spread of AIDS and other sexually transmitted diseases.

Sergei threw the condom Muriel handed him into the waste-basket and told her furiously that things like that were "women's business," and that she should get herself some "paste" if she needed it. Contraception was her problem, he yelled. When Joyce told Pyotr that she was getting up from bed to insert her diaphragm he was shocked. "That female stuff—go do it and don't talk about it!" he snapped. He insisted that she always jump up and "wash" immediately after sex since, like many Russian men, he was convinced that "washing" was an effective means of contraception—and besides, he felt that after sex a woman was "dirty." Joyce would have much preferred to fall asleep in his arms, but he saw her reluctance as yet another proof of her poor hygiene.

Russian mothers rarely talk about sex or contraception to their daughters, and, even though most Russian doctors are women, many young women are too embarrassed to speak to them. Seventy per cent of Soviet women say they have never experienced orgasm.[15] Partly this is because many Russian men don't know, or don't care, what satisfies a woman, but another common reason is the fear of pregnancy and a widespread belief that female orgasm increases chances of conception. Moreover, the strains of work, family, household chores and standing in lines, along with the presence of in-laws or parents next door or behind a screen, do not make for relaxed lovemaking. Sergei was surprised to find how different Muriel was in bed once they were in America. "In Russia," he said, "she was so tense and nervous, waiting for me to get it over with. She was always afraid someone would walk in on us."

Privacy was hard to find in Russia. An unmarried couple could not check into a hotel, and apartments were crowded with parents, children and other relatives. Borrowing a friend's apartment or making nervous love in a park or hallway was not unusual. That, plus the weight of conservative mores, fear of the consequences of an affair with a foreigner, and logistic difficulties kept some Russian-American relationships platonic far longer than was customary in America. Julie Zapolskaya held off Tom Whitney for quite some time after they had started dating. In his memoir the American reporter recalled an evening when she had finally managed to get a friend's apartment:

> She looked at her watch.
> "Bozhe moi!" she exclaimed in Russian, "My heavens— It's midnight and you must be home before curfew."
> I stood up and she did likewise. We stood within a few inches of each other. Our lips almost touched. We were like this, for ten or fifteen minutes, and I started to put my arm around her. Julie stepped back just a bit.
> "Not now, Tomochka, not tonight . . . Not yet."[16]

The pressures of the war and its aftermath, and the dangers of harassment and surveillance added an extra element of excitement. Whitney recalled ducking into a doorway to get away from their tail: "We waited—a welcome chance to kiss in a dark stairwell— and then slipped out and went on our way."[17] Their relationship remained platonic until the evening she told him he could stay overnight at her apartment.

More than thirty years later, Susan Eisenhower experienced a similarly intense platonic involvement that slowly grew into a love affair. "It might seem surprising," she wrote of her romance with Roald Sagdeev, "that such serious discussions of marriage were going on in the 1980s, between two people who had a con-stantly chaperoned platonic relationship. More than once I mused that this was how it had been a century before, in an era when greater priority had been placed on knowing the person and the circumstances before jumping in with both feet."[18]

Once a relationship became sexual the availability of an empty room could put pressure on a couple to engage in sex whether or not they really felt like it. Nancy B. became involved with a Russian in the 1960s while she was on an exchange program studying Russian—discovering, as Erica Jong wrote in *Fear of Fifty*, "what so many American girls learned, that sex was better in a foreign tongue because guilt could be left at home."[19] "We felt we had to make love whenever we had a room to ourselves for an hour even if we were exhausted," Nancy said. "It was really weird after we were married, trying get into a normal pattern of behavior."

The couples also had to adjust to different kinds of behavior in bed. In Russia talking about sex—which many Americans take for granted—was for perverts and prostitutes.[20] This silence appears to have been a blessing for many American men, tired of being told what to do during every minute of lovemaking. Unless he were hurting her, a Russian would be horrified by his wife's telling him she did not like what he was doing, and would be even more shocked were she to tell him what he *should* do. Fyodor seemed to know more positions for sexual intercourse than the author of the Kama Sutra, and Carol had trouble adjusting to his silent sexual acrobatics, as he twisted her into a pretzel or flipped her over like a Russian pancake without a single word. One Muscovite whose marriage ended in divorce was repelled by his American wife's behavior. "She was unbelievably aggressive in bed," he recalled. "Always telling me what she liked and what she didn't, put my hand here and my tongue there, trying to program me as though I were a computer. And she never shut up. It was like being at a horizontal seminar, not like making love." "I think the most important part of sex is passion," said Sergei, expressing a sentiment with which most Russians agree. "The Americans are all rational, all brain and no heart." "You should feel as if you're being swept away by passion," Irina said. "There's no place for all this talk and 'now do this now do that' stuff." A young Russian wife had a fit of hysterics when her American husband calmly asked her if she would like to use a vibrator.[21] Efraim Savela, a Russian writer whose wife left him for an American, wrote that

America is a land of female psychopaths. Women get into bed with men almost on the point of tears, scared of not achieving orgasm (nor will they after that 220 volt vibrator). . . . A woman who is in a bad mood when she gets into bed with a man might well tell him it is his duty to "service" her.[22]

A woman who initiates sex is considered extremely forward. Fyodor was repulsed when Carol stroked his leg or showed she was interested in sex. "I kept thinking she must have had a lot of lovers to do things like that," he said. As Aksyonov has pointed out, the Russian language rejects the notion of an active sexual role for women:

> The female half of the erotic act has always been demeaned in Russia. Even lexically. In English you can say, "She fucked him," thereby acknowledging the woman's initiative. The equivalent in Russian sounds strange, almost ungrammatical. Yet Russian has no end of expressions to debase and defile women, slam them down spread-eagled under a mighty stud.[23]

It is the man who calls the shots. Even though Muriel had to get up early, Sergei insisted on having sex whenever he wanted, even at five in the morning after an all-night drinking bout. A man does not expect his initiatives to be rejected. "In the Russian tradition, my beloved should be happy and not resist, even if she's got a headache," one Muscovite said.

> As we Russians see it a woman, regardless of all her degrees or dissertations, is first and foremost a woman. And I expect a response to my caresses, a readiness to respond to my feelings. But when I try to arouse Mary I never can tell what her answer is going to be. She can just say "I'm not in the mood now." If I insist, she gets furious and says I'm insulting her. She wants an equal partnership with me . . . A Russian woman wouldn't behave like that. She'd see that she's wanted, that her guy is after her. That means he loves her. And that means she should respond. [24]

Despite this "chauvinist" attitude, Russians can seem very romantic to American women who have talked themselves hoarse about sex inside and outside the bedroom.[25] Aside from a whispered "Was it good for you?" or "Have you come?" punctuated by an occasional *milaya* (darling) or other similar brief endearment, even the most voluble Russians have little to say during sex. Igor Kon observed that apart from vulgar "men's language" there is no "erotic language" in Russian, and that the language barely has the linguistic tools with which to talk about sex. "Even married couples," writes Kon, "find themselves in terrible straits because they have no acceptable words to express their specific desires or explain their problems, even to each other."[26] "I thought she didn't love me," Mark said of Svetlana. "Out of bed she was cooing and lovey-dovey, 'sweetie, darling,' and all that stuff. But in bed— not a syllable." Svetlana was equally surprised by her American husband. "He's so concerned about how I feel," she marveled. "He keeps asking me if I'm all right and if I'm enjoying it. I never thought a man cared about that!"

Since Russian women have been brought up to think that displaying an interest in sex is indecent, many never dared say anything if a man ignored foreplay. Marina Oswald did not want to discuss sex with her husband, and was frightened when Lee told her intimate details of other people's sex lives. She begged him not to tell his friends about their lovemaking. Yet, she said, "The longer I lived with him the more I felt attracted to him." As opposed to Russian men, "He was willing to do anything at all to give me satisfaction."[27] After his death she resented being asked by American interviewers about their sex life. "Nobody asked Jacqueline Kennedy what Jack was like in bed."[28]

The former diplomat Arkady Shevchenko and the prostitute Judy Chavez were a vivid, if extreme example of the differences in Russian and American attitudes towards sex. The sophisticated call girl was amazed by the Russian's uptight attitude and verbal reserve:

He wasn't the kind who could say, "Wanna fuck, baby?" so I always had to read the signs. He was very repressed. When I tried to talk dirty to him to get him off sooner he didn't even understand. Andy was out of it to a degree I could hardly believe . . . It was always the same, from the same angle, and he didn't even want me to move. You could say get up on your knees, or let's try this, and he would just act stunned, like he didn't even know what you were talking about . . . Did you finish? That's what he called it. Finishing. Like it was something to get done. Lovers don't talk about finishing. And how could he ask me that? I hadn't even bothered to fake it. Sometimes I'd even push his hand down on his cock, but he couldn't do it. He was too inhibited.[29]

Actually, his single question was misunderstood, for, in Russian, the verb "to finish" means "to come." The contrast between silent Russian lovemaking and American orgasmic chatter led the émigré writer Aksyonov to comment that "American sex life knows no peace, only eternal flailing."[30]

Attitudes towards sexual fidelity also differ. In Russia, the shortage of men provides considerable opportunities for short and long-term affairs, and for Russian men infidelity is the rule rather than the exception.[31] An article in the Russian edition of *Cosmopolitan* magazine, addressed to its women readers, says sarcastically: "It's a man's privilege to spit in farewell, and to announce that you never understood that he is a genius and that you never could fry potatoes, while his new flame is wonderful at both."[32] Since men are at a premium, a wife may have to put up with her husband's having a permanent mistress and even an out-of-wedlock child. Such a "second family" is quite common, and a man is not criticized for it; in fact, he may be praised for keeping both women happy by not abandoning either of them. What will the wife gain by rushing off to seek a divorce? Having a husband—even a roving one—is better than being alone. Men will be men. But while it is fine for a Russian to be unfaithful to his wife, it is not acceptable for a woman to deceive her husband.

A Russian woman will not be criticized for leaving a husband who beats her or who is an inveterate drunkard, but male adultery is not assumed to be automatic grounds for the wife's walking out. When Tatiana Leshchenko-Sukhomilina returned to the United States following a three-month trip home to Russia in the 1920s, her American husband Ben informed her he had been unfaithful. "I started to cry," she said. But she did not rush to call a lawyer. "You're so charming and wonderful that I understand that everybody falls in love with you," she sobbed to her husband. "'Just don't let her dare to show herself to me.' Ben embraced me and I think started to love me even more."

A man is expected to be discrete, and to spare his wife's feelings by keeping his dalliances from her. The ideal of total honesty that is professed in many American marriages is alien to the Russian mentality. Muriel and Joyce were surprised that their Russian husbands did not tell them about their former girlfriends, and did not want to hear about their wives' previous experiences. "Those things are private," Sergei explained. "If you're married and you're attracted to someone else, you keep it to yourself. Otherwise you only hurt your spouse's feelings." Muriel's arguments about honesty got nowhere. "I'm not going to tell you what I do outside the house," Sergei retorted. "All this blathering Americans think is honesty only winds up offending everyone."

Perestroika and the collapse of the Soviet system have been rapidly changing Russian sexual behavior and attitudes. Pornography is legally available, premarital sex is common, sex is splashed all over the media, and sex education is slowly being introduced. The most striking changes are clearly visible in the behavior of the younger generation. Yet even modern young women are still bound by years of Soviet inhibitions. And even the best matched Russian-American couples may find sex a fertile ground for misunderstanding. The "universal language" of sex is perhaps not so universal after all.

Home, Sweet Home

❦

"I'm going off to my place," Sergei announced as he sat down at his desk in a corner of their tiny studio apartment and closed an invisible door between himself and Muriel. Accustomed, in Russia, to living in a two-room apartment with his parents, grandfather and sister, he was able to ignore Muriel's telephone conversations, the television and the clatter of pots and pans. "It's as though he builds an invisible wall around himself," Muriel said. "Their language doesn't even have a word for privacy, and in Russia there was so little of it that they simply create their personal space out of nothing."

For decades the Soviet housing squeeze forced newlyweds to live with the parents of one of the spouses. The tight quarters aggravated personality clashes, but there were some compensations. The arrangement provided a built-in baby-sitter and the mother or mother-in-law usually prepared meals and did much of the housework. In America a Russian bride is faced with running a household without such live-in help, while in Russia, American spouses have to cope with in-laws at far closer range than in the United States.

Americans do not give up their "personal space" lightly. Mary C. refused to have the living room in her St. Petersburg apartment double as a bedroom, and insisted on making the smaller room, which Boris wanted as a study, into the bedroom. "I'm not going to take the bedding off every morning and make the bed back up into a couch. The bedroom has to be separate." Though Boris agreed, so as to humor her, he did not really understand why she was so upset.

Finding decent housing was always a severe problem in Russia, and in 1990 there were still one and a quarter million people on the Moscow waiting list for new apartments.[1] One young woman gave the following description of her dream: "A happy marriage is when you love each other and have your own apartment."[2] Tom Whitney described the seven-year wait and interminable rounds of letters, memoranda, phone calls, vodka and cash bribes which finally got him and Julie a livable place of their own in a diplomatic compound. For Julie, "an apartment with at least a little bit of room," a properly functioning toilet, some furniture and a set of dishes was the height of bliss.[3] Marina Oswald's dream was to find "a man who had an apartment. That was the largest thing about marriage: your own apartment."[4] The Russian women to whom Weston Rogers wrote must have wondered what on earth he meant when he described his 1400 square foot, two-bedroom, two bathroom apartment—with a living room, billiard room, dining room and kitchen—as not big.[5]

Yet moving to the United States, with its availability of housing, can lead to complications of another kind. Many Russians don't understand why two people, even if they plan to have children, would need four or six rooms. On the other hand, owning a house has long been such an unattainable dream that Russians may rush to purchase without carefully investigating the real estate market. One Russian engineer fell in love with a New Jersey house because its porch and the trees in the garden reminded him of his Moscow dacha. Although the foundation was cracked and the plumbing would have to be replaced, he insisted that his American wife buy it, and the repair work nearly bankrupted them. Gelsey Kirkland found Baryshnikov's austerely furnished country house heavy, dark and oppressive, but he loved the place because it reminded him of Russia.[6] The Oswalds' first house in America was shabbily furnished and decrepit, but Marina was enchanted by the privacy and space.[7] Even a woman as sophisticated as Raissa Gorbachev was amazed by the spaciousness of the home of the American family with whom she had tea during her visit to the United States, and by the fact that each of the four children had his own bedroom.[8]

When everything is available, Russians can become incredibly demanding. Nothing but the best will do. A new house or apartment is treated as a home for life, for in Russia if you were lucky enough to find a nice place to live, moving again was furthest from your thoughts. When Carol and Fyodor wanted to buy an apartment they saw at least eighty places before Fyodor was satisfied. The rooms were too small or the lobby was unattractive, or there was no view.

When it comes to wallpaper, furniture, and china, the Russian spouse is likely to opt for the most colorful, extravagant, and expensive items. For a miniscule studio apartment Sergei insisted on a king-size bed.

The memory of hundreds of virtually identical Soviet interiors is engraved on Russians' minds. The standard set of glossy dark wood furniture, a couch doubling as a bed, a rug hanging on the wall, glass-enclosed bookcases, a large television set and a sideboard with china and crystal—all this is transferred like a decal to the new American home. Svetlana could not imagine doing without a hall with a large mirror for the ritual hair-combing that takes place the minute a Russian enters, or a rack for the boots and shoes that are exchanged for slippers when coming in from snowy streets. Irina wanted a leopard-pattern rug and curtains which reminded Fred of a movie set for *The Godfather*. He did not see why she insisted on a sideboard. "Everyone knows we have china," he protested, "and ours isn't even that good. It belongs in a kitchen cabinet." As Aksyonov wrote,

> Apartment hunting brings home the duality of émigré existence—you want something that reminds you of your former life yet something you did not have—could not have had—in that life.[9]

Judy Chavez was surprised how fussy Shevchenko was about the pillows, blankets, and kitchen utensils he bought for his apartment, considering that these quarters were rented for him by the FBI for a stay of only a few months.[10] She recalled that he could be terribly indecisive. "He could spend half an hour with two pots in his hand and not be able to decide which one to buy. Then as likely as not he would put them both back . . . and walk away."[11]

In the United States the couples' homes are apt to be an uneasy mix of flashy items bought by color-starved Russians and leftovers from the American spouse's previous house; in Russia the standard furnishings may be enlivened by an American (or more likely Japanese) stereo system and coffee tables, lamps and paintings brought over from America. "Mary keeps saying Russian furniture is gloomy," Boris complained. "But I don't really like that rug that looks as if it's from the Museum of Modern Art." "I didn't want the place to look like a Russian souvenir store," Joyce recalled. "Pyotr had all these clumsy wooden figures and nesting dolls, and cheap reproductions of Impressionist landscapes. I managed to stash some of them in the closet." Setting up a house that blends two personalities from different cultures is a challenge demanding a good deal of time, effort and compromise.

Looks and Manners

W̶hen Nancy Reagan met Raissa Gorbachev she found her spike heels and black velvet skirt thoroughly inappropriate for lunch and "a little déclassé." Nor did she approve of the silver fox fur and high-heeled suede boots the Russian leader's wife wore at the Reykjavik summit, or the satin-collar black crepe dress, rhinestone belt buckle, rhinestone-studded stockings and black high heels which she flaunted on the state visit to the White House.[1] Mrs. Reagan was equally critical of Mrs. Gorbachev's crudely tinted reddish hair and her endless harangues, her "damned monologue," as she called it.[2]

Fashion in Soviet Russia was long subject to the dictates of the Soviet regime, and strict adherence to proletarian clothing, manners and etiquette was firmly enforced. Colorful Western fashions were labeled bourgeois and decadent. Small wonder that when the regime began to crumble the long-suppressed hunger for color and style burst out in forms that often seemed *outré* in the West. The impact on Russian-American marriages has been pronounced.

Masha Scott described her mixed feelings about her first Western clothes:

> Everything became so gay and happy that I said I would have a silk dress. So I ordered Paris styles, wide sleeves and so on—beautiful dresses . . . But I felt not so comfortable. I was chic but at first I felt those dresses not necessary. What for? I asked myself this. I always had skirts and blouses and some simple dresses, and in a silk dress I felt as if you put a saddle on a cow. I felt it was something nonsense. But, after a while, later, I liked the dresses. If we went to a party I put on a nice dress and then I felt it pleasant.[3]

Like Masha and most Russian women, Irina was used to having most of her clothes made by a seamstress. She was surprised that in America only the wealthy had clothes made to order and that even affluent people bought off the rack.

The Russian wives thoroughly enjoyed their new access to chic apparel in America. When Fred complained that Irina ran up huge credit card bills on shopping sprees she protested that she had left her country for him, hadn't she? Didn't he want her to look pretty for his family and friends? Jo Durden-Smith wrote that "the worst ordeal that any Westerner . . . had to endure when dealing with a Soviet was trial by shopping."[4]

And what was attractive to one of the parties could be seen as overdone by the other. Pyotr insisted on wearing suede jackets with fabric inserts in the front. Irina had a taste for tight knitted jerseys, gold lamé blouses and high leather boots, making her look rather odd at American dinner parties. Tina Anderson recalled how starved she was for color when she left Russia in the early 1960s. "When Ray wanted me to wear a little black dress with pearls I thought he was being stingy. I wanted color. I was like a child who had seen the world in shades of gray and had never seen the rainbow. My total disorientation in America included color and clothes."

Customs brought over from the old country hang on. Sergei wanted Muriel to go to the opera in the suits she wore to the office, which would have been appropriate in Russia. Carol could not make Fyodor wear a tie—which, like so many Russian men, he detested—to anything other than a wedding or a funeral. Even when the Russian spouse was eager to adapt to American dress codes, the result could strike the American partners as all wrong. Once Fyodor had decided that it was the American thing to wear jeans, he wore them to the office, to the theater—everywhere, protesting when Carol suggested he put on something else for a friend's birthday party. In Russia men often wear boxer shorts and tank top undershirts at home, but Carol could not stand Fyodor's sitting around the house in his underwear. "I have a right to be comfortable at home," Fyodor argued. "But *I* don't sit around in my underwear," Carol remonstrated. "Of course not," Fyodor replied. "You're a woman, and you have to look pretty. A man has to relax." Many American wives were surprised to discover that undershirts and boxer shorts doubled for their husbands as night clothes, since men's pajamas are virtually nonexistent in Russia.

Nor do most Russian men use deodorant or change their underwear. Judy Chavez complained that because of the "crazy idea that water made your hair fall out," Shevchenko washed his hair only once every nine days. (When she refused to run her fingers through his greasy hair he "Americanized" and started shampooing daily).[5] Several Russian women commented that they had originally been attracted to their American spouses because they were so incredibly "clean" compared to Russians. When she first met him, Marina was impressed by Lee Oswald's constant bathing.[6]

While Russian men may be remiss on hygiene and pay little attention to clothes, the women spend hours primping in front of the mirror, styling their hair and freshening their makeup. "It takes Svetlana two hours to get dressed to go to the grocery store," Mark complained. "Just think what it's like when we're invited to dinner." Joyce disliked the way the Russian wives of Pyotr's friends constantly criticized her hairdo, suggested a different lipstick color and talked for hours about where to find the best bargains in clothes. "I couldn't stand them always combing my hair and adjusting my collar," she said. "It was like Mommy getting you ready for school when you were six years old."

In the Soviet era trying to look attractive and feminine was not easy. Obtaining fashionable clothes was both incredibly difficult and incredibly important, and Americans were often amazed by the time and energy that educated Russian women devoted to rounding up western clothes and makeup. Francine du Plessix Gray remarked on how this intense interest in an

> impeccable, coquettish appearance has little or nothing to do with narcissism; that it is more akin to the compulsive

grooming instinct of a healthy bird or cat; that it may be the only way of cheering the uniform drabness of Soviet life, and establishing a status in its complex hierarchy.[7]

Looking good was a way of asserting control over oneself, and over life in a controlled and drab Soviet society. As one Russian woman asked,

> How are you going to keep up your morale if you work all day long and have a family and no mother to help out at home, and your combined work load is sixteen hours? Your only way not to fall apart is to put on your prettiest things every single morning of your life.[8]

Today much has changed, but high prices mean that many Russians still have relatively few clothes. Laundry and dry cleaning facilities are still poor, expensive and inconveniently located, and Americans are often surprised to see their Russian business associates wearing the same clothes day after day. These clothes are patched and repatched until they fall apart. Joyce had to throw out a threadbare shirt behind Pyotr's back because he refused to part with the disintegrating fabric. He still had clothes from his university days, and thought it was extravagant of Joyce to buy new clothes every season and to throw out things that were out of fashion. When the laundry lost an old and ragged undershirt, Pyotr was convinced that this cherished piece of clothing had been deliberately stolen.

Anne, a young American woman who lived with her Russian husband in Moscow in the 1980s, had a different problem. To avoid arousing the jealousy of her Russian women friends, she wore her oldest clothes and had two outfits sewn for her by a Russian seamstress. Actually, her Russian friends' reaction was quite the opposite. Did she have no taste or was the couple having money problems? they wondered. What kind of American woman walked around in baggy print dresses? Today Anne does not bother to dress down, since so many young Muscovites are wearing foreign fashions. "Before," commented a Moscow boutique owner, "if a woman dressed well, it meant that she was an airhead; it meant she spent all her time just putting herself together. Now it means that she is efficient and businesslike."[9]

While Russians still feel they are lagging behind in the world of fashion, they often find American women badly dressed. "With all the stores bursting with clothes, they run around in torn jeans and T-shirts with those silly advertisements on them!" Svetlana exclaimed. "I don't understand them." Mary C., while living in Moscow, felt that Russian women were sometimes better dressed than she was.

Regardless of the pressures of housework, jobs and standing in line, Russian men expect their wives to be well groomed, their hair perfectly set, their nails manicured and polished. "You'd think we were going to a fancy dress ball when we're going to a neighborhood movie," Joyce lamented. "Pyotr won't go out until he likes the way I look, and he always finds something wrong—my skirt's too short, my blouse is wrinkled, or there's a run in my panty hose. Meanwhile he wears jeans and the same damn T-shirt he bought three years ago." "My T-shirt and jeans are always clean," Pyotr retorted. "Besides, I'm a man, so I don't have to worry about things like that. All you American females yapping about liberation, always in a rush—you look as if you came off the garbage heap! No wonder you couldn't find an American husband!"

One of the couple's stormiest scenes occurred after Joyce had gone to work for an entire week wearing a down coat with a button missing. At 2 A.M. one night, after an argument about her messy hair and the messy apartment, Pyotr exploded. "How many times have I told you to sew on that button? You're a married woman, and you look like a whore off the street!" Trembling with rage, Joyce jumped out of bed, grabbed the offending coat and threw it out of the tenth-floor window. Pyotr pulled on a pair of pants, rushed down the stairs and retrieved it. In Russia a down coat could be worn for life.

Fyodor could not understand why Carol refused to paint her toenails bright red the way many Russian women do. "It makes me look like a whore," she said. Sergei and Pyotr disliked their wives' habits of kicking off their shoes, walking around barefoot, and sitting on the floor. Aside from being "unaesthetic," walking barefoot meant catching cold, and sitting on the floor was guaranteed to produce all kinds of feminine pelvic problems alluded to in somber whispers.

Manners are another potential mine field.[10] Marina and her friends were much taken with Lee Harvey Oswald's behavior. "My aunt liked his modesty and politeness, also the fact that he was very neat," she wrote.[11] His coworkers, however, were not impressed by his habit of putting his feet up on the desk.

And it can cut the other way around. Russians of the older generation, or who have not had much contact with the West may do things at table that strike Americans as unmannerly. Pyotr speared and ate potatoes and peas off the end of a sharp knife. He never put a plate under a soup dish or used a place mat. Sergei ate cottage cheese straight out of the container, and Irina took pickles from the jar with her fork rather than placing them on a dish.

At dinner the Russians did not wait for the hostess to start eating before diving in. At first Muriel was too embarrassed to say anything, but her friends' puzzled glances prompted her to talk to Sergei. "You dare to tell us, a thousand-year-old culture, how to behave," he sniffed. "In a country where women sit on the floor and people walk around the street dirty and barefoot." But the next time they were invited he ate the potatoes with a fork and waited for the hostess to begin before starting to eat.

Their American friends found Sergei and Pyotr rude because they hardly ever said "please" and "thank you." In Russian, polite requests are expressed primarily through a rise and fall in intonation, or through expressions such as "be so kind." Sergei was very polite in Russian, but "Give me this" or "Pass the bread" sounded extremely rude to Muriel's American friends. Nor do Russians use a pen to say thank you. One Russian bride had to be pushed by her American mother-in-law to write thank you notes for the wedding gifts. "Russians don't write them," she said in exasperation.[12]

Fyodor was offended when people he had just met addressed him by his first name. So were Boris's Russian friends when Mary C. addressed them by their first names instead of by the first name and patronymic. "I can't remember everybody's father's name!" she wailed. "It's hard enough remembering all the first names in this impossible language!"

Gestures and body language can also cause misunderstandings. For an American a smile on being introduced signals pleasure at making a new acquaintance, and a willingness to engage in conversation. Russians do not smile on meeting people. When Carol first introduced Fyodor to scientists who could be professionally helpful, his face was locked in a scowl. "Why should I smile at someone I don't know?" he asked her. "I'm not a clown. If I'm ready for a serious conversation I have to look serious." In Russia a smile on meeting a stranger may be interpreted as a sign that the person is not serious about the upcoming talk, or that he has a hidden agenda under a superficial and hypocritical smile. Carol explained to Fyodor that his refusal to smile made colleagues think he was being cold and unfriendly. As an American professor of Russian observed, Russians are accustomed to using an unsmiling expression as a barrier between themselves and the outside world:

> The Russians' lack of personal space at home in their apartments, on public transportation or on the job causes them to erect their personal space boundaries next to their skin. Therefore it is common for Russians to have deadpan or frozen expressions on their faces. We tend to perceive this as unfriendly and it may ruffle our feathers.[13]

Russians tend to gesture far more than Americans. Muriel thought Sergei was upset when he waved his arm or hammered his fist on the table, but this was merely nonverbal punctuation. Pyotr's habit of shaking his index finger at her, as though scolding a naughty child, infuriated Joyce. "Cut it out and stop lecturing me!" she snapped. "I'm not lecturing you," he protested, surprised. "I'm just saying be sure you lock the door when you leave."

Muriel had to explain to her girlfriends that when Sergei moved very close to them during a conversation, he was not making passes. He would stand eight inches away, much closer than the distance at which Americans feel comfortable: it's the Russian way. Nor was he trying to look soulfully and romantically into their eyes. Russians are in the habit of looking directly and unblinkingly at the person they are addressing. Fred had to tell Irina not to "stare" at his American friends, who were uncomfortable when she concentrated her gaze on them. Body language situations are particularly tricky because the problem remains unstated; the American does not say "You're standing so close I feel uncomfortable," and a Russian does not ask "Why are you looking away from me?"

On meeting and parting there is far more embracing, kissing and holding hands among Russians than among Americans. Carol explained to her girlfriend that Fyodor was not trying to flirt when he took her arm while escorting her to a cab after dinner; he was being a gentleman. She, in turn, could not get used to the way the Russian wives of her American friends took her arm in the street. Sergei learned not to embrace or kiss American men on meeting or parting, a friendly Russian gesture which can be drastically misinterpreted by American men.

Then there are differences in conversational style. Russians tend to talk in lengthy, uninterrupted monologues, and find the American style of short answers and repartee brusque and rude. Americans normally talk about their activities and experiences— what they have done, where they have gone, whom they have seen. For Russians, anything and everything is grist for the mill: people, ideas, politics, books, movies. "They can even analyze a borshch," Muriel commented, "as though it were a theoretical problem, like the existence of God."

When answering a question, Americans get straight to the point. Russians tend to go back to the beginning of time. "Every time someone asks Fyodor how he likes America, all he has to do is say 'fine,'" Carol sighed. "Instead out comes a doctoral thesis on the history of the United States and what's wrong with the country." "When my aunt asked Pyotr how his mother was, he gave her the woman's entire medical history," Joyce said. The Russian feels it is discourteous to give a short answer. The American resents being held captive to a long monologue. Americans feel that simplicity and brevity are the soul of wit and wisdom. For Russians, a valuable idea is a complex idea.

Muriel phoned a friend for some information and spent only a minute or two on pleasantries before getting down to business. In Moscow there would first have been a long conversation about the family, the weather, and so on. Starting off with a request, or responding with "What can I do for you?" would be rude.

Susan Eisenhower recalled her impatience when a member of the Central Committee, Nikolai Shishlin, came to see her and Roald Sagdeev the evening the couple intended to tell him about their marriage plans, and to sound him out about possible reactions in Soviet government circles. They knew that Shishlin was in a hurry, and, as Susan wrote, "The shortness of time was made worse by the fact that Roald couldn't seem to get to the main subject. Not until Shishlin said he had to go did Roald finally get to the point."[14] Sagdeev's behavior, of course, was deliberate. While Susan sat nervously on the edge of her chair, Sagdeev understood that putting the question earlier would have been counterproductive, as it would have contravened the unwritten rules of Russian behavior.

To American spouses and friends, the endless Russian stories that are a staple of Russian get-togethers can be boring and pompous. Americans like to save time and get to the point. The Russian prefers to go around in circles, lacing his speech with literary, mythological or historical allusions. As the cultural anthropologist Edward Hall noted, "Americans are often uncomfortable with indirectness . . . Most Americans keep their social conversations light, rather than engaging in serious, intellectual or philosophical discussions, a trait which especially bothers Europeans."[15] "I'm wasting my time with your friends," Sergei grumbled at Muriel. "I keep trying to tell them something interesting, and they sit there fidgeting and interrupting."

Years of living in fear of the secret police make Russians hesitant to state their ideas explicitly, and they often seek a veiled or subtle way of conveying a thought. If the listener is intelligent, he should understand what is meant, and it is insulting to spoonfeed him. For the American, speaking intelligently means speaking directly and clearly. "I feel like they're talking in code," Joyce complained of Pyotr and his friends. "Why can't they just say what they mean?" Many Russians see their mates as childish and unsophisticated.[16] "I can see my American friends' eyes glaze over when Sergei gets going on one of his half-hour philosophical diatribes," Muriel said. "That just convinces him even more of how superior he and his friends are to all of us."

The well-known American psycholinguist Deborah Tannen wrote that:

> I would wager that the much-publicized antipathy between Nancy Reagan and Raissa Gorbachev resulted from cultural differences in conversational style. According to Nancy Reagan, "From the moment we met, she talked and talked and talked—so much that I could barely get a word in, edgewise or otherwise." I suspect that if anyone asked Raissa Gorbachev, she would say she'd been wondering why her American counterpart never said anything and made her do all the conversational work.[17]

Barbara Bush was close to the truth when she wrote of Raissa's asking why Nancy Reagan didn't like her. "She almost answered her own question, by saying that she did not know our customs and was trying to learn. She did dominate the conversation, but maybe she thought that was what she was supposed to do."[18] She thought it was her duty to "entertain" the American First Lady. That is precisely the kind of failure of communication that ordinary Russian-American couples experience day after day.

Two Kinds of Time

◦ೋ✣ೋ◦

"Tamara was not on time for that first date, and now, after ten years of being married to her, I can say she's never been on time on any single occasion since then," wrote Eddy Gilmore.[1] When Sergei had a doctor's appointment at 3:00 he would show up at 3:30. When he and Muriel were invited for dinner at 7:30 she would tell him they were due at 6:30, and they would get there by 7:45. When they missed a bus from New York to Philadelphia there was another Greyhound an hour later, but when their plane to London had to be held for them at the gate at Kennedy airport, Muriel was beside herself. Joyce, Mark and Fred all had similar stories to tell.

Being late seems to be part of the Russian makeup. The anthropologist Edward Hall has described two types of time, monochronous and polychronous, each true for one culture but not for another. The United States goes by monochronous time, meaning that an American gives his undivided attention to one event before proceeding to the next. He takes deadlines seriously, values promptness, and attaches importance to short-term relationships. Russians basically live in polychronous time, in which a person deals simultaneously with multiple events and is very flexible about appointments. He is always ready to change his schedule at a moment's notice to accommodate a friend or relative, since he attaches more importance to long-term relationships than to short-term ones.[2]

Muriel would make lunch appointments with magazine editors three weeks ahead. Sergei would call up a busy executive in the morning hoping to see him that afternoon. Who knew what might happen three weeks hence? Fyodor thought it was ridiculous for Carol to invite guests to dinner two weeks in advance; Carol found it odd when his Russian friends called up late Friday night to invite them to dinner the next evening. As Ronald Hingley observed, "To the excessively time-geared Westerner, Russia still seems to operate in an atmosphere relatively emancipated from the clock."[3] Fyodor hardly ever wore a watch unless Carol reminded him that he had a very important appointment. He canceled a promising job interview because his best friend from Russia, whom he had been seeing almost every day during the man's month-long visit to America, called up that morning and said he needed to talk. If a friend or family member needs something, appointments and business commitments go by the board. Such an attitude does not go over well in American offices. Fyodor's boss threatened to fire him because of his chronic tardiness, and only an alarm clock set forty-five minutes ahead forced him to change his behavior.

Americans naturally quantify time. They will meet a friend in ten minutes, finish a project in five months, and apologize if they are more than five minutes late.[4] The Russian concept of time is porous. Joyce finally figured out that when Pyotr said "I'll be ready in an hour" he meant two hours; "in twenty minutes" translated into forty-five; "right away" or "immediately" meant in fifteen minutes. The vagueness of Russian time expressions can drive American spouses crazy. "He'll come during the second half of the day" means anytime between 1 P.M. and 6 P.M., while "around seven o'clock" covers the period from 6:10 to 7:50.

This elasticity also applies to the telephone. After marrying Irina, Fred got a second phone line because her calls to her Russian friends averaged one and a half hours and his business associates could not get through. Call waiting was no solution, as Irina refused to interrupt a conversation for any reason whatever. "If they could," Carol said, "the Russians would canonize Alexander Graham Bell."

For Russians, the telephone is sacred. If a friend calls, the fact that dinner is ready, guests are ringing the bell, or the plane is leaving take second place. When Joyce protested that dinner would be ruined, Pyotr would bring the phone to the table and go on talking between bites. During a Russian spouse's first years of life in America, talking to other Russians is a comforting retreat. "The Russians talk for hours and at all hours," Susan Eisenhower mused. "And why do they call so late?"[5]

To Russians, Americans seem time-obsessed. In English, they note, the expression is to "spend" time, as if it were money to be saved or squandered, while Russians can only talk of "passing" the time. Americans are forever seeking devices to economize on time spent working, shopping, cooking and cleaning. "I try to keep the nonsense stuff and housework to a minimum," said Joyce. "But Pyotr can sit for three hours writing a letter to a friend about what's wrong with America in general, and with American women in particular, while business mail goes unanswered." "Time is money" is alien to Russian thinking.

In the Soviet period one of the few ways of defying the regime with impunity was by refusing to follow its schedules. Showing up late for work made no difference in terms of salary, and was not regarded as grounds for disciplining. A young American who was hired as an English-language research assistant at an Academy of Sciences institute discovered that if she showed up on time at 9 A.M. the only people to talk to were the guard at the door and the coatroom attendant. Being late was a way of showing contempt for the system and of asserting the self—and of squeezing in some shopping and errands as well. The social and political roots of this chronic tardiness are not much consolation, however, to the American spouse when the couple is an hour late for dinner at the boss's house.

Margaret Wettlin found that "Russians find the importance of punctuality greatly exaggerated. Russians look upon appointments as guidelines rather than anchor chains. Applied to dinner engagements, this is exasperating for the hostess, as I have experienced more than once; as applied to business, it is disastrous."[6] Joanne Turnbull was so used to her Russian guests being late that at 7:30 one evening she was still in her bathrobe when the Americans she had invited to dinner showed up precisely on time.

At eight one evening Sergei went out into the New York night for a drink with a friend, telling Muriel he'd be back in an hour. When he returned at five A.M. she was hysterical. Sergei did not understand why she had been calling the police. "You knew I was with Oleg. What's the big fuss for a couple of hours?" An extra hour—or four or five—made no difference to his elastic sense of time. "Why didn't you call?" Muriel wailed. "I didn't want to wake you," he said. "What are we—small children who have to be back home to mama by nine o'clock?"

Fyodor and Carol invited two American couples for dinner. Earlier that afternoon a Russian friend dropped by for a drink. Forty minutes before the dinner guests were expected Fyodor took his friend to the bus stop; he was away for two hours. "Guess I was a bit delayed," he said, as Carol clenched her teeth trying not to scream at him in front of their hungry guests, whom she had been entertaining with Scotch and peanuts while glancing nervously at her watch. "There was something personal Igor wanted to talk about," he explained to Carol. "Between men. Things he didn't want to say in front of you." As long as Russians are dealing with other Russians, their clocks are beautifully synchronized. But in the monochronous United States, Russian time is badly out of joint. In post-*perestroika* Russia, however, attitudes are changing as people discover that making money means maximum use of time. Dick G.'s clients now arrive during business hours to get their video tapes instead of banging on his door late at night. And Nikolai Formosov has gotten so used to Joanne's punctuality, and the punctuality of their American friends, that Russian lateness now annoys him more than her.

On the Job

He who does not work does not eat, said the Marxist slogan. It is not easy to find a job, let alone a good one, while adapting to a new country and language. "Why should I write a C.V. about myself?" Irina asked Fred. "Putting down all my previous jobs, where I went to school, languages I know—that's boasting. If you just bothered to tell Professor Jackman about me—and you know him so well—I'm sure he'd get me an assistantship teaching Russian a few hours a week!"

In the Soviet Union you relied on the government to find you a job; résumés and job interviews were alien to the Soviet mentality. Even today Russians tend to assume that jobs are obtained through personal connections, and that skills play a secondary role. Fyodor expected Carol to make phone calls on his behalf to companies where he was applying for a job. Carol tried to explain that this would only work against him, since the laboratory heads would think he couldn't speak English or was incompetent, but all she got were accusations that she didn't care about him and was too busy with her own work. When a Russian is given a number to call—someone who might be of professional help—the answer tends to be, "That's awkward." Fred and Irina had furious fights when he suggested that she make these calls herself. "How can I call someone I don't know?" she said.

In Russia about 90% of all women are employed. Coming to the United States, some Russian wives get bored being without a job for the first time in their lives. Svetlana, who had taught music in Russia, got tired of watching television, reading magazines to improve her English, and having coffee with neighbors.[1] She started giving Russian lessons, and spent hours in a university library doing research for articles on Russian music for scholarly publications. Once her children were in school Tina Anderson thought she would die of boredom sitting home in her suburban house while Ray was at work at the *New York Times*, and he encouraged her desire to start a new career as a conference interpreter. "He thought I was better off going to work than going crazy."

For American spouses living in Russia, job opportunities have expanded far beyond those days in the past when the only kind of work available was English-language typing, editing or radio broadcasting, or doing translating at a few publishing houses such as *Progress* or *Novosti*. That work was frustrating, at best. "I kept trying to translate Soviet articles into normal English," Anne said of her stint with one such publisher. "But the editor kept changing things back to clumsy Marxist jargon. When I'd say that nobody would say 'the worker joyfully went off to his place of work in the morning,' the editor snapped, 'That's the way we say it!'" In the 1990s the mushrooming of foreign firms, foundations, government organizations, magazines and newspapers have provided a fertile field for varied jobs. Robert Coalson, the former Cornell University scholar of Russian literature, is now a journalist; Paul Kindlon, a former actor and teacher, is a college administrator; Steve Gutterman, a former student of Russian, works for United Press International. These Americans married to Russians say frankly that their jobs in Moscow are better than anything they could hope for in the United States.

Americans raised with the work ethic grow up knowing they will have to find a job to support themselves and their families. For Russians under the Soviet regime the idea was to get away with as little work as possible. Salaries had ceilings, there was no real threat of being fired, and working harder merely led to more work. The only workaholics were career-minded bureaucrats or ivory-tower scholars. Fyodor regularly took days off on the pretext of illness or urgent family business. For a Russian intellectual the worst possible fate was a nine-to-five job. One Russian history professor who married an American and moved to the United States could not believe that the American university that hired him expected him to see his students and serve on committees, even on days when he did not teach class.

For women in the Soviet Union the workplace was a place to chat, sell each other clothes, exchange tips on where to get things like shoes and coats, and organize shopping lists so that one woman could go out and buy things for all of them while they did a little work.

Pyotr kept telling Joyce how hard he had worked in Russia as a dentist, when, in fact, he used to spend much of the day chatting with the nurses. Whenever he had a hangover, which was rather frequently, Sergei did not go to his Moscow studio to sculpt. Such easygoing behavior goes back to the 1930s. Zara Witkin recalled his visit in 1932 to a broken-down agricultural machinery plant in Rostov:

> The woman guide conducting us through the plant had married an American engineer. He was chief inspector of the plant. Apparently he had succumbed to Russian habits. Instead of being at the end of the production line, checking machines, we found him in the office. Comfortably propped up in his chair, he told us about many of the conditions of the plant, in a guarded fashion. Occasionally his wife stopped him when he came too near the real causes of the confusion we had seen.[2]

Paula Garb recalled how she and her American coworkers earned the resentment of their Russian colleagues in publishing houses whenever they worked long hours or took work home.[3]

These habits often survive emigration to the United States. When Muriel got a job with a scientific publishing house, Sergei made it hard for her to go to work on time, keeping her up late into the night talking and drinking with him and his Russian friends. After several weeks of being late she lost the job—on which they were wholly dependent. This, of course, only served to confirm Sergei's stereotypes about materialistic America.

Today in Russia's private sector hard work pays off, and the Western firms that have set up shop in Moscow expect Western-style dedication to the job. Younger Russians married to Americans have a much more positive attitude toward work and are eager to "make it." Boris, the television journalist married to Mary C., spends long hours driving all over St. Petersburg covering news stories, and brings home an overstuffed briefcase every night. "He and his friends are turning into real American-style businessmen," Mary C. said. With the advent of Russian capitalism the younger Russian and American spouses' attitude toward work is rapidly becoming increasingly similar.

Dollars and Rubles

Right from the beginning, money—the rustling of the bills, and the jingling of the coins—settles comfortably in the corner of that which we call our soul. Bit by bit it drives out friendship, love, family ties. Why does that happen? How does it happen to us, such friendly, kind, noble, good people?[1]

These questions were asked by a Russian woman married to an American. Before *perestroika* most Russians never gave much thought to money, for under the Soviet regime salaries and what there was to buy were limited. Today, however, shops are filled with expensive goods and money is the key to food, clothing, housing and the good life.

Coping with the way Americans handle money is a difficult task for a Russian spouse. As late as 1994 a Muscovite girl broke up with her American boyfriend because she thought he was too greedy and concerned about money.[2] Aksyonov commented on how money matters were totally confusing to newly arrived Russians, since personal finances had not changed much since the days of the Mongol invasion.[3] Even today, checking accounts are virtually unknown and credit credit cards are not widely used.

Sergei, Irina and Fyodor arrived in America with less than fifty dollars in their pockets, and had to rely on their American spouses for cash for all their daily expenses. Such dependence put a strain on the marriage. "I felt like a child being handed its allowance," Fyodor said. "Even though Carol was very nice about the financial situation, and was always asking me if I needed anything, I kept my spending to a minimum until I started earning my own money. It was tough."

Couples who met during the American's trip to Russia or the Russian's trip to America did not see their mate in a work situation, and often got a distorted picture of their partner's finances. "I thought that if Carol could afford a trip to Russia she must be very well off," Fyodor admitted. He was surprised to discover that her salary as a university instructor barely covered the rent.

An article in the Russian edition of *Cosmopolitan* magazine warned Russian women against spending too much of their American husbands' money. "Many of our girls were poor as children, and then lived in dormitories," wrote the Russian journalist. "Once they get to civilized conditions, they simply lose their heads. One American told me that a Russian wife is a very expensive proposition. You have to pay for her English language courses, her driving courses, she has to be dressed from head to toe."[4]

Many Russians spouses had always dreamed of buying a house and were all too willing to take on mortgages, sometimes larger than they and their American partners could cope with. Once Svetlana and Mark had taken out a mortgage, however, she worried over every cent, hesitating to buy an ice cream cone because "we owe $100,000 dollars." She insisted that they pay off the loan as fast as possible, refusing to go on vacation or to buy new clothes to avoid giving the "robber banks" any more interest than was absolutely necessary.

In the Soviet era prices were fixed by the state, and bargain-hunting was a waste of time, but once Svetlana had seen the range of American prices she spent days looking for cucumbers that were five cents cheaper or shoes that cost a dollar less. She didn't know that what is cheap is usually of poor quality, and was surprised when the T-shirts she had proudly bought for three dollars each disintegrated in the wash.

Fyodor at first thought that the laboratory in which he worked was cheating him because the salary on his paycheck was lower than in his contract. No one had explained to him that in the United States taxes and Social Security are withheld, and in the USSR income tax was small and there was no system of deductions. Muriel and Carol are still doing the income tax on their own, as the intricacies of the Internal Revenue Service are beyond their Russian husbands' comprehension. Even an ordinary checking account is a new experience, as in Russia virtually all transactions are made in cash. "I still don't really understand why, when I write a check to the phone company, it manages to find its way back to me," Fyodor confessed after a year in America.

The idea of savings is also new. Since education, health care, vacations and retirement pensions were provided by the Soviet state, no one gave much thought to savings. Today in Russia prices are so high that people can barely get by, let alone save. Years of shortages made people buy things whenever they were available, and planning ahead was impossible. Saving or "hoarding" money was seen as eccentric. "At first I didn't understand why Fred insisted on taking out an IRA and life insurance," Irina said. "It seemed to me a waste of money that could have been better spent on things for the house. Life insurance seemed so morbid— thinking about when you'll be dead. But now with the kids, and the cost of school here, I see that he's right." Joyce, however, did not succeed in getting Pyotr to buy life insurance after Maria was born. "You hope I'll drop dead!" he screamed at her. "You just want to have a lot of money and enjoy life without me!"

Russian and American ways of talking about money are as different as their spending habits. Carol had great difficulty convincing Fyodor that questions about salary were expected during job interviews, and that it would be considered rather odd if he didn't inquire about the prospective pay. Pyotr kept embarrassing Joyce's friends by asking them how much they made and how much income tax they paid. He could not understand why Americans openly discussed the cost of vacations and schooling and how they took deductions on their income tax, but not how much they earned or paid for their homes. "Your friends prefer discussing what they do in bed to what they do at the bank," he complained to Joyce. As one Russian wrote,

Our countrymen who fall into capitalism have to go round and round in circles, break with the old, and play the game. Not everyone can withstand that change. The need to count every penny hardens your heart, but here in America, count they do, rich and poor alike. Thus, the "lessons of capitalism" fall on fertile soil.[5]

Arkady Shevchenko was stunned by Judy Chavez' "hardened heart" when she arrived in his room right after he had learned that his wife had died suddenly in mysterious circumstances in Moscow. For the call girl, as she remarked in her book, business was business and money was money, and the diplomat was stunned that his personal tragedy did not change Chavez' attitude towards him.

> He started crying and I put my arms around him. Then when I'd played some music on the radio and calmed him down a little I asked him for the money.
>
> "What? You ask for money at this time? Is that all you care about, your money?"
>
> "No," I said. "It's just that I like to get it over with so we don't have to worry about it."
>
> He . . . came back with a handful of money and threw it on the floor. I went over and picked up my five hundred and left the rest there. It must have been well over a thousand . . . and there must have been four thousand more in an envelope, but I didn't take any of it. I've done almost everything else to my customers, but I've never stolen from them.
>
> That night he didn't want to have sex. He just wanted me to lie there in bed with him while he held me and cried. The next morning the bills were still scattered on the floor.[6]

Though the relationship between the prostitute and the diplomat is hardly typical of Russian-American couples, the difference in their attitude towards money is telling, for different attitudes towards finances affect many mixed marriages. Fyodor was surprised that Carol insisted on their having separate bank accounts. He didn't mind her keeping her name when they got married, since many Russian women do this, but the two accounts were to him a signal of distrust rather than of independence. A Russian émigré was taken aback by the way his American wife insisted on her financial independence:

> Despite her kindness Elizabeth once let her husband clearly understand that there were areas (generally of a material nature) which were not his business. Like most women, she occasionally complained that she had nothing to wear. "But your closets are bursting with clothes," Igor remonstrated. "Why buy anything else?" Elizabeth answered something to the effect of "What business is that of yours? It's my cash I'm forking out." As Igor saw it, there was no point in his getting mad at this or at her other comments. The difference in upbringing and in the concepts of the two cultures was insurmountable, anyhow.[7]

Another émigré gave a friend the following advice:

> Remember, don't take anything from anyone, and don't give anything to anyone. Don't lend anything, and don't let anyone borrow anything from you. That's America. It's just not done. Here, you know, a boyfriend takes his girlfriend to a restaurant, they eat, have a good time—and each one pays his own way.[8]

Sergei wasn't too concerned about running up large bills because in Russia there had always been a parent or a friend ready to come across with a loan. (The Russian language, in fact, has only one word for the verbs "to borrow" and "to lend"). At first Muriel's parents were willing to lend a few hundred dollars, but when the figures started running into the thousands they balked and asked to be paid back with interest. Sergei was dumbfounded. "Such nice, warm, people—how can they be so heartless to their own child?" He did not understand the American tradition of financial independence from parents. When he tried to borrow from two of her friends and they asked that the loan be put in writing he wrote them off as mercenary capitalists, for in Russia setting such a condition would have been an insult. No one would hesitate to borrow money from a friend, dates for repayment were casual and flexible, and few people refused a request for a loan unless the borrower was known to be broke or a drunkard.

For Russians the ultimate sin is being "stingy." Despite her stormy relationship with Baryshnikov, Gelsey Kirkland was touched by his generous offers of money whenever he thought she might be in need.[9] The Russian edition of *Cosmopolitan* warns its readers that American men tend to be tightfisted, and that "while treating you to ice cream, your beau is making the agonizing choice between simply cheap and very cheap."[10] Dick G. remembered that when he checked the addition on a restaurant bill his Russian wife and friends were put out, thinking he was being cheap. If you're inviting friends out for dinner, looking for little mathematical errors is unseemly.

Over Muriel's protests, Sergei invited his sister Nadya to stay with them for three months in their tiny studio apartment, and Nadya's shopping sprees pushed Muriel even further into debt. When she demurred to her husband, Sergei was unsympathetic. Nadya had to buy presents for his mother in Russia, didn't she? All Muriel had to do was to raise the spending limit on her credit card.

For couples living in Russia it was often, paradoxically, easier. The American spouse who had a job with an English-language radio program or publishing house was paid partly in dollars, and this hard currency made an enormous difference. "It was so easy in Moscow," Anne sighed, recalling the years when she worked for a Moscow publisher. "With my dollars we could buy all kinds of fancy foods in the hard currency stores and have wonderful dinners for our Russian friends."

With rising prices, this advantage is being whittled down. Foreign-owned stores and supermarkets charge double and triple the prices in Russian shops. "I'm not against making my life here a bit more comfortable," said Mary C., "and of course the foreign stores are much nicer, cleaner and less crowded. But Boris and I feel ridiculous paying eighteen dollars for a three-ounce piece of Swiss cheese in the Irish supermarket when the neighborhood store has domestic cheese at a quarter of that price. Things certainly have changed here as far as shopping goes." Also, Mary C. can't get used to the pervasive bribery, something which goes way back in Russian life. "You shouldn't have to bribe the plumber just to get him to come, since you have to give him more once he's finished." Paula Garb observed that the Americans found the bribery insulting both to the person to whom the money was offered and to themselves.[11] Today Anne says: "I never know to whom to give it to and to whom not to give it. But I've never met anyone who couldn't be bribed if the sum were big enough."

Today, younger Russians are free from the older generation's apprehensions that wealthy people have undoubtedly made their money illegally. They see huge sums of money changing hands, and they are eager to get rich quick; this attitude often follows them to the United States. Muriel had to keep stopping Sergei from rushing into shaky schemes and fly-by-night swindlers. Irina kept pushing Fred to make more money. "At least I don't have one worry rich American girls have," she said. "I know that Fred didn't marry me for my money, because there wasn't any."

"You Marry the Family"

⚜

"Pyotr sometimes phones his mother four times a day," Joyce complained. "When she calls, it doesn't matter if we're in the middle of dinner or having guests. She still keeps him on the phone for half an hour."

"Muriel's mother calls only once a week," Sergei confided to Pyotr. "We see her parents only once a month. They're always busy entertaining or traveling, and they check in with us the way her father checks in with his clients."

Few areas of family life are as sensitive and highly charged as that of spouses' relations with each other's families. In the past many Russians were terrified by the political consequences of their child's marrying an American. Tamara Gilmore's mother was frightened by her daughter's exile and ostracism, and did not see her American son-in-law for several years. Julie Whitney's mother was at first afraid to have Tom Whitney in the house, and Irina McClellan's mother rightly foresaw severe problems, if not the eleven years of separation the couple endured. When Svetlana married Mark in the 1980s, however, her parents were distraught— not because of political consequences but because of the extended separation from their only child.

Nor was the reaction of American families uniformly enthusiastic. Fred's parents were terribly upset about his marriage to a "Red," though once they got to know Irina they became very fond of her. Lee Oswald's mother commented to him after she met his wife: "Marina, she doesn't look Russian. She is beautiful."[1] One family was so horrified at the idea of their daughter's marriage to a Russian that the girl's parents were the only family members who came to the wedding and the groom's nationality was hidden from the other relatives for as long as possible.[2] A Russian woman who married an American journalist discovered that her new in-laws were certainly not crazy about a penniless Moscow bride for their son. It took years and two children before they accepted her.

In-laws are an unavoidable fact of Russian life because of the housing shortage that prevents many young couples from having a place of their own. When Anne started living in Moscow with her husband Ivan and his mother Nadezhda, she was quite nervous about having a live-in mother-in-law. The older woman, however, proved an invaluable source of information about shopping and getting around. When Anne got a job as an English-language translator, she very much appreciated Nadezhda's willingness to do most of the shopping and housework. "I realized that she was just as afraid of me as I was of her. It took us about a year to understand that we really liked each other. Once Andrei was born I don't know what I would have done without her. She was absolutely great in helping with the baby so that I could keep on working. I don't think I'd be able to have this kind of relationship with my own mother—I certainly couldn't live with *her* and Ivan!"

An expatriate American journalist married for seven years to a Russian woman found, on the other hand, that adapting to her family was more difficult than he had expected. "It took me time to get used to making large sacrifices for a circle of friends and family," he said. "The North American family is more atomized."[3] A young Russian woman who met her future husband in the Moscow synagogue in 1984 during Passover, and joined him in California, also had a difficult time adjusting. "I still have Soviet customs and I'm not used to living without my parents," she said.[4]

In Russia living with a spouse's parents is the norm rather than the exception, and many couples rely on the parents for help with household chores, child care and financial assistance in purchasing major items such as cars, refrigerators or winter coats. The situation makes for close family ties, but naturally gives parents a major say in the young couple's decisions and creates strong financial and emotional dependence. Russian women, as one observer commented, express an extraordinary degree of closeness to their parents, consider them a central influence on their values and tastes, and remain highly dependent on their families of origin, both psychologically and materially, well into adulthood. [5]

The Russian tradition of parents aiding or virtually supporting their married children may lead Russian spouses to expect similar behavior from their American in-laws. Sergei could not understand why Muriel was reluctant to ask her parents for money, and Irina did not understand why Fred's father did not help them with expenses when they began setting up house. The American notion of raising a child to become independent—and move out on his own— is diametrically opposed to the Russian notion of parents supporting their children as long as possible and the children becoming their mainstay in old age.

"Pyotr's mother had absolutely no respect for his privacy," Joyce commented. "He was over thirty years old, and she was still reading his mail and listening in on his phone calls. I'd be hysterical if my mom did that, and he just says 'Well, she's my mother.'" Joyce at first thought that Lidia was a selfless old lady willing to do anything for her son and his family, but she soon discovered that the price for the shopping trips to the supermarket and the pots of borshch simmering on the stove was the expectation that her slightest whims would be obeyed. Lidia's "selflessness" was the way she bought Pyotr's willingness to give up a planned weekend in the country because mama had a little cold. "You may wind up having more than one wife but you only have one mother," she never tired of telling Joyce on each of her frequent and unannounced visits. She criticized Joyce's looks, cooking, housekeeping and the way she was raising Maria. Pyotr, for his part, never said a word in his wife's defense. One day after a violent quarrel with Joyce he rushed out of the house. Later, he claimed to have spent the evening dancing with a Russian girl. In fact, he had gone to his mother's house for cabbage pie and consolation.

After his fights with his mother, Lee Oswald would tell Marina not to allow her in the house. "She's your *mother*," Marina would object. "How can I not let her in?"[6] Even when Oswald hit her for refusing to obey him Marina could not bring herself to lock his mother out.

Raising children is another source of stress. Paula Garb said that the totally different approaches she and her Russian husband had to child rearing were a major reason for the failure of their marriage.[7] Such differences can make themselves felt even before the child is born. In Russia, women try to avoid going out in public while pregnant, and are amazed by American wives who work until a day or two before their due date. Pyotr thought it was improper for Joyce to go to a restaurant with him once her pregnancy began showing. Horror stories of labor pains handed down from generation to generation fill the Russian women with terror during pregnancy. And these fears are not entirely unfounded, for according to recent statistics only 25 to 30 percent of women in childbirth have normal deliveries in Russian maternity hospitals, which tend to be unsanitary and short of basic equipment, food and blankets.[8] Infection is rampant. No wonder Russian wives of Americans want to give birth in hospitals in the United States.

In Russia, husbands were not permitted to enter the maternity ward. "Visitors were not allowed to come into our room," John Scott's wife Masha recalled. "We went into a visitors' room, when we were able. Our husbands talked to us through the windows."[9] Eddy Gilmore recalled banging on the locked door of the hospital in twenty-below-zero weather to bring Tamara apples, candy, cognac and letters.[10]

Russian women—and men—find the idea of having the father in the delivery room revolting, and this is not allowed in most Russian hospitals. "The very idea is so alien in the Soviet Union that almost every Soviet woman and man I talked to has said they would not even consider such a thing even if it were permitted," Paula Garb wrote.[11] "I wouldn't feel 'feminine,'" Irina said. "I wouldn't have my make-up, and if I were in pain I might scream or curse at Fred." "I couldn't have slept with Joyce again if I'd seen her in labor," Pyotr said. She had wanted him to videotape Maria's birth. "That really disgusted me," he said. "It would have been like photographing her on the toilet." A Russian who witnessed his daughter's birth in an American hospital, at his American wife's insistence, was sickened by the sight. His wife, who had opted for natural childbirth, screamed in pain. "Everything was dripping, crawling," he recalled. "For a month and a half afterwards I couldn't look at our daughter. The memory of her appearance on this earth made me nauseous."[12]

Choosing a name for the baby can be cause for more than normal disagreement. Many couples settle on neutral names such as Gregory or Maria, which are common to both languages. Joanne and Nikolai named their daughter Anna, which sounds fine in both English and Russian. Feeding and taking care of the infant can lead to more arguments. For a mother to breast feed her baby in public is about as acceptable among Russians as doing a striptease. Pyotr was horrified when Joyce took Maria to work and nursed her in her office, though Joyce protested that there were only women on her floor. He thought Joyce was insane to take a two-week-old infant out for a breath of fresh air. "She'll catch pneumonia," he exclaimed. Even in seventy-five degree weather the child was wrapped up as though for the dead of winter, and Pyotr kept the windows closed out of fear of drafts.

Irina was impressed by Fred's behavior after their son was born. "He's so helpful with the baby. He even changes the diapers. And those disposable Pampers are wonderful." She greatly appreciated the absence of those damp cloths that hung in rows in every Russian bathroom following the birth of a baby. Most Russian men do not have the faintest idea of how to change a diaper. Igor Kon rightly commented that because of the the deaths of so many men in the purges and World War II many Russian men were raised without a father. As a result, they do not know how to function as fathers, and are minimally involved with raising their children.[13]

Caring for children brings deep-rooted traditions and beliefs to the surface. For Irina the standard cures for childhood ailments were mustard plasters and raspberry tea. She could not understand why American doctors didn't make house calls, and why a feverish two-year-old had to be taken to the doctor's office. "Any Russian doctor would make a house call," she told Fred. Nor could she understand why Fred wanted to take the six-month-old with them to a restaurant, for in Russia a small child would not be allowed in the door. Paula Garb observed that Russian spouses tend to pick up a crying child and forbid toddlers to crawl around barefoot, while Americans are much more easygoing about giving children freedom to roam around and dirty themselves.[14] American spouses also provide children with more freedom of choice. Joyce asked Maria if she wanted chocolate or vanilla ice cream, while Pyotr handed her the cone he had chosen. Maria quickly sided with Joyce.

The question of language arises soon after the child is born. Does each parent speak his own language to the child, or that of the country in which they are living? Joanne found that after three years of living in Russia, with a Russian nanny caring for little Anna, the girl had trouble communicating with her American grandparents during visits to the United States. Maria sometimes confused Latin and Cyrillic letters and wrote in a combination of both. She liked Russian fairy tales but hated speaking Russian, a language she associated with boring afternoons with Pyotr's mother, who kept telling her not to do this or that. Irina discovered that her seven-year-old son was avoiding bringing his school friends home because he was ashamed of her Russian accent. Though he understood Russian perfectly he began refusing to speak it, answering his mother in English whenever she addressed him in Russian. Since their mothers only spoke English to them, Paula Garb's and Sara Harris's children are bilingual, but because they attended Russian schools and did all their reading and writing in Russian, they had difficulty writing English properly.

An inevitable problem, for child and parent alike, is the dominance of the culture of the country of residence. McDonalds, Ninja Turtles, computer games and pizza were all "American nonsense" to Pyotr, and wrong for his daughter—who loved cheeseburgers and video games and hated the cabbage soup and buckwheat groats he wanted her to eat. When Anne visited her relatives in the United States, little Andrei refused to eat hamburgers and kept asking his American grandmother for *mannaya kasha*, a Russian cereal much like cream of wheat. Irina wanted to dress her children in "nice" clothes, while they insisted on wearing jeans, T-shirts and sneakers like the other children in their class.

In Russia there were numerous play and child care facilities—to say nothing of the ever-present granny—to keep an eye on the children. In America many firms do not provide the lengthy maternity leave granted in Russia, and American child care centers can be expensive. Nor do Americans display the communal spirit and sense of shared responsibility shown by Russian neighbors and friends. It is as hard for American parents to adapt to the Russian collective spirit as it is for Russian parents to adapt to American individualism. For one thing, Americans are not used to getting gratuitous advice on child rearing from relatives, neighbors, and perfect strangers. Tracy Kuehn, a young American married to a Muscovite, described to Paula Garb her experiences with her son, Philip:

"I can't tell you how many times a grandmotherly type has come up to me to tell me what I should or should not be doing with Philip. It's well meant, but there are times when it's annoying. I've gotten very good at listening politely and then walking a little farther away and continuing whatever I was doing before." The common situations in which Tracy finds herself the object of unsolicited advice is when Philip is not wearing a hat (both in hot and cold weather) when other children are, walking barefoot in the summertime, collecting rocks in his little pail (because the rocks are dirty), sitting on the ground (because it's too cold), and running (because he could fall down).[15]

Sara Harris had her baby in her arms when a woman came up to her in the street and yelled at her for not supporting the baby's head properly. How she was raising her children was taken by her neighbors as very much their business.[16] For children in Russia there were always playmates in the courtyard in front of the house, where they could run about freely under the watchful gaze of elderly grandmothers installed on benches where they spent the day gossiping. In America, Irina and Joyce had to arrange "play dates" for their children, and playing in the street was not for "nice" children.

The child's education provides more ground for argument. Under the Soviet system of free education the schools had identical curricula. In America, from kindergarten to college, a plethora of public and private schools offer a wide variety of programs at varied costs. Pyotr told Maria's teachers he disapproved of their teaching methods and of the way the school was run. If Maria was doing badly, that was the school's fault. The children had far too little homework, and there was no respect for teachers; instead of doing homework the kids wound up in front of the television set. Joyce was upset by the way Pyotr constantly criticized America to Maria. "We're all living here," she said. "Yes," he retorted, "but that doesn't make everything that happens here right. In Russia—" "We're not living in Russia," Joyce cut him off.

An American journalist and his Russian wife got a gripe from their son when they moved from Moscow to the United States. "I don't like American girls," the boy told them. "They're all so screwed up. Always talking about their problems and about themselves. Not like the Russian girls! They were interested in me and in other people!" Russian parents are inhibited in talking to their children about sex. Nor is sex discussed in school. Pyotr threw out a children's book about the birds and the bees that Joyce had bought to answer Maria's questions about where she had come from. Irina was so embarrassed when her son began asking about sex that she burst into tears, leaving Fred to answer the boy's questions.

Irina had been raised to expect that life would be difficult; Fred wanted his son to be raised expecting the best. "He's got to think positive," he argued. Irina was upset at the way Fred encouraged the little boy to smile and told him jokes. "He'll become a silly clown," she worried. "Nonsense," argued Fred, "he'll have a much easier time getting along with people. A smile and a sense of humor are the best things anyone can have. That's for keeps and doesn't cost anything." A Russian journalist remarked with surprise that American parents believed "a child must feel as many positive emotions as possible; until the end of his days he should be charged with optimism, with a 'positive attitude toward life.'"[17] Pyotr wanted Maria to be prepared for the worst. "Life is hard," he snapped. "Raising her to think things are easy will only get her into trouble."

With older children there are conflicts over money. Fyodor did not understand why American parents pay their children for doing household chores, which in Russia they do as a matter of course. He was very surprised that American college kids were eager to take on jobs as waiters and cashiers. Anton would not allow his daughter to work summers as a waitress. What was the matter—he couldn't support her? And everyone was supposed to see this disgrace? How could rich American parents sit by and watch their children do such demeaning work—and even encourage or force them into it? While American adolescents are accustomed to earning their own money to buy clothes, stereo equipment and cars, Russian parents often support their offspring even after the children have children of their own. Raissa Gorbachev was surprised when Barbara Bush told her that the Bush children had bought their own homes by working hard, saving and taking out mortgages with no help from their parents.[18]

On top of these fundamental differences about child rearing, the problems—for Russian parents—of protecting a child in the U.S. from the temptations of consumerism, "immorality" and excessive individualism, loom so large that some couples feel a child could put their marriage at risk. Muriel and Sergei, and Fyodor and Carol made conscious decisions not to have children. "I felt a child was the only thing which could seriously threaten my marriage," Carol said. "I can live with all Fyodor's annoying little habits and ignore all his dogmatic and intolerant ideas. But I couldn't take his constantly telling a child all those things, or that Americans are dumb idiots. Though he's the most intelligent, kindest human being I know, having a child would be really risky—and the one thing I don't want to lose is this marriage." In spite of the material difficulties of the Soviet era, American-Russian couples living in the USSR seem to have been more willing to have children than those living in the United States. Paula Garb, Tracy Kuehn, Sara Harris and Joan Turnbull all raised children who, they felt, were better behaved and more studious—if more pampered—than would have been the case at home in America.

As the children of these mixed marriages grow older, the issue of their identity becomes more acute. Are they Russians or Americans? Reading a child Russian fairy tales doesn't make him a Russian. For a child living in America, Russia may be a planet twinkling in outer space, and for a child growing up in Moscow, America may be in never-never land. Children's reactions to their mixed identities differ enormously. Margaret Wettlin's son, who played hooky from school riding streetcars and pretending he was on his way to America, asked her later, "Why in God's name did you ever come to this wretched country?"[19] Yet Paula Garb's son Andrei, who was raised in Russia, said to her, "Mom, I've had a terrific life. It couldn't have been better."[20] He was a bit nostalgic, however, for things he remembered from his early years in America. "As a kid," he said, "I missed the bubble gum, Coke and Hershey's."[21] Sarah Harris's son told her that he would always feel "about seventy per cent Russian."[22] As he matured, however, his attitude towards the Soviet system, in which he had been raised, began to change. "If you did a little digging and used a little common sense you'd realize it was all bullshit in the textbooks," he said. "It makes me cringe that I took it seriously."[23] In 1986 he moved to the United States, but missed Russia so badly that three years later he returned to Moscow.

An American court recently enjoined an American woman hired by the U.S. Embassy in Moscow from taking her three children with her on a three-year assignment. Her ex-husband's lawyer successfully argued that "in Russia there would be no 'Baby Sitters' Club,' no Barney, no Jurassic Park, no Macy's Thanksgiving Day Parade, no fireworks on the Mall on the Fourth of July," and that the children's health would suffer from Moscow's poor air quality and long winters.[24] Joanne Turnbull, however, is quite happy to raise her daughter without Barney and Jurassic Park, and feels that American consumerism and individualism are far more dangerous for Anna than Russian air and snow.

With the end of travel restrictions, mixed couples can easily travel back and forth between the two countries. Expatriate American parents are understandably afraid that their children will become foreigners. On the other hand, some Russian spouses living in the United States want their sons and daughters to assimilate to American life as soon as possible. Others, like Pyotr, feel that America is ruining their children and that they are engaged in a hopeless battle to prevent it. The complications are endless and there is no general rule. "My ideal," Anne said, "is for Andrei to learn how to live in both worlds and how to move back and forth easily between them. But it's going to be his choice."

"Friend" or *"Droog?"*

❧

"Will you please tell your friend Igor," said Carol, "that he is not to come by without calling! This is the second time this week he's rung the bell because he 'happened to be in the neighborhood.' It's just plain rude and I'm tired, and don't feel like making dinner again for that bum!" "But he's my friend," Fyodor protested. "We've known each other for twenty years. I'm sure his wife Olga would be glad to see me if I dropped by their place." Russian spouses in America often miss their friends more than their families. "In Russia I could share everything with Kolya and Anatoly," Sergei said. "No matter how much I love Muriel, she can't replace them. A man needs his male friends." Especially in a foreign country with another language and a whole new set of people he may or may not find congenial.

"Friend" means different things to Russians and Americans. The difference may be tied to the collective spirit of Russians and the individualism of Americans. In English, the word "individualism" has a positive ring, and in Russian a pejorative connotation.[1] The group—even if the group is two friends—can be more important to a Russian than the individual, and the individual's business is his friends' business. This means that friends may drop by at all hours of the day and night—to the American wife's dismay.

But, as Muriel discovered, there is a positive side to it as well. Once in the small hours, when she and Sergei, Joyce and Pyotr and a Russian couple were returning home from a party, Pyotr's car got a flat tire. While Sergei and Pyotr put on a spare, the Russian couple stood around waiting. "They could have taken a taxi," Muriel said later. "And leave their friends?" Sergei said. "They couldn't do that."

The closeness and caring nature of Russian friendships can be very appealing after the "me-first" attitude of many Americans.

Susan Eisenhower recalled her feelings toward their Russian friends as she and Roald Sagdeev prepared to leave Russia.

> I looked out the window of the little apartment and felt a rush of emotion. Despite the restrictions and the constant worries, there was a closeness and warmth in this country that I would miss dreadfully. Those who constituted a circle here could count on the support, love, and constant concern of the rest of their group. Their mutual involvement was in stark contrast to the way American society seemed to be evolving. In Washington, anyway, there was a disconnectedness because everyone was so busy. Even among the oldest of friends you seldom had time to be in touch, to stay engaged.[2]

Americans are used to moving frequently, leaving old friends behind and making new ones. They have friends from the office and friends from clubs, sports centers or churches. "Fred talked about a friend from the gym and couldn't even remember his name," Irina said. "What kind of a friend is that?" Americans tend to see friends as people with whom they engage in activities, such as tennis or golf or going out to dinner. In Russia friends talk. And talk and talk and talk. About serious subjects. Pyotr and Sergei were appalled to hear Americans talk for hours about the weather, sports, office politics, and what they'd eaten at a neighborhood French restaurant. Fyodor startled Carol's girlfriend Hilary by launching into a discourse about the significance of aging ten minutes after being introduced. Her American friends thought he was a bore. "He goes on for so long and doesn't let anyone get a word in," Hilary said.

Americans live in the present and future. Russians take everything back to the past. "If you ask Sergei how he enjoyed his trip to Italy, he'll tell you the history of the Roman Empire," Muriel said.

To Russians, this American impatience with the background of things seems unnatural. If Sergei tells Pyotr about an argument with Muriel, he must first explain what they had both been thinking and doing the day before, who said what to whom, and their reactions—doesn't he? If you are seriously exploring an idea, or telling your friend your deepest feelings, you take as much time as you need. Interruptions, aside from a sympathetic nod or a commiserating grunt, are disrespectful of the speaker, and trying to change the subject is like switching lanes on an expressway during rush hour.

The intensity of Russian relationships tends to surprise American wives. Pyotr and Sergei argued loudly in front of their friends, not sparing each other's feelings, and raising their voices in ways Americans would consider rude. The Americans present tried to smooth over differences of opinion, and prevent things from getting too heated, or simply changed the topic. To Pyotr and Sergei, however, this reaction seemed superficial and hypocritical. Arguments about matters of importance are part of friendship, and the more heated the better.

When his marriage to Joyce started running into trouble Pyotr refused to go to a marriage counselor. He could discuss anything with his Russian friends, so why should he go to an American stranger? That Joyce and her friends went to therapists was to him a sign that they had no friends. To Joyce, on the other hand, his constant turning to friends was a sign of weakness. In America you try to be self-reliant and cope, and if you can't cope you go to a professional. "In America," one Russian woman said, "you run to psychiatrists because you do not have the tradition of close every-day friendship that we have in Russia . . . We share everything with one another, hiding nothing or very little. We like to share our sorrows, we love to feel sorry for and help one another."[3] Tom Gillett, a divorced American advertising copywriter, who found his Russian wife Marina Volokhonskaya through a lonely-hearts ad in the New York émigré newspaper *Novoye Russkoye Slovo*, liked the way Russian women turned to their friends for support. "I've noticed with Russian women there's really a willingness to tell what went on before in their lives, a willingness not to cover anything up or hide anything. The neuroses that exist are a lot different from those among Americans. You'd never find anybody in therapy, for instance. If you've got a problem, you go to friends . . . I love that way of being."[4]

A male friend is a brother, a drinking companion, a soulmate and a bulwark against the outside world. A girlfriend is a confidante with whom a woman can share things she may not tell her husband or mother. Russian female friendships are as intense as male ones, for the women see each other as comrades-in-arms against weak men and a hostile world. "No Russian woman expects to find a man who listens to her as another woman does," remarked one Russian girl.[5] American women can have difficulty establishing such extraordinarily intense friendships with Russian women. Joanne Turnbull at first had some trouble making female friends, both because of the demanding nature of these relationships and because of the different lives she and the Russians were leading. "They have their own problems and difficulties in coping with life here, and these are not the same as ours," she said. But over time she has become close friends with some Moscow women.

Under the Communists, a friend was someone who could be trusted absolutely and would never betray a confidence—at a time when an imprudent remark or a political anecdote told to the wrong person could lead to the loss of a job or imprisonment. As one Gulag survivor put it, "Russian friendship was more similar to war camaraderie than to the Western kind of social friendship—no wonder, because Russian life was always a kind of war."[6]

The word "friend" is not used lightly. There are separate words in Russian for a casual acquaintance (*znakomyi*), a closer acquaintance or friend (*priatel'*) and a real friend (*droog*). Carol was amused at how when Fyodor met another Russian the two would size each other up before launching into "real" conversation. "Like dogs sniffing each other," she remarked. Such reticence is part of the legacy of suspicion and fear engendered by the Soviet system of mass informers. Americans take minutes to make friends. Russians take months or years.

And a friendship once made is not lightly shared. Sergei did not want to introduce his Russian friends to Muriel's American acquaintances: he was afraid they'd be stolen from him. When there was a falling-out Sergei would sulk for two or three days, refuse to call the offending party, and expect a formal apology before making up.

Russian wives are generally surprised by the friendship patterns of their American husbands. "Fred has no men friends," Irina said. "I was so surprised he didn't know any of the neighbors. He plays golf with two men, and sometimes has a beer with a friend from college, but they're not friends the way men were back home." In Russia friends were there to help out when the system got in the way, to help you get a job, fix a car, or lend you money. Irina could not understand why Fred's American friends refused to cosign a loan for the house she and he wanted to buy. "If they're friends money shouldn't be an issue," she sniffed as Fred tried to explain the concept of legal financial responsibility and why a young couple with a baby and two small incomes had refused to take on the responsibility for cosigning a large loan.

Russian spouses initially enthusiastic about the open and friendly attitude of Americans are often disappointed. They feel let down when what they see as serious friendship overtures— asking for a home phone number, suggesting lunch, expressing an interest in their lives—are followed by weeks of silence. That a broad smile and a warm handshake may not be an invitation to closeness is something the Russian arrival needs time to learn.

The notion of "meeting people" and "making new friends" as a cure for psychic ailments seems odd to Russians. One doesn't make or lose a friend in a day or on vacation. As one observer wrote, friendship for Russians means an "obligation of almost constant companionship and the rejection of any reticence or secretiveness."[7] Few Americans have the time or patience for relationships requiring such intense commitment and loyalty. In Russia one keeps up with friends. If there is no chance to see them there are hourlong phone calls. Joyce was surprised by the flood of calls from Pyotr's Russian friends for Easter, New Year and his birthday. Forgetting to call a friend on a holiday or birthday was taken as a slight. "The more you give, the more they take," Joyce commented. "They think they own you. They smother you." Even some Russians, such as the writer Tatyana Tolstaya, find these friendships overpowering:

> When Russians become friends they think they can burst into your house at any time without a phone call, if they have a problem they make you feel responsible, you must immediately give money, help, everything, they totally invade you.[8]

This is the opposite of American friendships, based on respect for privacy, and on give and take. In her book on French and American cultural differences, Raymonde Carroll wrote that American friendships are jeopardized by "all that we could summarize by the words 'too much' . . . anything that threatens the balance in the relationship, which is based on equality and exchange, on taking turns."[9] Russian friendships are based on just that notion of "too much."

Mixed couples find that American friends do not always react positively to the Russian spouse. Muriel's friends could not understand why she wanted to be married to a Russian who was not interested in earning money and who lectured them incessantly. Joyce's friends could not tolerate Pyotr's stubbornness and his rudeness to her. Fyodor, however, loved being with Americans and practicing his English, and tried to cultivate as many of Carol's American friends as possible. Mark and Svetlana developed a large group of friends, since her English was good, and on the university campus they found both Russians and Americans who shared their interest in history and music.

In their search for new friends in America, the Russian spouses seek out other Russians, and the American spouse can thus wind up acquiring a whole new group of Russian friends.[10] Armand Hammer described how his wife Olga's unhappiness, poor English and few friends made her "want to spend a lot of her time with the expatriate Russian community in New York, talking about the old days . . . [She] often went to the Russian restaurants and nightclubs. The incessant nostalgic talk in those places bored me."[11] The Russian spouses often encounter other Russians from completely different backgrounds, with whom they would never have chosen to associate at home, and a musician may find himself socializing with a mechanic.

American spouses in Russia also have a limited choice of fellow-countrymen with whom to socialize. A young scholar of Russian literature spent most of her time with lawyers and businessmen. "In the U.S. I'd be seeing university professors. But here, if I want to spend an evening with other Americans that's it—take it or leave it. These people don't have time for real friendships in the Russian sense, or even for the kind of friendships I had in the U.S. They're all busy making money." Margaret Wettlin recalled that she so desperately needed a close friendship with an English-speaking person that her relationship with the British writer Ivy Litvinov began to come between her and her Russian husband Andrei:

> My friendship with Ivy had hurt our relationship a little. I could not resist the joy of her company. Her wit, talent, and above all her identity with literature, *English* literature, provided the stimulation needed to counteract the disillusionment of the past years. Andrei found his stimulation in the theater and in his flowers. I did not share his interests with the same intensity I gave to Ivy's, and he felt it. It hurt me, too, for anything that weakened our relationship diminished the significance of our lives together.[12]

In the Soviet period, fear of associating with foreigners kept many Russians from trying to develop contacts with Americans. Paula Garb felt that this was one reason why she would never have the same kind of friendships in Russia as she had had at home:

I knew I would not be able to relate to my Russian friends the same way as to American friends, and that this would cause some inner tension. There is a psychology behind language; speech and even body language very often determine a relationship. The way of relating is simply different in the two countries. Another aspect of feeling alien in the Soviet Union would be due to the Stalin-era legacy—many people would be cautious about associating too closely with foreigners, guided by the philosophy of "you never know."[13]

"My Russian friends were envious because I could leave the country when I wanted and I could shop in the hard-currency stores," Anne said. "My privileges as a foreigner put a barrier between us that wouldn't go away. Some of them thought we were crazy to live here when life was so much easier in the West. In a way, though, they respected us for staying. Despite the fear and envy, there's a warmth and closeness you just don't have in America."

Though today the fear of associating with foreigners is gone, friendships with Russians still can be difficult. Several American wives living in Moscow said that they had trouble making friends with Russian women. "They seem to be off in another world with problems I can't share," one young woman remarked. "I know and like my husband's friends," Patty Montet said. "But for some reason I haven't been able to form close relationships with Russian women."[14] One young American claimed that his two Russian business associates were also his best friends. Though these Russians certainly did not see him as their best friend, these friendships were far closer than any he had had in the United States. Mary C. resented Boris's friends, with whom she had to spend long evenings, listening to them carry on in a language she barely understood. "They treat me like a centerpiece," she complained. "For them I'm just a pretty woman, not a human being. They don't seem to take anything a woman thinks or says seriously."

Trips back home can also cause tensions between a spouse and friends. When Mary C. first took Boris to visit her friends on a trip to the United States they found him a bit of a Martian, caught up in Russia's problems and barely interested in them or in America. After nine years in America, Fyodor took Carol to Russia to visit his old friends. She quickly sensed, however, that they had their own lives to catch up on, and made her own plans so that Fyodor could spend several evenings alone with his friends. He was upset to discover that many people he knew had gone into business, and no longer had time to chat for hours. "They're turning into Americans," he said sadly. In the last few years the transition to a market economy in Russia has led to a change in friendship patterns, for people now have far less time for endless talk. Problems with transportation, fear of crime, the long working hours required by Western firms and the expense of food and alcohol for entertaining have put a damper on the endless talk sessions.

"My best friend is my wife—or my husband"—is a common refrain of the mixed marriages, for it is the partner who sees the spouse through the bumpy adaptation period, who encourages, teaches and consoles. Yet it is during that period that the Russians particularly miss their old friends. Until Sergei began meeting Russians in New York, Muriel's phone bills for his calls to friends in Russia were astronomical. Five or ten years later, it is still their friends whom the Russian spouses miss the most, and with the passing of time these relationships take on an even rosier glow. In the meantime new friends, both Russian and American, become part of another area of married life—entertaining.

Eat, Drink and—Relax?

"Pyotr didn't really appreciate the *blanquette de veau* or the *crème caramel* I made for him," Joyce said after six months of marriage. "All he really wants is a big well-done steak, and lots of greasy fries." Likes and dislikes concerning food are deeply rooted in childhood memories and traditions. For Russians, the revolution, the Civil War, World War II, famines and constant food shortages made getting and preparing food a daily obstacle course. Sophisticated cuisine was out of the question, as it was never clear what would be available that day. "Go find yourself a girl who knows how to cook," Marina screamed at Lee Harvey Oswald. "I work, I don't have time to prepare cutlets for you. You don't want soup, you don't want kasha, just tasty tidbits!"[1]

In America, a Russian spouse can become very fussy. Sergei insisted on selecting fruit at the store himself, carefully checking each item and telling Muriel she was throwing rotten apples and peaches into the shopping basket. Arkady Shevchenko insisted on going to expensive specialty stores because the spices in ordinary shops were not fresh enough for him.[2]

Table manners also reflect cultural differences. "Pyotr sits down and throws himself on the food," Joyce said, "chomps away in silence, and only starts talking towards dessert." For Pyotr and Sergei dinner without guests was a way of satisfying hunger, not a social affair that combined eating with conversation.

Eating required a special kind of privacy. Irina avoided sitting near the windows of restaurants, where passersby could see her eat, while Fred and his friends enjoyed sitting by the window people-watching. At a birthday party after a few drinks Pyotr got quite loud and rude, but refused to be photographed while eating: that would be "undignified."

For Russians, getting together over a meal is not a way of doing business, and a "power breakfast" or "business lunch" seems strange. When he was first invited out to business meals Fyodor either left his food untouched or refused to talk business until his plate was clean. The idea of saving time while eating, or getting to know one's interlocutor in a relaxed situation seemed odd to him, though today's younger generation of Russians is adapting quickly to this custom.

Russian husbands expect three meals a day to be put on the table in front of them. One marriage ran into trouble over the husband's expectations that his wife would always cook. "Igor doesn't hide that his wife despite all her qualities—kindness, calm temperament, respectful attitude toward people—didn't live up to Russian marital standards," wrote a Russian journalist. "In particular, she didn't put cabbage soup on the table. Sometimes she cooked, and sometimes she didn't."³ None of the Russian men knew how to cook. Sergei could fry eggs, Pyotr could boil frankfurters, and since he had mastered the art of adding milk to a can he proudly boasted that he could "make soup." When left to his own devices for dinner he would make a meal of a package of cream cheese and chunks of ham on thick slabs of pumpernickel, which reminded him of Russian suppers of black bread, salami and cheese.

Muriel was used to grabbing a sandwich at lunch and having a full meal in the evening, while Sergei expected "dinner"(*obed*)—at midday– including salad, soup, meat, potatoes or noodles, and a dessert. Soup was a must; Russians cannot understand how people can go for days without soup at lunch.⁴ Side dishes other than potatoes, noodles or rice were infrequent in Russia, and Sergei rebelled against spinach, asparagus, or other green vegetables. With a Russian spouse around, bread consumption is high. From earliest childhood Russians are taught to "eat with bread," and everything—soup, meat and salad—is accompanied by a slice. Fruit is expensive in Russia and often not available, and the abundance of fruit in the United States comes as a delight. Shortly after Svetlana's arrival Mark found his refrigerator overflowing with bananas. "I'd rather have raspberries or peaches than ice cream or cake," Irina exulted.

The most important thing—a collective memory from the hunger of the wartime and postwar years—about food is that there be enough—and enough is never enough. Sergei would panic when he and Muriel ran out of anything, even a staple such as bread or milk. On his first visit to a supermarket Fyodor wanted to buy ten jars of dill pickles, sure that such a delicacy would not be available the next day.

"They had everything," Irina said about a dinner in a Russian household to which she and Fred had been invited. Fred did not agree. "Everything" to Irina meant smoked fish such as sturgeon, salmon and sable, a dish of red caviar, a plate of herring, and a large bowl of boiled potatoes smothered in butter. Sour cream is as ubiquitous on Russian tables as butter or margarine. Judy Chavez was turned off when Shevchenko would gobble down a can of corn with huge gobs of sour cream and a chunk of bread.[5]

Despite the profusion, in America, of dozens of products that were scarce in Russia, many Russian spouses dislike American food. Irina and Fyodor didn't care for pumpkin and mince pie, and found American cuisine bland. "No sooner do they feel at home in this world of plenty than they start reminiscing about the glories of Russian cuisine and criticizing Americans for their pale palates," wrote Aksyonov.[6] Differences in palates can lead to misunderstandings. After their first night together one Russian decided to surprise his American girlfriend by treating her to breakfast:

He put on the table everything he himself liked: fried eggs with fatback, sausages, creamed cottage cheese. She looked at the pieces of fatback in horror as if she were seeing live frogs. "You eat that?" He answered that he always did, and with pleasure. "And egg yolks?" "Of course." "But yolks have cholesterol!" She also turned down the cheese. "It's got four percent fat!" "And how much should there be?" Fyodor was confused. He had never counted up those percents and didn't even know they existed . . . Mary also rejected the sausages—"Garbage." She refused both tea and coffee: "I don't drink caffeine." She ate only an apple washed down with a swallow of orange juice. Then she set off for work.[7]

Foods that are "caloric" in America are considered healthy and desirable in Russia, and Sergei was horrified to see Muriel skimming the fat off a pot of chicken broth—"the best part." Today, however, young Russian women have become more calorie-conscious and are making an effort to cut down.

The only foreign cuisines most Russian spouses knew were those of the former Soviet republics, or of Eastern Europe. Fyodor found Chinese food "slimy," and sushi revolting. Most Russians saw a restaurant as a place where a group of friends went to celebrate a special occasion such as a birthday. In the Soviet Union a couple did not ordinarily go to eat out by themselves, as it meant standing on line, sitting with strangers, a limited menu, deafening music, and excruciatingly slow service. In New York, Sergei quickly developed a fondness for small French and Italian restaurants, and his insistence to Muriel that they go out to dinner several times a week poked more holes in their already tattered budget. He even developed a taste for dim lighting, which most Russians avoided, being used to restaurants that were garishly lit.

American spouses living in Moscow acquired Soviet reflexes regarding food. They saved any and all containers for storing foods, and went to markets rather than stores for fresh fruit or vegetables. "In the old days it was nice not to have to compare prices, since they all charged the same thing," Anne said. "But we missed fresh vegetables and fruits, and it was hard to get good meat. I always used to bring back cold cereal and peanut butter from the States, and lots of instant coffee. But there was no way you could bring back asparagus or pizza." The American wives shopped at the "dollar stores" which had a decent but limited assortment of meat and delicacies such as Algerian orange juice and French pâté. Most important, these stores had no long lines.

In the 1990s, with the opening of Irish and Austrian supermarkets, shopping for food became much easier. The choice of products was now much larger, but prices were sky-high; a pound of beef could cost fifteen dollars, and finding a variety of decent fish and meat was still a problem. The situation with restaurants has vastly improved, as Moscow now features a range of Chinese, Indian, Italian, Swiss and other eateries, including some 24-hour establishments; though, aside from McDonald's and pizza places, most of them tend to be fairly expensive. "We don't go out that much to eat," Anne said. "The restaurants are too expensive and a lot of them are full of Mafia types showing off their guns."

Entertaining at home brings out other differences. Irina was taken aback by American pre-dinner cocktails with peanuts; in Russia, drinking is done at the table, not before the meal. During cocktails at a fancy dinner party Sergei got so hungry that he made himself a cheese sandwich in the kitchen. The notion that less is elegant is alien to Russians, and a buffet dinner consisting of a main course and salad is considered stingy. "Fyodor and his friends hate buffets," Carol said. "It's not just the inconvenience of balancing plates and serving themselves. For them the whole idea of an evening is that everyone sits around one table, and there's one big conversation." The idea of talking to someone for five minutes over a drink, and then moving on to another person, runs counter to the ideal of long and soulful conversations. The goal of such American gatherings, Nikolai Formosov commented, seems to be to prevent people from really talking to each other. Invited to an American wedding, Sergei was surprised to see the guests seated at ten round tables. "What kind of a wedding is that?" he demanded. "There's no chance for people to talk to each other!" In Russia even a wedding party of seventy people is seated at a single horseshoe or T-shaped table.

Joyce and Muriel learned that if Russian friends were invited there had to be at least six *zakuski* (appetizers), including several

salads consisting of lots of finely chopped ingredients, smoked
fish, pâtés and cheese, followed by soup, meat and potatoes,
and two or three kinds of cake. Anything else was penny-
pinching. For American wives in Russia who did not have
food processors and dishwashers, these dinners were even
more daunting. Nothing could be worse than having too
little or just enough, for extra helpings are repeatedly prof-
fered by the hosts. Both as hosts and guests, Americans
must play the traditional Russian game of "have-some-more,
no I can't, just-a-little, well-just a-bit." "It's hard for me to
keep pressing food on guests in our house and to avoid insulting
the hosts when we're invited," Mary C. said. "I just can't eat
that much!"

Lavish Russian hospitality is a deeply rooted tradition. A
description of Russian sixteenth-century entertaining states that

> Feasts were the usual social form of bringing people closer
> together . . . The distinctive feature of a Russian feast was the
> enormous abundance of food and drink. The feast was a kind
> of a war between the host and guests.[8]

Susan Eisenhower commented that after several years of living
in America, Sagdeev would suffer from indigestion on visits
back to Moscow because he was no longer used to eating such
huge quantities of food. "I know Russians come to our house and
criticize," she remarked, "but I can't cook that way."[9] Nor do
Russians throw anything away. Carol and Muriel complained of
the quantities of leftovers from those huge meals, and of the
chunks of moldy cheese and acrid sausage that desiccated for
months in the depths of the refrigerator. The only way to dispose
of them was behind their husbands' backs.

Not much help is forthcoming from the men, who usually
do not budge from the table to fetch or clear anything. Though
Sergei was willing to help with the dishes, he was not used
to detergent. He would run a plate under cold water, take a few

half-hearted swipes at it with a fork, scratch it with the tines in the process, and consider the dish clean.

Birthdays are an occasion for pulling out all the stops. As Paula Garb noted, Russian adults hold birthday parties far more readily than Americans.[10] "I always invite Fyodor's friends for his birthday," Carol said, "because if I don't they're likely to come by anyhow, expecting to be wined and dined." Joyce once invited Muriel, Sergei, and another mixed couple, Igor and Beverly, for Pyotr's birthday, which fell on a weekday night. Though invited for seven, the guests showed up after eight. They all brought flowers, which for Russians are *de rigueur*. As soon as the couples had taken off their coats, the Russians lit their cigarettes; for, regardless of any warnings or antismoking campaigns, Russians of all ages continue blithely to puff away.

The conversation consisted of serial monologues. Pyotr told a very long story about his sister's cousin who had come to visit them in Odessa from the village on the Volga where he lived, how difficult it was to get food in the village, and how removed the village people were from the country's cultural and political life. When he was through Sergei and Igor took over for another twenty minutes each. The Russians felt they were "entertaining" the guests. The American wives found them boring and rude.

At 1:30 in the morning, after endless vodka and cognac toasts, Pyotr saw Muriel and Beverly off in a cab, and the three men continued sitting at the table. At 2 A.M. Joyce excused herself, as she had to get up early the next morning for work. At four o'clock she was awakened by thunderous pulsating music and found the threesome in the living room debating the words of a song on a tape they were playing—verses by the Russian poet Osip Mandelshtam, sung by the popular Russian singer Alla Pugacheva. They were distinctly annoyed when Joyce asked them to turn down the sound. When she got up to go to work at 7:30 the three were still at the table, now drinking tea instead of cognac, and when she came back at lunchtime they were still there, eating cheese sandwiches and downing bottles of beer. "What on earth have you been doing all that time?" Joyce demanded. "Doing? Talking, of course," Pyotr shot back. After that there were no more weekday birthday parties. "These Russian get-togethers are called a way of 'relaxing,'" Muriel said, "though I think they're anything but. Sergei feels exactly the same way about an evening with my American friends."

Drinking habits are also very different. In Russia, alcohol was for years the only form of legitimate deviance, and there was great indulgence for drunks. Under the influence you could say what you wanted, and it wasn't held against you. Drinking was a way of withdrawing from the Soviet system into a fuzzy, friendly world at home. There was a dark side to this retreat, however, for by 1989 there were more than 21 million alcoholics in the country, and drinking remains a major cause of divorce, birth defects, illness and accidents.[11] Yet, as Ronald Hingley commented, few other countries show such reverence for drinking. He noted the

> high regard, tenderness and even affection with which the average sober Russian seems to regard any intoxicated person. One would think . . . that to achieve a condition of helpless alcoholic befuddlement was a feat not only meritorious, but also extremely arduous and only attainable after years of unremitting self-sacrifice and dedicated apprenticeship.[12]

Sergei could go through a bottle of vodka at a sitting, and during one evening he put away so much cognac that he passed out in the subway on the way home. "When Sergei arrived in the U.S. he only drank vodka and cognac, and never touched wine," Muriel said. "The wines in Russia are awful, but now he's starting to develop a taste for Chardonnay." Vodka vs. white wine, canned corn and sour cream vs. peanuts and pre-dinner cocktails—three times a day the mixed couples are vividly reminded of their gastronomic cultural differences.

How Are You Feeling?

"When my aunt asked Sergei how he was feeling," Muriel said, "all she really wanted was a two-minute answer. Instead, he went on for twenty minutes about his sore throat and cough." Nothing brings out stronger feelings than illness, and the way a sick child is treated by his parents sets the stage for his adult expectations of how he believes he should be treated—and how he will treat others—when ill. Fred and Irina, who rarely had serious arguments, had screaming fights on the subjects of health and medicine, each accusing the other of being a relic from the Dark Ages.

In America, illness is to be avoided and gotten over as soon as possible. Joyce called in sick only when she was really ill. As an American management expert noted, "In today's economy, with companies being downsized all the time, there's a real concern about not appearing weak. You don't want to acknowledge you may be ill."[1] Sergei and Irina, on the other hand, had used illness throughout their lives to avoid doing anything even slightly unpleasant. Were you hung over from too much vodka? You called in sick. Was your report late? Sick. Was your friend about to get a reprimand at a Party meeting and you didn't want to vote for it, or to stick your neck out by defending him? Sick. Since there was no incentive to work and no real threat of being fired, getting sick was the universal solution.

Both real and imaginary illnesses were taken with deadly seriousness. Pyotr and Irina thought their spouses unfeeling and slightly crazy because they did not take every sniffle as a threat of hospitalization, and went to work even when they were really ill.

Because health is taken so seriously, Russian spouses are extremely attentive to a sick mate. Margaret Wettlin was touched by her husband Andrei's tender care when she was pregnant and ill with typhoid fever. "He spent every hour free from professional duties at my bedside. His steady gaze at the height of the battle assured me I would win it."[2] When Muriel broke her arm, Sergei did household chores for three months, and cared for her in ways she never thought him capable of. When Pyotr sprained an ankle and Joyce did not fuss over him night and day he went off to his mother's house to get chicken soup and plenty of attention. Gelsey Kirkland was amazed by Baryshnikov's solicitude while she was suffering from a painful skin rash. "I expected him to turn around and leave," she wrote, "but he surprised me. He was gentle. He stayed and offered consolation. He even sprinkled baby powder on my tender skin. This was the prince with whom I had fallen in love."[3]

"It's so hard to know when Fyodor is really sick," Carol lamented, and her complaint was echoed by many American spouses. "Any little scratch is gangrene, and a cough signals the beginning of pneumonia." "It's like the boy who cried wolf," Mark said. "I'm always telling Svetlana not to think about her aches and pains, and yet I'm afraid I won't know when she's *really* sick because of the constant whining about her health."

Complaints of various aches and pains do not necessarily mean the same thing to the two spouses. Russians moan about "pressure," certain that their blood pressure is affected by every change in the weather, humidity and moods. "I'm feeling my pressure" can mean a headache or fatigue rather than high blood pressure. Liver complaints can cover everything from hangover to heartburn, and "my heart hurts" can translate as "I'm feeling low," rather than as cardiac trouble. It is also a useful euphemism. The first time Svetlana told Mark she was having heart trouble he wanted to call an ambulance, thinking that in such a young woman chest pain must be a serious symptom. Svetlana refused, and when he pressed her she admitted she was feeling tired and having her period, but had been too embarrassed to tell him.

Though Russians can discuss illness endlessly, certain health problems such as "female troubles," dentures or mental illness are considered so personal that the Russian spouse may avoid raising them even with the partner. Mentioning such complaints to a third party is as reprehensible as a public recounting of the couple's sex life. In response to Barbara Bush's question as to why she had not asked Nancy Reagan how she was feeling after major breast cancer surgery, Raissa Gorbachev replied that in Russia no one would mention such an operation.[4] A reference to something so personal would have been extremely tactless.

Russian popular beliefs can seem rather odd to American spouses. Pyotr was convinced that sitting on the floor led to female infertility. Sergei believed that eating honey caused low blood pressure, and Shevchenko repeatedly told Judy Chavez not to drink too much water because that would lead to a cholesterol problem.[5] If you had a cold all the windows had to be closed, because fresh air could kill you.

Some reactions to illness were conditioned by the differences between Russian and American medical care. The Russians were in the habit of dropping by the neighborhood clinic with any and all complaints, and were accustomed to doctors who made house calls. Under the Soviet regime all such care was free of charge, and what the medical personnel lacked in modern equipment, CAT scans, MRIs and medicines they made up in brains, diagnostic skills and human warmth.

The inadequacy of medical equipment and the shortage of medicines made many Russians resort to diagnosing themselves. "Pyotr thinks he's dying, goes to the doctor, gets an antibiotic and then refuses to take it," said Joyce. "He always thinks he knows better." In the USSR patients dreamed of getting foreign medicines; in America, Russians long for their old familiar pills. "Every time someone goes to Russia, Fyodor asks them for Seduksen," Carol reported. "With all the excellent tranquilizers such as Valium that you can get here!" In a new world the familiar is reassuring. "When Sergei had the flu, I found him taking pills some Russian émigré had given him," Muriel said. "He didn't even know what they were, but they were from over there."

Joyce had to stop Pyotr from calling the doctor three times a day to check what time to take his medicine or beg for one more day of sick leave. "That's what doctors are for—to take care of you!" he argued. "The doctor can't drop everything to keep holding your hand," she retorted. "Of course he can't," snapped Pyotr. "He's a doctor for dollars—not for people!"

It is hard for Russians to get used to the brusque style of American doctors. "That doctor only does his job for the money," Fyodor complained. "No real discussion of how I am, no questions about my family." The American doctors' fear of malpractice suits was also new to the Russians, as well as the fact that physicians feel bound to tell a patient the truth about his condition. Pyotr could not understand why the doctor insisted on informing his mother that she had cervical cancer, for in Russia, patients were never told directly that they were seriously ill; the doctor informed a spouse or other close family member. Cancer was a no-no word. "How can you hand someone a death sentence?" Pyotr wondered. "If a person thinks he's going to die he'll never try to get better." From the Russian viewpoint, the moral issue of telling the patient the truth and the question of the doctor's legal responsibility do not cut much ice.

The American spouses in Moscow lived in perpetual fear of Russian hospitals, which were breeding grounds for infection, and where patients had to bring their own blankets, bandages and food. By the 1990s good treatment and drugs could generally be obtained only through huge bribes. Though in the last few years a few American clinics with modern equipment have opened up, American spouses tend to go home when serious illness strikes. In the event of an accident, however, first-aid treatment must be rendered on the spot. When Mary C. broke an arm in Moscow the X-ray equipment in the clinic where she was examined was thirty years old, and the slings consisted of dirty pieces of gauze. "At least they didn't charge me anything," she said, "and the doctor spent two hours reassuring me that the fracture wasn't serious."

Back in the 1930s, John Scott's wife Masha commented that knowing how much an American hospital cost made her feel sicker:

> In Russia I never worried that I had to pay. If I got sick, I knew they would take care of me. But here once when I was sick for three days in hospital, I felt not good, because I had to pay . . . how can I know if I am really sick when it is to doctor's advantage for me to be sick? So I cannot enjoy hospital here . . .[6]

The Russian collective spirit was evident in Masha's attitude towards her hospital stay. Most Americans long for privacy in a hospital ward. "When I was in hospital here in New York once John had for me a private room and I found it very bad," she wrote. "I was so lonely I cried all the time!"[7]

THE MINDSET

❧

While most mixed couples eventually resolve arguments about how to eat a potato or being an hour late for dinner, the basic values inculcated in childhood remain a source of latent friction.

In Soviet Russia the sense of collective responsibility was highly developed. Lee Oswald's first Russian girlfriend, Ella, was surprised when he did not move to help a woman on the street whose pocketbook had been stolen.[1] "Carol only thinks about herself," Fyodor complained during the first year of their marriage. "I never thought she was such an individualist. It's always what she wants to do, what's good for her, all this stuff about realizing and fulfilling herself. I seem to be an accessory to her 'personal growth plan.'"

At home and in school, Americans are taught to rely on themselves. From first grade on, school children are told to "do your own work" and "keep your eyes on your own test paper." Letting another student look at the answers to an exam is grounds for expulsion. When Irina took an advanced English-language exam, she naturally assumed that the students would copy off each other's papers, the way they always did in Russia. Her teacher, an American of Russian background, explained the consequences.

"That's unfair," Irina protested. "It's *wrong* not to help your friends. If I help Olga by letting her copy my paper, the next time she'll help me!" The argument that that this was "dishonest" did not convince her. "What if you can't write a business letter because you've copied Olga's paper and never learned how to do it yourself?" the teacher asked. "Oh, I'll ask Olga to come over and help me," Irina replied.[2]

Involvement of the collective in the affairs of strangers was part of the fabric of Soviet life, and it took many Americans a long time to see such meddling as an expression of concern.[3] It is not easy to be constantly admonished by self-righteous individuals, however well-intentioned, proffering all kinds of unsolicited advice. Susan Eisenhower described a night with Roald Sagdeev and some friends at a concert in Moscow, when she desperately wanted to talk to him in private:

> Even though these gatherings had been pleasant enough, all I could sense was time ticking away before my departure and no resolution to our difficulties. The tension between us was palpable. That cold windy evening I wasn't wearing a hat. One of the women in our party admonished me for not having one. After several efforts to get me to borrow hers I finally exploded: "I don't want a hat!"[4]

The spouses' expectations of other people also differ greatly. Joyce and Muriel had been raised to "look on the bright side," to expect things to turn out well, and to assume that people's intentions are basically positive. The Russians' reaction was precisely the opposite. Whenever Joyce suggested they go to a movie, Pyotr's first reaction was, "It's probably a piece of junk." Mark asked Svetlana why she didn't seem happy when her first article was accepted for publication in a prestigious American music journal. "They'll probably change their minds and not publish it," she answered. In the light of the hardships their country has endured, the Russian spouses' pessimistic attitude is understandable, though the persistent gloom sometimes seems excessive to the Americans. When Carol proposed going to a Japanese restaurant, Fyodor replied that it was probably awful. "Why do you always have to be so damn negative?" she exploded. "Does that make life more fun?" "Look," he responded, "if you think something will be awful, and it turns out to be good, you're pleasantly surprised. If you think something will be good, and it turns out to be awful, you'll be very disappointed."

If things are bad, Americans try to make them better. Carol was upset when she failed her driver's license exam for the third time, but she immediately set a date to take the test again. Sergei's favorite response to any setback was, "So what can I do about it?" A Russian expects things to go badly. A corollary to this negativism is the conviction that the world is a fairly rotten place populated primarily by rotten individuals who are out to cheat you. The paranoiac legacy of Stalinism decrees that everyone is guilty until proven innocent, and many Russians who reject the tenets of Soviet Marxism continue to view the world through the lenses of its dogma.

Norman Mailer remarked that Marina Oswald "always suspects the motives of the new people to whom she speaks."[5] Fyodor was convinced that the bank deliberately made mistakes on his statements, to cheat him. Pyotr was sure that any hotel room he was given was undoubtedly the worst one in the building, and checked out the furniture and the bathroom fixtures as though he intended to move in for life. Irina was convinced the accountant was trying to deceive her and Fred. Judy Chavez describes how Shevchenko infuriated movie audiences by constantly standing up to look for another seat, sure that other people had a better view.[6] For Russians, who are chronically suspicious of human motivations, the determination of whether someone is a "good" or a "bad" person becomes a critical criterion for deciding on any future relationship.[7] The American characterization of people as intelligent, outgoing, sensitive or fun strikes them as rather superficial.

The assumption that things will inevitably get worse in a world over which one has no control can lead to passivity. Why write a letter to the newspaper? No one will publish it, and anyhow, it won't make any difference.[8] The Soviet system in which the individual had no say engendered a laid-back, *laissez-faire* attitude in millions of Russians. Muriel kept trying to get Sergei to write his résumé, cover letters, and get on the phone with people who could help him professionally. "If someone is interested he'll find me," Sergei replied. Svetlana at first refused to send any of her articles to music journals because she was so sure they would be rejected.

The expectation that things will get worse also leads to an unwillingness to change anything that works. Irina did not understand Fred's interest in new computer software. If a program worked, why get another which might wreck the computer? If the Chinese restaurant down the block was good, why try the one across the street which could be worse? Such apprehensions were even stronger regarding changing apartments or switching jobs. The known was preferable to the unknown.

The Soviet system engendered a disdain for meaningless rules and regulations. Laws were respected only if breaking them entailed serious consequences. Otherwise, you got away with what you could, particularly if the damage done was to the state rather than to your neighbor. Obeying laws meant that you were part and parcel of the detested system. If you were stopped for speeding, you could bribe the policeman; if he took away your license, you could buy another one around the corner. You didn't steal from your friends, and stealing from the state was of no consequence. Sergei kept urging Muriel to take nonexistent deductions and cheat on her taxes. It was *her* money the state was taking away, wasn't it? If she were audited the accountant could surely invent something, if he were paid enough. When Pyotr wanted to borrow a friend's medical insurance card to avoid a hefty doctor's bill, Joyce had great difficulty in convincing him that this would be unwise.

The Soviet system also fostered a reflex response of lying. Americans are raised to believe in honesty and, barring proof to the contrary, usually believe that people are telling the truth.[9] The Soviet government and press lied to the people, bosses lied to their subordinates, who paid them back in kind, and husbands lied to their wives about everything from infidelities to drinking up the household money. And while most Russians sincerely believe that honesty with a spouse about extra-marital affairs is hurtful and destructive of the marriage, the atmosphere in the Soviet Union encouraged a general attitude of sidestepping the truth which included sexual relations along with nearly every other aspect of life. People said one thing in public and another in private. Lying became second nature, a form of self-defense.

Muriel was frustrated by Sergei's instinctive reaction of telling a falsehood to get out of an embarrassing situation. When they accepted an dinner invitation from some friends, forgetting they had theater tickets for the same night, he wanted her to call and say she had to work that evening. "And when we run into mutual friends in the theater, what do we say?" she asked. Her response was to call their friends, tell them the truth, apologize, and make a date for another evening. Muriel tried to explain to Sergei that in America once you are caught in a lie it is enormously difficult to regain lost trust. In Russia, people were quite understanding with a person caught in a blatant falsehood, since the next day the same thing could happen to them.

The Russian spouses found certain aspects of American honesty extremely peculiar. When Carol's girlfriend told her she had confessed to her husband that she had had an affair, Fyodor was dumbfounded. "The stupid fool! The affair is over, and she wasn't about to leave him. He'd never have found out! So what's she got now? What kind of a life can she have with him?" "But she was honest," argued Carol. "I'm sure he appreciates that she came clean with him. Otherwise she'd be living a lie." "You Americans are so naive," Fyodor sighed. "You think being honest makes anything all right. If she really cared about his feelings she'd never have told him!"

Sergei quoted to Muriel the words of the Russian poet Tiutchev: "A thought that is spoken is a lie." "Things are much better left

unsaid," he argued. "Your American friends are wrecking their relationships with their husbands with all the yak-yak about 'commitments,' and all that talk with psychiatrists." "*You* should talk,"
snapped Muriel. "All you Russians ever do is talk and talk." "Yes,
but there are some things we never say," Sergei replied. "Such as 'I
don't like what you're doing in bed,' or 'You look terrible in that
dress.' Sometimes being silent isn't lying—it's being sensitive."

The worst thing a Russian spouse can say about a person is that
he is "dry," meaning that he is cold and lacking in emotion. As
Tatyana Tolstaya wrote, "Logic is seen as dry and evil, logic comes
from the devil. The most important thing is sensation, smell,
emotion, tears, mists, dreams and enigma."[10] At the start of his
romance with an American girl a young Russian was shocked by
her coldness:

> She looked into my eyes. As though she were boring into
> the most hidden depths of my consciousness. Then she said
> flatly and calmly, "I love you." It was the tone of a TV
> announcer's weather forecast.[11]

While Russian intensity can be attractive, it does not make for
easy living. "I'm a person who shows her emotions and feelings,"
said Viktoria Fyodorova. She complained that her husband "doesn't
show his feelings unless we're alone. Even a kiss on the cheek was
taboo."[12] Russians do not believe in doing things halfway. Out-
pourings of emotion in private life are balanced by extreme
restraint and suspicion in public life. As Hedrick Smith commented, "They adopt two very different codes of behavior for
their two lives—in one, they are taciturn, hypocritical, careful,
cagey, passive; in the other, they are voluble, honest, direct, open,
passionate."[13]

Ideas are as important to Russians as deeds, and the more complex and abstract, the better. Anne's husband Ivan planned to
submit to a publisher a project for a four-volume series on the
history of Russian music, and found her suggestion that he first do

a one-volume proposal small-minded and petty. Irina was going to revolutionize the way the Russian language was taught all over America, not just in her school. Russians are convinced that great ideas are born in the dialectics of talking. "I can't tell Fyodor I want to buy a chair," Carol complained. "I get a lecture on what's wrong with American aesthetic taste in furniture and on the evils of a capitalist system which only produces shoddy junk."

Sergei's favorite answer to Muriel's question, "What are you doing?" was, "I'm thinking." Irina could think for a week about where she wanted to go for dinner Saturday night, and Svetlana waited five years before deciding how to decorate her living room. A Russian psychiatrist noted that "Russians can look at an object all day and reflect on it but take no action."[14] Fred found Irina irritatingly slow, while she accused him of constantly rushing into things without thinking. There were also accusations of a lack of "seriousness." If you took things "seriously," be it buying a pair of shoes or inviting a friend to dinner, you thought it over carefully and talked it through. "You Americans never think through the consequences of your actions," Pyotr complained to Joyce. "And you Russians," she replied, "never do anything— you only talk, and sigh, and complicate the simplest things in life."

The American spouses had trouble with the way their Russian mates were "assured of certain certainties." Marxist ideology and historical materialism were so deeply etched into the minds of the population that even the most virulently anti-communist Russians were affected by the Soviet mindset. Aside from religious fundamentalists or mad scientists, Americans tend to reject the notion that philosophical systems can explain everything, and that there is always a "right" or a "wrong" answer; several options should be explored and the best choice made. From elementary school on, Americans are trained to preface their views with, "In my opinion," "You may be right, but," or, "We might look at this another way, too." Saying, "You're wrong," is discouraged. For Soviet believers, there was only one answer. They were right and everyone else was wrong. Margaret Wettlin recalled how over-powered she was by her husband's self-assurance.

> He was never troubled by doubts and misgivings, always certain of the rightness of his ways and choices . . . circumstances arose that led me to question the legitimacy of such overweening self-confidence. I was fully aware of his rich gifts and lofty aspirations and suspected he was prevented from giving them fullest expression by his insensitivity to the moods and responses of others.[15]

One foreigner described this mentality as that of people who had "the unstoppable, unsteerable certainty of a child's noisy windup toy."[16] Many Russian spouses, however, are blissfully unaware that they are engaging in this type of behavior. "At first I was irritated that Margo never expressed her opinions," one Russian said of his American wife. "And then I understood that she simply never had a chance to voice her views. I would interrupt her."[17] The Russian spouses had all the right answers, be it to the future of America or the dramatic qualities of a Broadway play. "There are no shades of gray for Irina and her Russian friends," Fred commented. "Everything is right or wrong, good or bad. They know everything about everything, from politics to art."

Joyce hated going to movies with Pyotr and her American friends because they could never have a real discussion afterwards. "This was a bad film," or "the director was not successful," Pyotr would announce. Differing points of view were greeted by "That's wrong" or a condescending smile at the obvious stupidity of the comment.

As the psycholinguist Deborah Tannen has noted, "Many cultures see arguing as a pleasurable sign of intimacy."[18] Arguing with Americans, however, was no fun for the Russian spouses. Everything was "I think that" or "perhaps." Couldn't they state their position forcefully and stick to it? The Americans found the Russian style of debate aggressive and confrontational. The

Russians found the Americans weak and indecisive. In the United States arguing is not considered a sport, and disagreement is something to be resolved by various means, including compromise.[19] In Russian, however, "compromise" has a pejorative flavor, implying going back on one's principles and retreating from a correct and justified position. As an observer of Soviet behavior noted about the Russian view of arguments,

> If one gives in too easily . . . the winner will not respect the loser. Perhaps more importantly, he will not trust him. How can a man's word be good, if his mind can be changed that easily? And if I can change his mind that easily, so can someone else . . . What seems in private conversation to an American to be a reasonable respect for the other person's opinion, may appear to a Russian as, at best, wishy-washy, at worst, contemptible. In referring to a man she didn't like, a Russian woman said, "He has no opinions of his own. . . . He is like a sausage: what you stuff him with—this he carries around."[20]

One of Shevchenko's favorite expressions, "No, that's totally unacceptable,"—which he applied to any and all situations—became a standing joke between Judy Chavez and the FBI agents.[21] Some of Muriel's and Fred's friends called their Russian spouses "Communists," meaning not believers in Marxism but dogmatists so convinced they were right they would not listen to any opposing views. One Russian married to an American woman remarked, "Psychologically it's not easy for a former Soviet citizen to become an American. I don't even know if it's possible. I think I'm the best adapted of all the people I know of my age in the U.S. . . . But I'm still sometimes too categorical—Soviet style."[22]

Pyotr could get away with expressing dogmatic views about a movie, but he got into trouble at a dinner party with his confident assertions that "Everyone knows all homosexuals are sick," and "Blacks are intellectually inferior to whites." Many Russians have few compunctions about making negative remarks or jokes about people of various races, nationalities, sexual orientations and disabilities. On several occasions Sergei and Pyotr were left facing dead silence at the end of an anecdote they found hilarious and their American friends found glaringly bigoted (the Russian spouses, in turn, often found American jokes incredibly vulgar or stupid). In the interests of preserving domestic harmony, one mixed couple simply decided that they would never discuss blacks or homosexuals—a "compromise," as the Russian husband sarcastically put it.[23]

Ironically, Russians who disagreed with the Soviet system could be just as doctrinaire in their thinking as their Marxist opponents. Pyotr and Sergei, who were violently anti-Soviet, were as stubbornly dogmatic as any orthodox Marxist. As an expert on intercultural marriage noted, no matter how negative a spouse's feelings about his society, that culture is a part of him—and therefore of the marriage:

Generally, people who enter into an intercultural marriage have already distanced themselves somewhat from a strict adherence to the predominant values of their own societies. But, at the same time, they are what they are because of their society's value orientation. Whether they personally believe in those values or not, they were shaped by a society which espouses them.[24]

The authoritarian mindset can carry over to family life. Pyotr thought the family was his fiefdom to rule as he pleased. His one justification for his behavior was, "I said so and that's it." One young émigré girl, complaining about how her father had forced her as a child to learn ice skating, ballet and classical guitar, remarked sadly, "My father constantly speaks against the dictatorial reality of Soviet totalitarianism. But . . . totalitarianism can penetrate the fiber of a people and infect every facet of their lives, even family life."[25]

Despite the spouses' dogmatism, virtually none of the mixed couples had a problem with religion. Most people raised in the Soviet era were not believers, but many had religious grandparents, and were rather tolerant of their spouses' beliefs. Sergei went to church only on Russian Easter. Today the Russian Orthodox church is rapidly gaining believers in Russia, and many younger Russians are returning to the religion of their grandparents. For most of the Russian Jews, religion consisted of bits of tradition and superstition. All Pyotr knew of Passover was eating gefilte fish and matzo, and he was happy to join in Joyce's traditional family celebration.

Only when a couple had children did religion become an issue. Fred wanted his children to go to the Presbyterian church, in which he was raised; Irina was apprehensive about their starting to believe in "all kinds of strange things." For many Russian spouses, superstitions were far more important than religious beliefs. Sergei would not shake hands with a visitor across the threshold, because the power of the icon in the corner of a Russian house ends at the door and the devil is right outside, waiting to cause a quarrel. Pyotr insisted on sitting down before going on a trip, and Irina refused to buy baby clothes before the child was born because that could mean bad luck. Even highly sophisticated Russians were not immune to these folk beliefs.

National identity and patriotism were far more important to the Russian spouses than to the Americans. For Sergei, a third-generation Italian-American was an Italian, not an American. Whether or not they became American citizens, the Russians remained Russian. Though they might bitterly criticize the Soviet system, Russia remained the center of the universe. They could talk for hours about their homeland. "Sometimes I feel as though there are three of us in this marriage,—Sergei, me and Russia," Muriel remarked. "Irina is always criticizing the U.S.," Fred said. "With all the stores and clothes, you'd think she'd be ecstatic. But the only articles she reads in the paper are the ones about Russia, though when she lived there, all she thought about was how to get out." Even after years of life in America, when Russian spouses said "our country," they were usually referring to Russia, not the United States.

Because patriotism was so important to the Russian spouses, they also valued it in their American mates. As much as they might dislike various aspects of the capitalist system, they expected their spouses' attitude to America to resemble the loyalty they felt towards Russia. When Maria wrote a school composition imagining how President Clinton spilled orange juice on his pants and dropped a chicken on the floor, Pyotr was horrified. "She'll get into all kinds of trouble!" he shouted at Joyce. "She has no right to show such disrespect! This country is full of bad things, but she's an American, and he's the President!" Convinced that the child would be expelled from school, he was flabbergasted when the teacher praised Maria's imaginative writing and read the composition to the fourth-grade class.

Today, following the collapse of the totalitarian system in the USSR and the subsequent influx of Western notions of individualism and the rules of the game of a market economy, the collective spirit, paranoia and passivity of the past are gradually being eroded. Fyodor was amazed by the ambition and spunk of his nephews in Russia, and at how freely they spoke their minds to friends and strangers alike, often to the horror of their older relatives. Deeply rooted attitudes and fears, however, do not change overnight, and the stultifying grip of decades of fear and passivity cannot be fully loosened in only a few years. Nor has the entire system—and the thinking of the population—changed as radically as many Americans would like to believe. The Russian national character and the entire nation had been forming for centuries before the advent of Soviet Marxism, and are still marked by the influence of the Russian Orthodox Church and Byzantium, the Mongol invasion, Slavophile nationalism, the Westernizers and the opening up to Europe under Peter the Great, the Napoleonic invasion—the list could be continued indefinitely. While the future Russian spouses of Americans may well be free from the paranoia, passivity and blind dogmatism born of the worst aspects of the Soviet system, they will still be Russians—the proud and patriotic products of centuries of Russian history and culture—and not Westerners.

Of course, as far as Russian and American spouses are concerned, the situation today is very different from the years when Russians left the Soviet Union with no hope of return, and were treated as traitors to the motherland. Once in America, Russians who had desperately wanted to leave their country became equally desperate to see it again. The knowledge that "you can't go home again" made the yearning even stronger. Though today travel and contacts are no longer restricted, and couples are free to live in either country, the question of identity remains unresolved for many of them. When Viktoria Fyodorova began living in Connecticut with her American husband, she wrote, "I am in the United States, but I am not yet American. I have left Russia, but I am still Russian." When she took her baby on a visit to Russia in 1977 she felt like "a Soviet citizen, but an American wife." She realized that her interests had become completely different from those of her Russian friends, who did not understand her new life. "It was nice to see them, to chat, but after a while you don't know what to talk about."[26] Elena Safonova, a Russian actress married to a Frenchman, commented that when she was in Paris she missed Moscow—and when she was in Moscow she missed Paris.[27]

This feeling of not having a real home is voiced by many spouses torn between two cultures. One Russian wife who was unhappy in America, and went home to visit her family and friends, found that in Russia she was equally dissatisfied. "Home is only *home-for-now* to me," said Viktoria Fyodorova. "I do not know the deep meaning of that word, because life has left me too fearful that what is good will not stay, and what is bad will return."[28] Intimate involvement with two cultures can result in a richly bicultural life. It can also create a person who feels homeless in both countries.

LOVE AND MARRIAGE
DOT-COM

"Russian ladies, truly beautiful, want to meet you!"

From glossy brochures, slick videos and colorful catalogues with pictures of hundreds of girls, the message blares out in lure of the American male, promising meetings, adventure, happiness. Over the past five years there has been an explosion of dating agencies in the United States specializing in bringing American men together with women in Russia and Eastern Europe. In the business of mail-order brides, which goes back to the frontier days of the old West, the Russian contingent has shot up, placing second only to Filipino women in the number of "fiancée visas" granted by the U.S. immigration service in 1999.[1]

And the way the meetings take place has undergone a sea change. Many Americans and Russians of both sexes still meet by chance and fall in love, as in the cold-war decades, though they no longer have to struggle with their governments to be united. But in a lot of cases today, the meetings are arranged by dating agencies or on web sites and preceded by exploratory correspondence between the man and woman on the Internet as a result of a calculated decision on both sides. An on-line American list server, the Russian Women's List, boasts a membership of more than

1200 men, who swap information on everything from the women they have met and the problems they encountered to recipes for borsht and the best hotel deals in Minsk.

What has developed is a whole industry. Of the 200 to 250 international dating agencies in the United States, at least 80— European Connections, Anastasia, Foreign Relations, A Foreign Affair, Russian Connections, Scanna International, Elite Match- making, Marriage Club Classic, to name just the biggest—focus on women applicants in the former Soviet bloc, and in Russia some 400 agencies, more than 100 of them in Moscow, service their Russian and American clientele. European Connections alone claims a catalogue readership of more than 70,000 men and a file of some 7,000 Russian women.[2] The phenomenon has been providing grist for both serious newspapers and pop magazines, as well as for television specials ranging from investigative studies to splashy sensationalism.

Interestingly enough, few American women seem drawn to this marriage market; those with Russian husbands met them, for the most part, while traveling or at work or through friends. The boom in e-mail brides has been attributed to the American male. What manner of man, then, provides the demand for the currently plentiful supply, and what makes him look abroad, and particu- larly at Russia, for the gratification of his desires?

The word from European Connections is that most of the men who sign up for the agency's get-together tours across the demol- ished iron curtain are between 30 and 55—the bulk around 41 or 42—and are evenly divided between lifelong bachelors and divorced men; nearly a third have a child. On one trip to Russia the oldest man was 74 and the youngest 27.[3] In my interviews and correspondence with dozens of Americans looking for Russian wives, I found them, for the most part, to be well-educated WASP professionals in their thirties and forties. Significantly, perhaps, a high percentage were computer and software experts.[4] Most of them had devoted all their time and energy to making it in their fields, and woke up one day to the realization that if they wanted a family it was time to "do something." But why, then, not do it in the United States?

"What do these Russian girls have that we don't?" sadly asked an American wife whose American husband of twenty-three years had left her for a young Russian woman with a child.

To this question there are many answers, but the one most frequently heard revolves around the word "feminine." Among the men in question there appears to be a widespread feeling that the feminist movement in the United States has gone too far in stripping the American female of those qualities of warmth and piquancy that make women attractive to men. A *Philadelphia Inquirer* reporter who tagged along on an agency trip to Russia wrote that what seemed to unite the men on the tour "was a strong conviction that American women were materialistic and had been corrupted by feminism. They saw themselves as victims."[5]

Here's how it was put by Edward, a computer engineer, married to a Russian: "During the seventies I supported the equality and equal opportunity for women that they worked for. And I still do. It's the way I was raised. Somewhere in the seventies the women's movement was hijacked. 'Women of the world unite against bourgeois-proletarian male domination!' The net result was that women were taught to view all male-female relationships as power struggles where somebody wins and somebody loses. Every American woman I met at some point turned our relationship into a struggle for power. They thought things couldn't be any other way."

The complaint is pervasive. In a how-to book, *"Your Bride Is In the Mail!,"* the author comments on his search for an American wife: "It seemed as though I were fishing for trout in waters populated only by barracuda."[6] Conversely, a subscriber to the Russian Women's List rhapsodized: "I just married the most devoted and caring woman I ever met. Russian women are simply better at being women than American women." "These Russian girls are beautiful, faithful and perfect women," said Sam, another eager suitor. Undaunted by his Russian fiancée's leaving him two months after he brought her over, Sam signed up for another tour to find another Russian bride.

And he had company. A surprising number of American men abandoned or divorced by their Russian wives remain so captivated by their femininity, appearance and intelligence that a poorly groomed careerist American spouse will no longer do, and they sign up with an agency in search of a Russian replacement. Perhaps the ultimate case of persistence is of a gentleman who offered up to $100,000 to anyone who could introduce him to his "special Russian woman." He was planning, at the time, to go to Russia and wait for the lady to be found.[7]

By no means, however, is disillusion with American women the sole reason for going Slavic. There are, clearly, a number of other factors at work. Some of the men in question, it seemed from my research, were carried away by the enticing photos in the agency catalogues; one of them was quite frank about it: "I wanted a drop-dead gorgeous woman in her twenties. In the U.S. my chances were zero, but in Russia you're batting close to hundred percent."[8] Others, with more modest expectations, came from small towns where the pool of potential wives was tiny or nonexistent. A few classed themselves as "losers"—too shy, or too plain-looking, or too set in their bachelor ways, and having trouble attracting a woman in the United States. Others had a yen for the exotic, for exploring a new world with a woman of a different culture. Some knew exactly what they wanted—a mature woman raised on conservative values or a certain kind of religious belief—and thought such a woman would be easier to find in the former Soviet Union than at home.

Another widely shared wish was for a homemaker who would place family well ahead of career, and again the feeling was that there were more of her kind left in a more old-fashioned society such as Russia's. The agencies are aware of this preference, and their literature on their "Russian ladies"—it is always ladies rather than women—makes a point of their "family oriented" and "traditional" upbringing. Some men, in fact, specify an interest in a ready-made family—a woman with a child past the diaper age.

Whatever the reasons given, the spectacle of American men chasing after younger Russian women—the age difference averages out at about 13 years—has come to the attention of American women's groups, and the reaction has been largely skeptical. "It's not a normal love interest that's driving them, it's fantasy," was one comment; or it's "the dream of being the 'all-provider.'" An even less positive assessment was that these men are "stiffs, weirdos and those who drink too much."[9] And from talking to people who have returned from their Russian tours, it does appear that in a few cases the search across the seas is for a good time and a week of sex. One participant avowed that "being an optimist," he took along a "variety sampler" of 75 condoms. A few others have spoken of husbands cheating on their American wives. "They are all kinds," was the view of a dating network administrator in Belarus. "From people with real good reasons for wanting a foreign wife to just plain losers with no chance back home and the wild idea that they can buy a girl."

So much for the American men; what about the Russian women?

The videos produced by the major agencies reveal an assortment of hopefuls from all walks of life, some evidently on the make, some who have obviously been around, some apparent innocents from the provinces, and a smattering of older women whose thick makeup is a mask for fatigue and quiet desperation. More than half of them, according to agency claims, are between 18 and 30; almost all have a higher education; about half are divorcées; almost a third have a child; pulchritude abounds. What, then, makes a beautiful, educated young woman (the average age is 29) send her photo and bio to a dating service or web site, present herself at a "meat market" lookover by platoons of American men, even sleep with one of them at the risk of his disappearing the next day, and at best meet and marry a perfect stranger, most likely considerably older than her, giving up country, family and friends for a new life in the United States?

As in the case of the men, there is one overriding answer. The economic collapse that has reduced almost half the Russian population to dire straits, with poverty, malnutrition and poor health care endemic across the country, has been especially hard on women. A 1999 survey of living conditions in Russia found that women account for 70 percent of the unemployed.[10] And the burden of this social and economic breakdown has fallen with devastating effect on the institution of marriage. In my interviews with Russian women, the complaint voiced again and again was that, in the current slump, Russian men seem to have lost their sense of responsibility for their wives and children; they cannot hold down a job and drink up their earnings.

"One must live in Russia to realize how deep is the crisis there between men and women," one woman said.[11] While the woman may be taking a chance on an American husband in a strange land, "she escapes from what appear to be even worse alternatives—no husband, or a Russian one."[12] Thus, though the principal motive is unquestionably one of exchanging extreme hardship for reasonable security in the America—few of the women are naive enough to dream of a pot of gold at the end of the rainbow—it also holds out the hope of acquiring a responsible and sober husband. One young woman's parents, who had lost everything in the August 1998 crash of the Russian banks and markets, were actively urging her to seek out an American husband and take them with her to the U.S.[13] Not surprisingly, ads for the dating firms try to convince prospective American clients that the Russian women are really interested in love and marriage, and not solely motivated by a desperate desire to leave the country and better their economic situation: "The vast majority of these ladies would only marry a man with whom they were deeply in love and with whom they believed they had the highest chances of building a happy marriage and family,"[14] one firm glibly proclaims.

A contributory reason is that the pressures of bare survival have made Russian women acutely vulnerable to sexual exploitation. Prostitution rings proliferate. Many newspaper ads for secretarial jobs are thinly disguised solicitations: girls "without complexes" wanted. For many a young secretary, sleeping with the boss is considered part of the job. And for many Russian women, a brush with this reality is the final straw that makes emigration via marriage seem a better way out. As quite a few women who would like to marry someone from their own country have discovered, a good Russian husband can be hard to find.[15] Despite the sexual revolution, a Russian woman who goes to a bar or other public place will most likely be seen as a potential one-night stand rather than as a possible marriage partner. Such factors make the agencies all the more appealing to Russian women. "While it's OK for a man to go to a bar," a young Russian girl said, "and to strike up a conversation with a woman, it's not all right for a woman to go out to a place like a bar in search of a man. So she goes to an agency instead."[16]

Marriage to an American, rather than a European, is preferable in her eyes. American men have a reputation in Russia of being more sensitive and caring in their relationships with women. "Russian men are drunkards, not physically fit, not very good sexually . . . while Western men seem to be leaner, more responsible and fit," commented the head of the St. Petersburg Center for Gender Issues.[17] The willingness of American men, in most cases, to take on a wife with a child—which many Russian men apparently will not do—is a definite plus. Desire for a better life for their children, with a stepfather standing by, is a powerful inducement for many of the women, particularly since a lot of Russian mothers today worry about their sons being called up in a war such as the one in Chechnya.

There are, inevitably, the sharks—the so-called Natashas—whose search is for American sugar daddies with furs, jewelry and Jaguars to hand out, but they are mostly fashion models and the quota is small. And there's another small group that reflects sadly on conditions in Russia today—widows whose businessmen husbands were gunned down by the Russian mafia and who do not relish the prospect of going through the same tragedy again.

Such, then, is the group portrait of the American men and Russian women who have been entering into these arrangements; how, though, does the system work?

For the man, the first stop is usually the dating agency, which sends him its brochures and catalogues with the photos, descriptions and biographies of its female assortment, and, for a fee, provides him with the postal and e-mail address of the woman he selects. To get on these listings, the woman in Russia pays a small fee to a local Russian agency in business with the American one. Or the man can go directly to the web site of one of the e-mail pen-pal clubs, specifying the type or relationship—language practice, friendship, marriage—desired.

When the man has made his choice, there is usually a period of phone conversations and correspondence by letter or e-mail, with the agency providing translations when needed. For Nina Rubasheva, the director of Vesta, one of the Russian agencies, this phase of getting acquainted is all right but shouldn't go on too long. "You have to get them together as fast as possible. Many men and women who met through the Internet or catalogues and corresponded for years have been bitterly disappointed when they finally met in person and felt they were duped and had wasted a huge amount of time. It's all in the personal chemistry."[18] The chemistry gets its chance in a couple of ways. Once the couple has met—usually after the man has made one or more trips to Russia—the American suitor may apply to the U.S. Immigration and Naturalization Service for a fiancée visa, and then wait for the woman's arrival. Some 2,700 such visas were issued to Russian women in 1999 (compared with 747 in 1997); the recipient has 90 days to marry the person who made the invitation, or leave the United States. The man who goes to Russia may have already selected his prospective fiancée or may go to look over the field. The bigger American agencies sponsor group or individual tours of one or more cities, with air fare, hotels, meals and entertainment included in the fee.

The entertainment may include "socials"—huge parties during which the 40-odd American clients may meet and try to size up between 600 and 800 Russian women, including some they've picked out of catalogues and corresponded with. One American participant in such a social spoke of it later as a male fantasy come true. "I was like a little boy walking into a candy store. I've never seen so many beautiful women."[19] Nor had he ever had so many good-looking women interested—or pretending to be interested—in him. On a week-long tour the men have an opportunity to date the women, sightsee with them if they're so minded, and it goes without saying, sample them sexually. The bill for the tour can run quite high, anywhere from $3,000 to $10,000. If he decides on a fiancée visa, there's also the lawyer's fee and the woman's air fare and her expenses during the prenuptial period in the United States.

How many of these tours end up in marriages? It's hard to know, since there are no general statistics covering all the agencies, but Art Steckel, co-director of European Connections, says that of the 2,000 or so men who have taken his agency's tours since 1992, about 75 percent invited a woman to the United States on a fiancée visa and about half these couples got married.[20] Other reports indicate that of the Russian women involved thus far with these agencies and dating services, some 10 percent to 40 percent found their American husbands.

How well have these marriages held up? Here the statistics are even sketchier. European Connections claims credit for some 800 successful marriages; Encounters International claims 104 marriages, five engagements and four divorces since it was founded in Bethesda, Maryland in 1993.[21] A lawyer who specializes in fiancée visas says he has seen some 600 marriages and 21 divorces in the last eight years. Listening to some of the parties involved in the marriages, or talking to their relatives or friends, or reading what they've written about their experiences, provides some insight into what has been going on.

One thing that is clear is that mail-order marriages between Russians and Americans pose at least as many problems as the more traditional kind of marriage grounded in love and passion. And while many of the unions arranged through agencies and web sites have proved successful—some very much so—the same problems of cultural difference and national character provide a challenge at least as difficult as in the more romantic past.

Beguiled by the woman's appearance of femininity, the American husband often discovers that the softness conceals a hard core. Russian women generally have strong views about their roles as mothers and homemakers; they are far from submissive, and as an article on French-Russian marriages complains, they are often prone to a cultural snobbishness—a Russian trait—that makes them hard to take.[22] "Russian women can be very, very stubborn and very, very demanding," wrote one American husband.[23] And another: "[They are] soft beautiful velvet over sharp steel."[24] The American may be aware from the start that he is taking a considerable risk marrying someone who does not speak English well and may be from a different social background. Only gradually may he realize that they are from two different worlds, with no basic values or interests. A case in point is that of a middle-aged postal worker who fell for a stunning Russian gym instructor on a Russian tour. Their marriage, featured on several American TV specials, quickly fell apart.[25] An example of discord reaching unbearable heights is that of an American who placed a desperate Christmas-eve call to his travel agent begging him to put his Russian lady on a plane back to Russia that very night.

Incompatibility is sharper without love to smooth its edges, and for the new Russian wife it can be compounded by her strange new surroundings. A woman accustomed to living in a city, where she had no trouble getting around on her own, may find herself deep in American suburbia, having exchanged grinding poverty for grinding isolation. Like as not, she cannot drive, and with her husband away at work she can go crazy from loneliness in a gilded cage with the latest freezer, dishwasher, washing machine and VCR, but no escape from her loneliness. Of course she can learn how to drive, but often this is not as easy as it might seem to someone raised in a car-dominated society. Dependent on her husband not only for getting out of the house but for all the ins and outs of a strange culture, she may find the whole experience too much. It was too much for Zhanna, a medical student from St. Petersburg who found herself in a Southern suburb. "I left him," she said, "because I was so bored in that dump I couldn't stand it."

While some young Russian women speak good English, others don't speak it at all, and are forced to communicate through smiles and gestures. If the wife lacks enough English to find a job, she must rely on an allowance for her daily needs, and put to the test, her reputed American free spender may turn out to be quite stingy. In general, however tempered by common sense, her expectations of American prosperity may have been inflated by Russian television ads for Snickers, Pampers and Pepsi, and she may not have understood that a $20,000 car and a $100,000 house did not mean her prospective husband was a millionaire. Disappointment can set in quickly. "I thought he lived in a beautiful house," said one young woman. "It was a mobile home."

In a few cases, her problems are far more serious: she discovers a violent side to her husband's nature and winds up abused. The dating agencies do not have the means to screen their male clients for criminal records or mental illness. The U.S. immigration authorities require the criminal record, if any, of the foreign applicant for a fiancée visa, not of her American sponsor.[26] There are some human-rights organizations that are trying to protect foreign brides from fraud and domestic violence. Nonetheless, although the cases are rare, the Russian woman can wind up abused, alone and frightened, with no one to call on for help.

There is a curious twist to this: Since battered immigrant women and children may petition for permanent residence on their own, a foreign wife could try to take advantage of the law by making a false claim of spousal abuse, dumping her husband and obtaining a "green card" permitting her to seek employment. She could then strike off anew, perhaps in search of a "better" spouse. Uncommon though they may be, there have been some scams of this kind. There have also been several cases of American husbands being pummeled in anger by their Russian wives. One apparent instance, which received wide media coverage, ended in the sudden death under mysterious circumstances of a 63-year-old American married to a Ukrainian girl 40 years his junior.[27] A few stories of couples who met and married through dating agencies or the Internet may provide a closer look at the problems they have faced and how well or badly they have been coping.

Robert and Zina met in Pskov in August 1998. He was 33 and had devoted the past 10 years entirely to his career as a computer engineer and software specialist, with a lot of traveling thrown in. What he wanted now was a wife who would build a home life for him. "I wanted the feeling that if I told the office to buzz off, I'm going home, there would be someone there at the door to make it worthwhile." To that end he had been corresponding with several Russian women through a dating agency, Zina among them.

Zina was 21. She spoke good English, had been to England and France, and did some translations for Robert—both of his technical documents and his correspondence with the other women. He reciprocated by relieving her of the attentions of a deranged American who had been menacing her by e-mail with such threats as, "I'll get you, you bitch." The persecution ended when Robert uncovered the man's identity and threatened to expose him to his employer. Zina agreed to meet Robert if he came to Pskov, and the courtship began.

What attracted her to Robert was his thoughtfulness, politeness and tact. He brought her flowers. They were married. "American women," she said in an interview, "are so stupid to have let such a nice guy pass by."

The couple live in Atlanta. She is studying at a state university for an M.A. in communications. One thing she appreciates about America is the relationship between the sexes. "In Russia," she said, "all the men know what women's obligations are—to sew, to cook, they know all that by heart. But they have no idea whatsoever of what their obligations might be. Here it's just the opposite. The men know what is wanted of them, and what their obligations are. In Russia, the men have been spoiled by women."

As for Robert, he has found the home life he sought. "We seem to be the most normal of couples," he said. "The age difference really isn't an issue, for women in Russia grow up faster. I don't feel that Zina is that much younger than I am. And we've got a lot of living ahead of us both."

A few years ago, Tamara was a 32-year-old secretary in Irkutsk making $60 a month. She was blond, blue-eyed and beautiful, but things had gone badly for her. Her marriage had ended in divorce. Her only child had died at birth. With only her cat for company, she felt that "there had to be more to life than this." But the situation was unpromising. "All the local men were drunks, or married. And then there were the suicides . . . such as my ex-husband's best friend, who killed himself because he couldn't support his family. The worst thing was the hopelessness, the feeling there was no way out . . . "

On a dare from one of her girlfriends, Tamara took her photo and bio to a dating agency. The response was a raft of letters from American men. But none of them seemed interesting. And then came a letter from Frank.

Frank was a stocky, balding, 47-year-old TV repairman, divorced, with a teenage son. He saw Tamara's photo in a European Connections catalogue, and instead of signing up for a tour with all its "socials," he took himself to Irkutsk to meet her.

For both of them, "something clicked." He proposed. She accepted. Her English was quite good. She took driving lessons. Now, married, in her new home in Virginia, she is considering getting a job or going back to school. Thinking back to when she accepted her girlfriend's dare, she says, "All our other girlfriends thought I was crazy. Now they're tearing their hair out from jealousy."

Alan, an engineer in a small town in Vermont, was 41 and divorced when he spotted Viktoria, a 23-year-old law student in Kiev, in an agency catalogue. So sure she was the girl for him, he signed up for a tour to meet her. She was beautiful and bright and seemed to fall for him as promptly as he had for her. Her family liked him and had him move from his hotel into their apartment. As soon as he got back to the U.S. he arranged for a fiancée visa.

When Viktoria arrived things seemed to go smoothly. She had a minimal grasp of English but learned quickly to make her way around. "She read every book in the house," Alan told me. "That girl knew more than I did about American history, and about a lot of other things, too. She'd read all kinds of books I'd never heard of."

But hardly three months had passed before she gave him a shock. "I thought I loved you," she announced, "but I only tried to love you. You're very kind, very understanding—and there's nothing there."

Viktoria is back in Kiev with her family, her friends, and her intellectual conversations. And Alan has signed up for another Russian tour.

For Peter, a 29-year-old engineer from Wisconsin, Tanya, 24, is "a dream come true." They met through the Life Partners agency, and everything seems to have worked out well. She has a three-year-old daughter from her first marriage, but that's all right with Peter. In Irkutsk she worked as a translator and her English is fairly fluent.

What made her go to a dating agency? "It's not that I was absolutely determined to find an American man," she said. "It's that I couldn't take Russians anymore. Russian men only care about themselves and their problems. Americans are kinder, more open. Peter listens to me. He calls me every day from work to see if I need anything. Very few Russians would do that."

Also, she said, there are the small things in her new life, like going to the movies, that she didn't have back home. "In Russia everything now is so expensive that I hadn't been anywhere in a long time. And things here are so relaxed."

Peter is enchanted: "She's so much more feminine and appreciative than American women. Besides, being with a Russian woman is never boring. It's like childhood all over again, because of the fresh way they see things. Even simple things, like going to the mall, are interesting."

A 35-year-old kindergarten teacher in Kharkov with a 14-year-old daughter from an unhappy first marriage, Masha lived with her parents, reconciled to her humdrum existence. When a girl-friend offered to fix her up with an agency and post her photo and bio on the Internet she thought it was a joke. "How," she asked, "can I find an American when I can't even find a Russian? And if he's someone like my ex-husband, who drank constantly and ran around with other women, who needs that?" Besides, another of her girlfriends had tried e-mail, and when she arrived in the United States on her fiancée visa her prospective husband announced that he had no intention of marrying her; with no money, little English and no place to go, she was forced to live and sleep with him for the 90 days until her visa expired and he had to pay for her trip back to Russia.

In spite of her misgivings, Masha went ahead. And when Paul began to write, she was won over. "He was so kind. I didn't need much English to understand that." Paul was a 40-year-old math teacher in an Indiana suburb, also divorced, also with a daughter, but he didn't see the child often; and when he arrived in Kharkov he was delighted to find in Masha's daughter, Dasha, the studious, talented child he had never had. He was much taken with Masha as well, and he made a hit with her.

But back in Indiana with his new family, Paul found he had more problems with his Russian wife than he had reckoned on. Lonely and depressed, she took out her moods on him when he came home from work, with a way of being offended for no good reason, or—her English being somewhat sketchy—because of misunderstandings. She admits it: "I was used to the old Russian idea of the wife. You know—tears, screams and wave the rolling pin around as you smash the plates on the floor." Partly it was psychological: she felt guilty about arriving with no money and being dependent on him for everything.

To help give her the independence she needed, Paul tried to teach her to drive, but it didn't work—they wound up fighting. "For a while," he recalls, "I thought this marriage would founder on the gear shift. Finally I paid for some pretty expensive lessons, but it was worth it."

Even in the beginning, however, things weren't all bad. She was pleased with Paul's attentiveness and patience with her. And there was an episode, early on, that made a big difference. Masha's Russian husband used to get drunk every night. "When we arrived at Paul's house and he got himself a glass of orange juice and poured in some vodka, I thought, 'Oh my God, I've done it again.' I'd never seen a man have just one drink and stop. But he was so considerate of my feelings about alcohol, and my panic over it, that he gave up his daily cocktail. That really touched me."

Even after getting her driver's license, Masha stayed home to work on her English, but now she's looking for a job. "She's remarkably frugal," Paul commented. "I thought she'd want me to buy her everything in the stores, but she's really used to 'doing without.' Soon after she arrived she asked me about my bills, my mortgage and credit cards. Boy, was she shocked! 'How can you owe that much?' she kept asking. I had maxed out a few credit cards to go to Kharkov to get her and Dasha, and to pay for their expenses. Now that we're saving to buy a house, she shops really carefully—I wouldn't have the patience to go around the stores like that comparing the prices of apples and milk." Both are sure they will stay together. "I know," she says, "that he loves me more than I deserve."

For another couple, though, there was no happy ending. John and Elena were brought together by desperate need, but their needs were different, and for that he paid a heavy price.

Beautiful but uneducated, having barely finished high school, and with no work experience beyond a brief stint at a candy factory, Elena was living with her parents in Minsk, in Belarus, where the family had moved from Russia. At 27 she had been left with a three-year-old son from a disastrous first marriage. Before they were married, her husband, a drunk, had beaten her during her pregnancy; after the wedding he began sleeping with other women. She left him and nearly starved. When the baby was born, she gave in to his pleas to go back to him, but the marriage quickly fell apart and he never showed any further interest in her or the child. Her parents were as badly off as she, having lost their jobs in a tool factory. Worn out and penniless, with only a part-time job to sustain her, she went on the Internet looking for an American husband—for the sake, she said, of her boy.

It was Elena's mother who picked out John's picture; she thought he had kind eyes. And kindness, Elena said, was all she wanted. John lived in Philadelphia. They exchanged letters for several months. When he asked her what she looked for in a husband, she replied: "It is important for you not to hit me."

John was 44. Divorced five years earlier, he had a demanding job in computer science, and was unbearably lonely. "What I needed most in my life," he confessed in an interview, "was someone who loved me. The woman who loved me, educated or not, would have my love." Impressed by some of the Russian women he met in the course of his work, he decided to gamble on a Russian wife.

Five days in Minsk was all it took to persuade him that Elena was the girl for him. He proposed as soon as he returned to Philadelphia. But because she lived in Belarus, it took a year and a half for the paperwork to be completed and for her to join him with her son.

They were married at the local City Hall, and it did not take long for Elena to change. She suddenly became impossible, screaming insults, accusing him of being cold to her and her child, and refusing to do any housework. She announced that she didn't love him and never had. "She admitted," he said, "that she always thought my letters to her were false, and that therefore she had also written falsehoods to me." And she proceeded to make his life miserable, trying craftily to goad him into hitting her. Clearly, she figured that as an abused wife she could get a green card without waiting for the end of the two-year residence period for foreign brides, and could then discard her husband and be on her own.

The marriage, which lasted four weeks after the expiration of the 90-day fiancée visa, ended in an acrimonious divorce. John found himself out some $4,000 for dental work for Elena to repair the damage done by incompetent dentists in Belarus, plus legal fees for both of them, plus the money he had spent to bring her to the U.S. To get her to drop further claims for support for her and the child, he bought his way out of the marriage, as he put it, for more than $20,000.

The experience left him financially ruined and emotionally devastated. What hurt most, he said, was the realization that he had been deceived. Would he try with another Russian woman? No way! "I wouldn't look for another relationship that way, not knowing who can be trusted and who can't." Meanwhile, trying to avoid deportation proceedings, Elena may well be looking for another American husband.

Katya was 15 when she discovered the Pentecostal movement in her hometown of Lugansk in the Ukraine. The Assembly of God movement had sent over a mission from the United States, and Katya, the daughter of a retired army colonel, attended some of its services and decided to "give my life to Christ." "I was amazed," she recalled later, "by the way the American missionaries treated their wives . . . The missionaries were always saying, 'Honey, could you please do this or that,' not snapping, 'Go get me some tea,' the way our men did. I felt that the Americans valued women more."

After doing some interpreting for visiting missionaries at a Ukrainian Bible school and spending a year studying in England, Katya, at 19, turned to the dating agencies for an American husband, "determined to marry only a real Christian." Of the dozens of letters she received in response, she liked Harry's best.

Harry was 33, the son of a Japanese mother and an American marine, a high-school teacher in a small Ohio town. After a failed two-year marriage, he wanted to try again, and signed up for some agency catalogues. "I had nothing against American women," he explained. "There just weren't any nice Christian girls around." He liked Katya's photo and her saying that religion was important to her. "It just happened—I guess because God wanted it to happen this way."

They corresponded by e-mail for a whole year; he went over for a two-week visit; they have now been married for two years. Theirs is a story of shared religious beliefs that made adapting relatively easy for both. She was surprised that Harry and his buddies preferred a T-shirt and tennis shoes to ties and jackets, and that "people here don't have close friends the way they do at home," but otherwise everything seems fine. With her excellent English, she is a journalism senior in an Ohio college, and deeply grateful for Harry's encouraging her to finish her education, remembering how many of her friends in the Ukraine had to go to work right after high school to help their families. She is pleased by Harry's willingness to help around the house. "We share the responsibility for our marriage and home."

"These Russian women," Harry observed, "have gone through a lot of hardship. Russians don't tend to take things for granted. They don't feel they deserve happiness, so when something good happens they are really appreciative."

Before looking at his first agency catalogue, Edward, 48, a software specialist ten years down the road from his divorce, made a thorough analysis of whom he wanted for his second wife. He decided to try for a Russian woman in her thirties who had been raised under the Soviet system, a woman with strong values, preferably with a child. A young woman, he reasoned, would make the age difference too great, and growing up in the era of perestroika would have exposed her to the corrupting influence of the West.

Edward set about studying Russian, made several trips to Russia, and dated one woman after another until he met Irina, a native of St. Petersburg, who seemed to fit his scheme. Irina was the right age, strong-minded, with a Ph.D. in chemistry and a little boy. As a bonus, she was tall and attractive. Her English was shaky, but that could be fixed. The first time he took her to dinner, she ordered a fairly expensive dish—not the most expensive but not the cheapest, either. That showed she had standards: he was pleased. When the bill came she insisted on seeing it. That pleased him, too: it showed she knew the value of money and wanted to make sure the waiter wasn't cheating him.

They were married and Edward is content. Irina's kind of strength, he explains, is quite different from his ex-wife's. "When I married Irina," he said, "a lot of my friends said, 'All you want is a docile, subservient wife. This woman is not as docile and subservient as you want her to be.' That was pretty silly, since it was perfectly obvious to me that Irina's a highly educated professional. And I don't need to emphasize," he added, "the absurdity of the idea that Russian women are docile and subservient. Stubborn, maybe. If I'd wanted a docile wife I sure as hell wouldn't have married a Russian Ph.D. There's quite a big difference between a suburban American woman who prides herself on being aggressive and a Russian woman who is polite, well-mannered—and truly assertive when she needs to be. She sees our relationship as a partnership, not as a power struggle."

Of course, he admits, it was not all peaches and cream. "Anyone who says the first year of marriage to a Russian woman isn't difficult is lying through his teeth." In the beginning Irina was going stir-crazy in their Denver home while he put in long hours at work. But then she learned how to drive, acquired a working knowledge of English, arranged for day care for little Vanya and took a job as a restaurant hostess—at which she did so well that she was promoted to manager. Today she is looking for a laboratory job in her specialty, chemistry.

The important thing, John says, is that she finally feels at home. "When Irina arrived she put up a huge map of St. Petersburg on our bedroom wall. She was spending almost all her free time e-mailing and phoning her friends and relatives at home. Six months later, I came home one day and noticed that the map of St. Petersburg had been replaced by a map of Denver. That said a lot."

As the above makes all too clear, the experiences of the American men and Russian women who have met and married through the agencies and the Internet run the gamut from debacle to happily-ever-after. For a woman who finds herself suddenly cut off from family and friends, dependent for money, support and warmth on a stranger in a strange land; for a man who after five days of meetings convinces himself that a younger woman living in poverty is in love with him—for both the hazards are immense, and it is surprising how many of the marriages have turned out tolerably well.

To sum up, the pressures of the agency-sponsored trips to Russia, during which a man often tries to decide within a week whether to offer a fiancée visa to a girl he barely knows, can lead to major mistakes. Nor do the ninety days granted by the visa provide a lot of time for making a final decision to marry. It is hard enough in one's own culture to make the right choice of the person with whom to spend one's life and raise a family. In a foreign country, without a common language, knowledge of the culture and of all the cues and gestures which provide insight into an individual's background, education and social status, such a decision becomes even more difficult.

Those who have found happiness in a mail-order marriage feel that all the expense, travel and red tape were more than worth it; those who have been financially battered and emotionally hurt feel deeply disappointed and duped. The more time the couples can spend getting to know each others' values, motivations, feelings and desires, the better their chances for a successful partnership. Otherwise the risk of becoming "wedded strangers" is real indeed.

PARENTS AND
CHILDREN

༺❧༻

Edward, who knew exactly what he wanted when he married Irina, has learned something else in the last year or so: "I know Irina married me in good part because of her son Vanya. If I'm a good father to him she'll stay with me even if she falls out of love with me, but if she felt I were not a good father to him she'd leave me even if she loved me." The rise in mail-order Russian-American marriages has led to the creation of many ready-made families. "In a way," mused one American husband, "it's not much different than adopting a Russian child. You just get the mother as part of the package."

At the start, the man often doesn't know what he's in for. Rarely does the American who has fallen for a sexy Russian blonde count on changing diapers or arranging for day care for Vanya or Tanya. And it cuts both ways. The woman is apt to be more interested in getting herself and her child out of Russia than in being a step-mother to little Tommy or Suzy, even if only on weekends and for three weeks in summer.

In several divorce cases the children were a decisive factor. John, who is trying to put his life together in the wake of his disastrous four-week marriage, has no illusions about Elena's ever having loved him: "She was only concerned about her kid."

Her concern about his own child from his first marriage was less pronounced. The boy, 4, who lived with his mother and came over on visits, had a roomful of toys that had Elena gasping. "I couldn't believe the pile of gifts at Christmas!" Whenever John refused to buy her son a candy bar—not wanting to be regarded as a Santa Claus rather than as a father—she accused him of being stingy, sure that he would have bought the candy for his own boy.

Where children are concerned passions run high. A husband and wife who can sit down and discuss their own differences fairly calmly can often wind up in a shouting match when the kiddies are involved. Both Russians and Americans tend to imitate—or react against—the way their parents raised them, and attempts by the foreign spouse to impose different values or disciplines on the child can be deeply resented. The children themselves can be affected by the unfamiliar. Far from home, which often included doting grandparents, a Russian child who cannot understand his stepparent's English may be frightened by a strange house, strange food, a strange language, and a stranger to whom Mama is devoting more time than to him. In Russia, small children have always been little kings; during the Soviet period many an American visitor would be led to the whimsical observation that it was the chubby little tikes bundled in their winter jumpsuits, rather than the dour Party bureaucrats, who were really running the country.[1]

A small child who cannot talk to his stepparent or step-sibling can lash out and be generally aggressive. John found himself defending his son Teddy against Igor's blows when Teddy couldn't understand what the Russian boy wanted. Cries of "Mine!" and "No, mine!" rent the air. Russian boys are taught from an early age to defend themselves, and hit back; in a Russian kindergarten, where there is one adult for as many as thirty boys, fighting is constant. Igor would grab one of Teddy's toys and pummel him when the other tried to get it back. As John saw it, Igor had been doted on so by his mother and grandmother that he did not know how to play with other children. But to Elena, Teddy's wanting his toy back was another example of "American individualism and selfishness."

Another source of conflict is disagreement bred of cultural differences as to what is healthy or unhealthy for the children. In Russia children are always being wrapped up against the cold, and fear of drafts is inborn. John could never understand why Elena bundled up Igor in warm sweaters and a woolen hat in warm weather. When she tried to do the same for Teddy, the boy howled that he was hot and tore off his cap.

Even playtime can be a problem. In Russia, children are allowed to play in that Russian institution, the courtyard of the apartment building, under the watchful eye of the old women who spend the day sitting outside on benches gossiping and knitting. Most American apartment buildings do not have courtyards; so where can the Russian child play? In the street? But for children from small Russian towns or villages, unaccustomed to watching out for passing cars, that can be dangerous. Igor regularly would burst into tears in traffic, even when John held him by the hand.

Scared of John and unable to talk to him, Igor clung to his mother. He insisted on staying up late, so as to prevent her from going into the bedroom with John, and she would wait until midnight or later for the boy to fall asleep. The result was an exhausted child and an irritated husband. Whenever John tried to discipline Igor, the boy screamed and ran sobbing to his mother, who comforted him with hugs and kisses.

When, as it often happens, the wife's devotion to her child is all-engrossing, the husband feels excluded altogether. That was Bob's experience. His wife, Zhanna, would not allow him to raise his voice at her rambunctious 15-year-old son or to discipline him in any way. She got him to buy the boy a car, but wouldn't stand for any criticism of the boy for refusing to help around the house or for leaving the front door unlocked. "It was love me, love my son," Bob recalled. "I had the feeling that the only reason she married me was to get her son out of Russia and away from military service. By the time the marriage was obviously on the rocks and she was refusing to sleep with me, she was still insisting that I adopt her son."

Even for Edward, who had found in Irina what he was looking for—a woman with a child—helping to raise three-year-old Vanya has "taken a lot of adaptation." The child proved to be bright but aggressive, prone to using his fists before his tongue. He was also used to having his mother's undivided attention. She put him into day care in the mornings, and that gave him playmates and a start on English, and she'd spank him when he needed it, but she would not allow Edward him to punish the boy in any way, and that made him feel she was keeping him from being the father he wanted to be.

Remembering how unsafe antibiotics could be for children in Russia, she was afraid to give Vanya the antibiotic prescribed by an American doctor for a flu and ear infection. As a result, she and Edward both caught the child's flu and Edward was out of work for 10 days.

Edward is philosophical about Irina's mother love and Vanya's jealousy of him. "For her everything—the whole world—revolves around that boy. I'm convinced she would sacrifice everything, including me, for that boy. But I'm fine with that. Vanya's an adorable kid and we have a ball together. And she and I love each other. Everything takes time. We've come a long way in a very short time, but there's still a long way to go."

For Paul and Masha, raising her daughter, Dasha, has been a positive experience. The 14-year-old spoke little English when she arrived two years ago, and threw herself into her schoolwork. "We had a major disaster on our hands when she came home with a B in English," Paul said. "She'd only been here a few months and she was crying because she wanted an A so badly." A whiz at her studies, she revealed a special talent for the violin, and her music teachers admitted that she needed more than they could give her. At considerable sacrifice, even though he and Masha are saving to buy a house, Paul is paying for her violin lessons.[2]

Dasha has been quick to take to American ways. Aside from her grandparents, to whom she speaks regularly on the phone, there is nothing about her old life in Russia she seems to miss. Even in the suburban area of Indiana where they live, Dasha has dropped her Russian friends.

Not surprisingly, Masha admitted that her first consideration in signing up with an agency was to secure a decent life for her daughter. "What it boiled down to was simple, and the way I feel about Paul is this: you're giving me a decent life for myself and my child, and so I'm giving you love. After all, what I was thinking about back in Kharkov wasn't where can I find love but will I have money today to buy bread for my child? And how can we get washed when there's been no water in the house for a week?"

Yet now, in America, she finds that these elements—love for her daughter and gratitude to her husband—are being fused. "How can I not love a man who's being so kind to me and my child?"[3]

Michael, an engineer for an American aerospace firm with dealings in Russia, was living in Moscow when he married Nadya in 1991. He was 34, she was 32 and had a three-year-old daughter, Polina. He moved in with her and her parents—and got a crash course in child rearing, Russian style. "I had been through a full-scale rebellion against my own parents, who were pretty strait-laced, old-fashioned people . . . I'm from California, and I grew up in there in the sixties and seventies. So I swore I'd never put my kids through everything I went through." In his new Moscow home, it upset him to see Polina's grandparents, who had both been in the military, treating the child "as though they were all back in the nineteenth century," and he did his best to counteract it, with little success.

Things came to a head, Michael remembers, on Polina's fourth birthday. "By eleven in the morning my mother-in-law was busy setting the table for guests who had been invited for two in the afternoon. She had Polina all dressed up in a velvet party dress, white lacquer shoes, and her hair swept up in a tight bow. The child was hot and sweaty in all those clothes, and she was getting fidgety and cranky. I took Polina into the bedroom, changed her into jeans and a sweater, and took her out. It was early June, and there was a playground next door, and hills you could slide down. So she and I had a great time, rolling down the hills, playing on the swings, and we ran around and played games. We came back around one-thirty. Polina was radiant, but covered with mud, with grass and twigs all over her hair. Her grandmother was so livid she could hardly speak. 'On her birthday—the child looking like that—and the whole house is going to know!'"

"I got the child into the shower, cleaned her up, dried her hair, and we dressed her up again. Polina was so happy, relaxed, laughing. But even though Nadya saw how happy Polina was, she didn't defend me when her mother started in on me. I guess she really felt that way, too, about how to treat a child."

The couple later moved to Colorado, but the problem was still with them. "God forbid Polina should run around barefoot," Michael said. "Nadya was like all Russians on that one. No way. And in America cold drinks come with ice. Polina loved ice. No: she'll catch a sore throat, she'll get sick. So here she is drinking warm flat soda while everyone else is enjoying a nice cold Coke." Yet Michael learned the virtues of compromise, realizing that Nadya's approach to child-raising reflected some of her attitudes toward life as a whole.[4]

Henry met Sonia while in Moscow six years ago, lecturing on political theory. Sonia was an administrator at the conference. They were married and he took her home to Washington. Sonia had a 12-year-old son, Oleg, and it took Henry some time to establish a satisfactory relationship with the boy.

"We told him he could take any last name he wanted—his father's, his mother's or mine. We were really delighted that he ultimately decided to use my name. He calls me Henry, but that doesn't bother me in the least. After all, he has a father in Russia." (Unlike many ex-husbands of Russian women who marry Americans and move to the United States, Oleg's father has stayed in contact with him.) "What's important," said Henry, "is how he feels about me and how we get on, not what name he uses."

The boy did present some problems, though. "In Russia," Henry said, "Oleg's grandparents were always there to cook, clean, shop and take care of everything. It took him a while to realize who does what and that he had to do his share in the household, too."

Oleg had a love of music, and his piano and violin lessons were expensive. "Sonia seemed to think it was up to the two of us to pay for every step the boy took, while I thought he could be out on his own making some money to pay for part of his expenses." That, Henry came to realize, was a novel concept for his wife and stepson. In Russia kids didn't work—not, at any rate, while they were in school. If they did, it meant their parents couldn't support them, or it looked like child labor. "But after a while, Oleg rather liked the idea of having his own money, and of not having to ask me for things all the time."[5]

The boy is seriously considering becoming a musician. He has traveled a good deal, and spent a year studying music in Paris. He has also been back to Moscow several times—feeling, he said, not that he was going home, but more as though he were going on vacation to visit his father and his grandparents. His Russian is still excellent, but his Moscow friends can catch him on slang expressions new to him, and sometimes they tease him about being "American."

"At first I didn't know what was 'American' about the way I've been behaving," he said. "Then I caught on. It's the way I walk. Standing up straight, looking straight ahead of me—facing the world."[6]

Don and Eleonora met when they were both working in a Greenwich Village restaurant. She had come to New York from Moscow on a student visa; he was working part-time to pay for computer courses; both were sculptors and graphic artists. They are now in their early thirties and have been married for eight years.

Eleonora was amazed when Don said he wanted to be present when she gave birth. Her Russian girlfriends warned her that he would be traumatized by the sight and would suffer, as one of them put it, a "permanent chemical imbalance" rendering him incapable of looking at her as a woman. But he insisted and she finally gave in. Since Don was there to hold her hand but did not witness the delivery, ultimately no one was traumatized. Their daughter, Anna, is now two years old. Eleonora is delighted with the way he cares for the child: Don adores the little girl and often feeds her and changes her diapers—prompting Eleonora's Russian girlfriends to accuse her of letting him take over her own job. When the girl misbehaves, Don is less of a disciplinarian than she. He'd let the child patter barefoot about the apartment, but she—never! Anna always has her booties on, for fear of her catching cold or picking up an infection.[7]

Don, who doesn't speak Russian, talks to his wife in English; she speaks only in Russian to the child. Anna's Russian nurse has no English, and Anna seems happy being addressed in both languages and responding as best she can in both.

Adriana is an American woman married to a Russian, Viktor; they have a three-year-old son, George. She speaks to the child in English, he in Russian, and the boy is doing nicely in both languages. When Viktor's parents come over from Russia on a visit George knows he is to speak to them only in Russian.

How long he'll stay bilingual is another question. Once placed in an American school, many a child born in Russia or raised in America with a Russian-speaking parent stops speaking Russian because of his longing to be like everyone else. Conversely, an American married to a Russian and living in Russia may find that after a few years in a Russian school his or her child may have trouble reading and writing in English. Raising a child to be truly bilingual and bicultural requires spending time in both cultures. And in today's world, bicultural children are becoming increasingly common. As they grow older, they are likely to discover how valuable their knowledge of two languages and two cultures can be, both professionally and for enriching their own lives.

THE CULTURE
CONFLICT

Potentially, all is transformed. Borders have opened up, Russians travel freely, the word émigré is losing its meaning—and Russian-American marriages blossom in both countries, with and without the aid of the dating agencies and the Internet.[1] But some things have not changed—the deep-rooted cultural differences between Russia and the United States. And these continue to bedevil many of the unions formed across the cultural divide.

Communication begins with speech. Edith, an American woman who speaks good Russian, found that she and her Russian husband had few problems during the two years they lived in Russia. But after they moved to the U.S. and switched to English, in which he is weak, they began having arguments based on misunderstandings. "One word misinterpreted could cause a whole lot of heartache," reported another American wife. The record shows that for a mixed marriage to be happy, both partners must try hard to break through the language barrier and see how the other spouse looks at the world. Often the effort is even more important than the result.

Then there is the issue of religion. Prior to the collapse of the USSR few mixed couples had any trouble on that score. Few young people had any religious education, and questions of faith were of little consequence for them. With the lifting of restrictions on religious observance, many young Russians have become interested in Russia's spiritual roots and in other religions as well. Many young Jews became aware of their religious traditions, Russian Orthodoxy underwent a nationwide revival, and American Protestantism rediscovered Russia as a field for missionary work. For many of the young, religion has begun to play a more important role in their lives, their choice of partners and the way they wish to raise their children.

Perestroika bred a sexual revolution, to considerable effect. Among the young polled in a recent survey, 70 percent favored premarital sex, and more than 80 percent had seen a pornographic film. The Internet and the Russian press have ads for sexual partners, birth-control devices are more available, and prostitution is rampant. Whether the spread of sexual freedom has made people happier is debatable. A recent study of happiness with sex life in 19 countries finds the U.S. in third place after Venezuela and Brazil, while Russia was way down the list with only 6 percent of respondents claiming contentment.[2]

For one thing, there has been little emphasis on making sex more enjoyable for the woman. "The whole focus on female orgasm is absolutely non-Russian," writes one commentator.[3] An American male reported that a Russian woman with whom he had slept was surprised by his concern for her pleasure; the Russian men she had had in bed felt that it showed "weakness" to worry about the woman's response. It may be, however, that she told him this to make him feel good: he was looking for a Russian bride and she was interested in "making a catch." True, most Russians don't go in for the "pillow babble" favored by so many Americans, but silence does not have to mean that the Russian man does not care what the woman is feeling. Still, cultural differences do play a role. As the linguist George Steiner says, "to make love in American English, say, is a completely different happening for the articulate from doing so in German, in Italian, or in Russian."[4]

A recurring major source of conflict is jealousy on the part of the Russian woman, based on her expectations of Russian men. Paul was astounded by how intensely jealous of him his wife, Masha, proved to be after they moved from Kharkov to Indiana. "I'm a forty-year-old computer geek," he said, "below average in looks, and have never, ever, had women lined up waiting to meet me. I am, however, kind, reliable, intelligent, a light drinker, and, in her eyes, a prime catch. So she thinks every woman must be trying to find a man like me."

Paul's computer job often required him to work late at night and on weekends to maintain the system and deal with crashes. "When a file server is down on a Sunday morning, I work for 24 hours straight or 800 engineers will come in Monday morning and twiddle their thumbs." Masha, however, would call him into the early hours to make sure he was there and not with another woman. "It got to the point where my boss telephoned her to explain that I really was at work all night."

To keep the peace, Paul turned down a promotion, a job with the *Playboy* magazine computer files involving still more night work. "I told her I'd be in a room with dozens of machines, but she had images of bars and bunnies." Finally he switched to another firm with no night or weekend work. He does have to travel occasionally. "And when I travel she calls me every night. Seems that every time her ex-husband had an evening at 'work' or a 'business trip' he was off with a girl. I have absolutely no intention of ever cheating on her. And I hope that after enough time has passed she will figure that out."

So accustomed was Masha to jealous scenes with her first husband that whenever the couple fought, she would try to provoke Paul into hitting her. "That's what she used to do with him," Paul said. "Then they'd make up. Once, after we'd had an argument, I went outside and decided to take a ride in the car to cool off. Masha charged out the door screaming, 'Go ahead and hit me.' She stood next to the car as I was backing up, yanking on the outside mirror, until finally I jumped out and yelled at her. And then everything was fine—she stopped screaming and calmed down. I remember how when a couple she knew in St. Petersburg argued till they came to blows, and when the woman showed up with a black eye Masha referred to this as 'Russian love.'"

It should be clear that this equating of wife beating and love applies in Russia only to some woefully ignorant men and women. For the average educated Russian of either sex, the notion is as repugnant as in any other civilized country.

Paul was able to cope with Masha's jealousies because he was aware of the conditioning behind it. In Russia, given the shortage of Russian men and the general acceptance of male infidelity, the situation he experienced is a widespread phenomenon. As the Russian saying goes, "A real man should smell of tobacco, wine and the perfume of another woman."[5] Moreover, sexual jealousy is closely linked to lack of trust generally, and the "distrust thy neighbor" reflex instilled by the Soviet system spilled over into marriages, as into everything else.

One 30-year-old American described how badly upset his Russian wife was by his having to go on business trips with a female colleague, a happily married woman in her early thirties with three children. He made the mistake, he said, of telling his wife that they had dinner together twice, between meetings. "But people on our team always do that, be they men or women. What are we supposed to do—sit at separate tables?" His wife, however, was convinced that he was sleeping with the woman. After all, most of her young women friends in Dnepropetrovsk slept with their colleagues and bosses if they wanted to advance their careers.

Another American came up against a variation on the theme. On leaving the house he told his Russian fiancée that a friend of his would be stopping by, and asked her to let the man in if he wasn't back in time. Absolutely not, said the girl. What if the man "tried to do something" with her? With bad experiences in Russia with her former boyfriend's acquaintances, she trusted no one.

Yet another American, Bob, told his Russian fiancée that when he was away on his long business trips, he had had a foreign exchange student, a young Scandinavian girl, living in his house to take care of his dogs and plants. "Nina was absolutely convinced that I was sleeping with the girl. How could I do that? First of all, I'm 47 and she was 22. Second, I would have been taking advantage of her." His fiancée's retort amazed him. "What a sucker you are," said Nina. "Since she was living with you, she had to sleep with you—nothing in life is free. If she wouldn't sleep with you, you should have kicked her out."

It would be wrong, of course, to see these examples as typical of Russian women generally—it all depends on the woman's education, social class, profession and lifestyle. Yet, since for decades in Russia trusting the wrong person could lead to political, professional and personal disaster, the legacy of distrust is difficult to overcome.

Jealousy and mistrust are not the only strong emotions on display. Many men, French and British as well as American, have commented on the Russian female's penchant for extremes. "She loves drama and invents it when there isn't any," one American husband said of his Russian wife. "She doesn't just have a headache—her head is splitting." Said another: "Her emotions change so that she herself sometimes doesn't know what she wants." And another. "In five minutes she can turn from a businesswoman into a little girl."[6]

So volatile are some of these women that American men can seem too tame for them. Back in Russia the men may have been infantile or passive in some respects, but they were "men who know they are men."

"The less macho American men, the ones beaten down by feminism, are too weak for these Russian women," said one American who had had a stormy relationship with his Russian fiancée, and who was obviously putting himself into that category. "Once when I cried while listening to a torch song, she said, 'I need a real man and you're a baby.' She kept telling me, 'Be a man.'"

Some American husbands have found their Russian wives too "strong," in a way. Daniel complained that his wife Marina kept telling him what to wear, straightening his tie and brushing off his jacket as if he were a schoolboy. "She continually interrupts me. And if she disagrees with me—which she often does—she'll say that little Alyosha needs to go to bed, or has a cold, in a tone implying a major tragedy is in the offing. Once, when I forgot to buy milk, you'd think I'd started World War III."

Here is a paradox—that of the beautiful, feminine creature who turns out to be to be psychologically stronger than her husband. In Russia there is the cult of the mother who does everything for her son, attends to his every need and passes him on to a wife from whom he expects the same attention. An American woman who lived for a short while with her Russian husband's parents in Moscow reported that it strained their relationship. "I had a lot more problems with his mother than with him. She kept saying I wasn't a good wife because I didn't wash his socks every day. And she did absolutely everything for him, including washing those socks. When we got our own place it took quite a while for him to realize I wasn't going to do everything his mother did, and that he had to do his share around the house."

The demographic imbalance created in Russia by 70 years of purges, famines and war produced strong women used to fending for themselves at home and at work. Yet these same women were expected to retain their femininity and looks or have their spouse wander off to one of the many single women who would be only too happy to have him, even on a part-time basis. As opposed to those American women who phone a lawyer at the first spat, the Russian attitude, as one woman put it, is, "So what if he's a loan shark, throws tea cups at me when he's angry, and goes three times a year into the blackest depression known to mankind; he's mine."[7]

The Russian woman feels sorry for her erring mate and stands by him, no matter what.[8] *Liza*, a Russian women's magazine, cited several cases of women who married cads of various kinds.[9] One husband turned out to be a drug addict and got his wife addicted as well. Another got a seven-year sentence for shady financial dealings and trading in stolen jewelry. In American inspirational stories of this sort, the woman escapes into a shelter for battered women or some such. But the Russian stories end with the first woman assuring her spouse she will always be there for him, and with the second standing in line outside the prison with a package for her man. Both reject divorce and remain faithful to their spouses, sure that tenderness and patience can turn these poor wretches into upstanding husbands and citizens. And there's an inverted—from the American viewpoint—kind of self-protectiveness involved. "What would I gain from throwing out that drunk?" one Russian woman asked. "I'd be working just to feed my children, have a few evenings out with my girlfriends, be forced to laugh in public and shed my tears in bed at night, and be bitter and unhappy at home for life."[10]

* * *

In spite of the judgments of many Russian women that today's Russian men make poor husbands, quite a few American women have shown their disagreement by marrying them (though rarely on the agency or e-mail circuit). What do they see in these men?

"I'd start out with one simple word: passion," said Julie, a young American woman married to a Russian. "These men are free from psychobabble, they're stronger than American men and yet they have a more feminine side. They aren't afraid of life. They know what they want. American men are always complaining; Russian men put up with what life gives."

Here too, of course, there are strong cultural differences and the difficulties they create. "Misha is not one to talk about his feelings," Laura said about her Russian husband. "As a pop psychology person, I'm used to discussing things and letting it all hang out." So it was hard, for her, at first, to understand his need for a "private zone" of personal feelings—that this did not mean he was shutting her out.

Caroline, a programmer who lives in Moscow, is happy in her marriage to a Russian tour guide. Yet she recalls with some nostalgia some aspects of her first marriage to an American. "American men are much more communicative and in touch with their feelings as compared to Russian men. Russian men seem to me much more chauvinistic and unable to discuss their emotions. My Russian husband's family is very kind to me, but I feel that they don't take women seriously; they're treated somewhat like the flowers or the china on the table, there for decoration."

"My Vanya has a lot more respect for other people than many of my American friends, who are so busy analyzing everyone's motives," said Linda, a 32-year-old manager of a chain of Moscow stores who has been married for six years to a 35-year-old Russian photographer. "He doesn't constantly analyze all his emotions, but he is extremely careful of my feelings and I have learned to show him the same respect."

A more common problem is the Russian male's aloofness from household chores. "Misha had never washed a floor or a dish before he married me, and he still has trouble helping around the house," said Laura, a 31-year-old American woman who works for an educational exchange program in Moscow. "His mother did everything for him. Now he's finally beginning to participate in household chores."

Adriana met Viktor while working as an interpreter in Moscow. For the eight years of their marriage they have lived in her home state of Indiana. "When Viktor and I were deciding to get married, I let him know I was *not* going to be a Russian wife," Adriana said. "Over the years we have learned to compromise: I cook, he helps with the dishes and the laundry . . . We knew that these issues would cause problems, but I think we've fared pretty well."

An illustration of this problem came up at a recent Thanksgiving dinner in Vermont. The buffet table was laden with a turkey roast, toasted marshmallows, cranberry, creamed onions, squash and all the other holiday treats. The host's daughter, Susan, is married to a Russian, and several of the guests got into an argument about this very book. "I don't like it," announced Leonid, the young Russian husband. "Visson is much too hard on Russian men—she treats them as if they were selfish male chauvinists." As the argument continued, Susan got up, filled a dinner plate with foods and resumed her seat on the couch.

"Is that for me?" Leonid asked, eyeing the turkey and cranberries. "No," Susan replied. "It's for me. You can get your own plate."

"What did that book you were discussing say about Russian men?" one of the guests inquired with deliberate sarcasm. There was a burst of laughter.

Leonid scowled. He was angry, both at his wife for not serving him, and at being the butt of the joke. It took Susan some effort to calm him down and restore the festive mood. Even though she was a historian who spoke excellent Russian, this Russian male attitude was new to her. "I explained to him," she said, "that I would have thought it silly to bring a grown man a plate, because he'd want to decide for himself which of all these dishes he wants. Since he's not a small child or an invalid, he's expected to get up and serve himself. But Leonid thought I was being selfish—typically American individualist selfish, as he put it."

One of the happiest marriages I came across in my interviews is that between Annette, a 39-year-old nurse living in Florida, and Iliya, a 42-year-old former Moscow circus clown from Kazan who has recently has been performing at Cypress Gardens with a circus troupe of expatriate Russians. A skilled portraitist-caricaturist, he is listed in the Guinness Book of World Records as the world's fastest quick sketch artist. At first glance, Annette seems an unlikely candidate for a Russian-American marriage. "How could you marry a damn Communist?" her politically conservative father asked in amazement, for to him all Russians—including those who had chosen to leave the USSR—were "Communists."

What Annette appreciates most about her life with Iliya is the sense that their family is a little community, both unto itself and as part of the Russian community of his performer friends. Together, they have a four-year-old daughter, and Annette has a 14-year-old girl by a previous marriage, and while the familiar problems of cross-cultural child rearing do come up, it all fades for her before the satisfaction of the family as a collective, with a collective purpose, instead of as two individuals pursuing two individual goals.

"In the typical American marriage," Annette said, "everything tends to be 'yours' and 'mine.' I sometimes tend to slip and say 'my' this and 'my' that, but in the overall picture all is 'ours.'" She loves the way Iliya and his Russian friends sit around the table for hours sharing their stories; and he has taught her how to roll out the dough for *pelmeni,* the Russian dumplings. "Americans sit down for ten minutes, swallow their food and do the dishes."

"Iliya respects me," said Annette, "and he treats me like a woman. I don't want to be treated like a man. I don't want to be my husband's 'buddy.' Flowers and a kiss are just perfect. Iliya holds his mother in such high esteem, and that's important, because the way a man treats his mother is the way he'll treat you."

Their admiration is mutual. "She's a great wife and mother and my closest friend," Iliya said. "When you've found your real wife you don't feel like gallivanting; you want to stay home."

Annette is impressed with how well Iliya has adapted to family life in America. "We had this child so that she could translate for us," jokes Annette about their daughter. "I want Tanya—she's named for Iliya's mother—to learn Russian, to know the heritage and culture of her father." Iliya speaks Russian to Tanya, who also spends a good deal of time with the Russian circus performers. She doesn't seem to have trouble with the two languages, though she gets mad when Annette can't read one of her Russian children's books. Like so many children of mixed marriages, she has an American accent in Russian.[11] And while Annette's daughter Stefani is sometimes embarrassed by having a stepfather with a foreign accent, "her friends think the circus is really cool."

Despite Annette's fears of how her Russian husband, who had a heavy work schedule, would manage the household and two children when she had to work for a week an out-of-town hospital, Iliya coped beautifully. "I made a big pot of borsht," she said, "and he managed very well with Tanya, who was then three, with Stefani helping out. When you're a real family, everything falls into place."

This Russian sense of family as community has been strongly felt by many an American married to a Russian "I find the Russians much more capable of being team players than most Americans could ever be," said one of them. "I see it in my wife's family and in many of the families I met there. Compared to American families, they are amazingly close. Here you can go off on your own and both survive and succeed. I was out the door when I was 19 and have been ever since. They all rely on each other."

When Joan, an English teacher, met Volodya, an artist and graphic designer from Moscow, "he stared at me so hard I told him he was making me uncomfortable." As she got to know the young man and his Russian friends, she got used to the intense way Russians gaze at people around them, especially new faces—and, besides, "there was something about him."

Joan, a petite, vivacious 24-year-old, is Irish Catholic, the daughter of an ex-priest married to a former nun; Volodya, tall and dark, with large green eyes, is from a Jewish family, nonobservant but with ties to Jewish traditions. When they went before a justice of the peace, she didn't tell her parents until a few days later.

"Our differences were striking," said Joan. "I was used to discussing relationships, as I had with all my former boyfriends. I needed to hear him say all the things he felt but didn't say. Since his English is so good, I didn't see why he wouldn't talk. I demanded attention, affection, and analysis of our relationship; he just put up a wall and ignored me."

In the year and a half of their marriage, Joan has learned to give his actions greater weight than his words. "I've learned to let things slide without analyzing or obsessing over everything. Now he doesn't have to tell me hundreds of times a day that he loves me, but he'll kiss me hello and goodbye just to make me happy. I've learned to respect his silences rather than be suspicious of them. I let him spend time with his Russian friends without me, so that they can talk about their old days in Moscow. And he's learned to cook and iron!"

Joan has become aware of some of the cultural differences embodied in what one says and doesn't say. "I've learned that Volodya finds it insulting for me to always be thanking him. And I've realized that though he doesn't always say please, that doesn't mean he's not trying to be nice or polite. In Russian you just don't use the word please that much, you express that through other words, intonation and gestures. I guess I've learned to take several breaths before I react to something he says that seems weird or annoying."

For example, when she asked him if he could pick her up in time from the dentist's office, when she'd be having her wisdom teeth out, he grunted, "Yes, sure," without writing the date down. It felt insensitive to her and she was hurt. For Volodya, however, picking up his wife from a doctor's office was something to be taken so utterly for granted that he didn't give the matter another thought. All Joan had to do was to remind him a day or two in advance.

Her parents like Volodya fine, and he is happy with his life in Philadelphia. "Here," he said, "I've got a feeling of responsibility. I'm responsible for myself, for Joan, for our family. I can control my life. In Russia you never had control of anything." Sometimes, though, the fast pace of American life depresses him. Americans, he complains, have no time to look at a painting or sniff a flower. And he has not made any close American friends. "You can't really rely on Americans as friends. People keep moving from one home to another, from one city to another." When Joan is out socializing, he prefers to stay home and draw. But whatever their differences, they are optimistic about the future.

Abigail met Artem eight years ago, when she was 23 and studying Russian literature at St. Petersburg University where he was a chemistry student. "I was unabashed in my pursuit of him," she recalled. Three months later they had a Russian wedding. Abigail's Jewish grandparents had emigrated from Belorussia in the early 1900's, and her parents worried that Artem was after America rather than her—that he was "just some sleaze ball who wanted to get out of Russia." Once they got over that fear, "they started to think of him as one of their own kids." Today, settled in the U.S., Abigail is teaching Russian at a small Midwestern college and Artem is working as a medical technician.

Artem's English was not all that good, and Abigail wanted to keep up her Russian, so they hit on a routine. "At home we speak Russian on odd-number days and English on even-number ones, though occasionally we get messed up when we have guests who only speak Russian or English. That lets each of us get to speak his or her native language part of the time, and keeps us from combining them into a Russian-English mess."

The psychological problems are more resistant. "At first Artem was dependent on me for nearly everything. I felt guilty because he had to work at some pretty low-level jobs here just because I didn't want to live permanently in Russia. But Artem did his best to adapt to America. He was upset, though, that I spent so much time at work, and he had to learn to deal with an occasional frozen dinner or heaps of unironed clothes. The biggest problem is that he hasn't made any close friends—he's still in contact with his friends in St. Petersburg."

Artem's mother, says Abigail, is pressuring the couple to have children. "And I think she'd have been happier if I were more of a 'Russian woman,' more of a stay-at-home type. But I've never considered myself a typical American, any more than Artem has ever considered himself a typical Russian. After all, he doesn't drink, doesn't smoke, and does more housecleaning than I do!"

Fundamentally, all is well with this couple. Now and then they socialize with some Americans who don't speak Russian and are married to Russian women they met through the agencies and the Internet. Abigail has only to see these women, "who don't have a clue whom they've married, who these men are," to realize how much she and Artem have in common and how well off they are.

Michelle Berdy, an American woman who has spent many years in Moscow, finds Russian men, with all their faults, preferable to the American species. The Russian men, she writes, make a woman feel like a woman.[12] They are frank in their need for attention and tenderness—and this is on a gut level, not as part of a rational American life program.

Michelle is not alone. One of the most enthusiastic letters I received was from a 72-year-old American woman with adult children and grandchildren. She had been married to an American; widowed, she went to Russia nine years ago with a peace group, staying with an elderly couple who spoke almost no English. It was the son who interpreted, and love followed linguistics. They are married; he is 42. "We feel blessed by every good day," she wrote. "Meryl Streep and Daniel Day Lewis could play our parts so well."

* * *

For Tom, who met Zoya while studying Russian in Moscow, a Russian wife was the logical consequence of his interest in Russia and its culture. He is now happily ensconced in an American expatriate community in Russia which has grown spectacularly in the last few years and has produced a large number of mixed marriages. Both are now working as translators, and say they would feel equally comfortable living either in Russia or in the United States.

Anthony has been living in Moscow for almost 10 years. Now 30, he manages the local office of an American firm. For the last eight years he has been married to a Russian woman, and they have two small children. Anthony has always been in love with Russia. "I think of Russia," he says, "as an incurable disease . . . I always knew I would marry a Russian." Yet marriage to Lena has had its bumps. "Her Russianness sometimes bugs me—she's always trying to tell me what to do, what to wear, interrupting me, quarreling dramatically, when presenting something calmly is much more effective."

But he finds that they are both changing. "Lena's now more reserved, slower to explode. I glow a little less, I trust people a lot less—the way Russians do. I'm quicker to think, and slower to act. But I caught myself wanting *tvorog* (cottage cheese) and *smetana* (sour cream) with sugar for dessert in the cafeteria the other day, and that was telling me I've grown more Russian."

Bernard, 29, personifies a laid-back younger generation that can live almost anywhere. He met Svetlana when she was 26, over from Russia as an exchange student. "It was at a dance club in Boston, and I thought she was the most beautiful woman there. When her visa was up, I quit my job as a radio technician and went back to Russia with her."

Svetlana now works as an English teacher in Moscow, and Bernard freelances for an American radio company. They both are careful who among the expats they associate with. As he puts it, "There are a lot of people here just to make money, there are some OK people who're interested in Russia, and there are all the disgusting men who are here just for sex." Otherwise, Bernard finds Moscow thoroughly enjoyable. "Our only surprise is that we're so much alike. We've been married over a year now and we've never been happier. I guess I'm not your typical American and she's not your typical Russian. We're both just human."

Some of the expats who feel equally at home in both worlds are nevertheless torn between them. Said Fran, who has been living in Russia for over five years: "I believe the biggest difficulty in our marriage is choosing between the two countries. Where is home?" And Susan: "For me Moscow is home, I go visiting to the States." And for one woman, who is married to a Russian and has lived in Moscow for several years, the whole experience is a puzzle. "Sometimes I think," she writes, "what does it take for a nice, normal American girl to do this? You have to be just a little crazy. But this is so exciting and intense that now I couldn't imagine being married to an American."

EPILOGUE

More than half a century separates the romance of Zara Witkin and the "Dark Goddess" from the marriage of Susan Eisenhower and Roald Sagdeev. During those decades the relationship between the two countries has moved from distrust and suspicion to a wartime alliance, cold war, détente, and an uneasy partnership. Yet even in the darkest periods of Soviet-American relations, despite the "image of the enemy," despite the dangers, threats and obstacles, Russians and Americans have been falling in love and marrying. Today with the collapse of the Soviet Union, the freedom for Russians to travel, the boom in dating agencies and the Internet, the increase in business and student exchanges, and the growth of the American expatriate community in Moscow, the number of new marriages has shot up. And the process has only begun.

Some of these marriages have been good. Others have ended in bitter recriminations, shattered lives and an undying hatred of the partner and the partner's country. The idealist steelworker John Scott, the journalists Eddy Gilmore and Homer Smith, the history professor Woodford McClellan, were all deeply attracted to Russia and to Russian women, won their battles to get their wives to the United States, and had successful marriages. Despite all their differences, Svetlana and Mark, Carol and Fyodor, and Irina and Fred are still happily married.

Zoya Fyodorova's romance with her American naval officer, Gelsey Kirkland's affair with Mikhail Baryshnikov, and Donald Davis's marriage to his Russian mail-order wife did not end happily. Unable to adapt to life in Russia, Mary C. has gone back to America and is ending her marriage to Boris. Joyce has obtained a divorce and swears she will never again date a Russian. "But in a way," she remarked, "Pyotr poisoned me. American men now seem so boring—even when they are perfectly honest and decent!"

The outcome of many other Russian-American marriages is still uncertain. Some Russians love America while others hate it, and there are Americans who love Russia and those who cannot stand it. In 1990 Marina Oswald made her first trip back to Russia. "When I flew back to Dallas, I knew I belonged here," she said. "I love America with all my heart."[1] Paul and Masha, Edward and Irina, Annette and Iliya, Joan and Volodya, are building their lives in America. Joanne Turnbull, Sara Harris and Anthony feel they are happier living in Moscow.

Despite the suffering the Soviet system inflicted on them and their families, many American spouses became deeply attached to Russia. "After Andrei died," Margaret Wettlin wrote, "I did not soon consider leaving Russia, because for 36 radiant, stormy, disappointing, jubilant, apocalyptic years Russia was the stage on which Andrei and I played out our destinies."[2] Some Russian spouses were surprised to discover that American streets were more often paved with garbage than with gold, and many Americans were repulsed by Soviet censorship, police harassment and the lack of basic creature comforts. Then and now, neither country has a monopoly on selfishness. Some Russian women, determined to improve their lives and those of their children are ready to make their way to the United States at any cost, including the American partner's broken heart. American men interested only in a pretty mail-order Russian wife may be blind to the wrenching difficulties confronting a stranger in a strange land. Other Russians and

Americans, brought together by chance meetings or by the dating agencies and e-mail, have built fulfilling partnerships through patience, compromise, humor and love.

While Americans are attracted by the emotional intensity, close relationships and cultural richness of Russian life, Russians are captivated by the free and easy climate of American society and the wide range of opportunities held out by the United States. Where Russian women look for strong, responsible and sober American husbands, American women fall for the romantic, passionate Russian male. And while some American men are attracted by the feminine, "old-fashioned" side of Russian women, Russian men are intrigued by energetic and independent American working wives.

Often bilingual, the children of Russian-American marriages should be better able than most to live in both cultures and interpret them to each other. And they should be able to benefit more than most from the best both countries have to offer.

Though the iron curtain is gone and ideas and people circulate freely around the world, the image of the enemy does not disappear all that quickly. It will take several generations to dispel the deeply rooted stereotypes Russians and Americans have formed of each other. Character traits and attitudes molded by centuries of national history do not automatically dissolve in the melting pot of the global village. Perestroika is only some 15 years old; Russian culture goes back over a thousand years. While today's Russian-American couples have a much easier time meeting and marrying, and know a good deal more about each other's countries than did the spouses of decades past, Ivan and Mary still bring very different expectations, values and traditions to their union.

In the past, Russians who married a foreigner fought for exit visas and left their country not knowing if they would ever be allowed to return. Today, these couples are free to enjoy the best of both cultures. For better or for worse, in the years to come, more and more Russians and Americans are likely to become involved in the most exciting and permanent of bilateral exchanges—marriage. The risks are great and the losses can be enormous. So can the rewards.

NOTES

INTRODUCTION

1. Quoted in Gordon McVay, *Isadora and Esenin* (Ann Arbor, Michigan: Ardis, 1980), p. 110.
2. Zara Witkin, *An American Engineer in Stalin's Russia: The Memoirs of Zara Witkin, 1932–1934* (Berkeley: University of California Press, 1991), p. 35.
3. Alexander Kabakov, "Pogovorim o strannostiakh liubvi," *Moskovskie Novosti*, 2/18/90, p. 11.
4. Eliza K. Klose, "Message," *Surviving Together*, Vol. 11, #3, Fall 1993, p. 2.
5. Kevin A. Sullivan, "A U.S.—Russian Formula for True Romance," *Washington Post*, 5/24/94, p. A10.
6. The couples include both Russian citizens and émigrés. Since many Russian Jews are highly assimilated to Russian culture, Jewish spouses have been included and are identified as such. Marriages of Americans to nationals of other former Soviet republics such as Georgia, Armenia or Uzbekistan, whose cultures differ radically from that of Russia, are not discussed. While some early Russian-American marriages are covered, this book is not intended as an exhaustive historical treatment of the subject, and my focus is on contemporary couples.

BREAKING THE ICE

Building the Future

1. Pico Iyer, *Video Night in Katmandu* (London: Black Swan, 1988), pp. 30–31.

2. McVay, p. 106.

3. See McVay, pp. 3–5, and Victor Ripp, *Pizza in Pushkin Square* (New York: Simon and Schuster, 1990), pp. 179–81.

4. Ripp, pp. 180–81.

5. Quoted in Ripp, p. 181.

6. Ripp, p. 100.

7. John H. Dick, "Soviet Images of America, or Where Do We Go From Here?" *Russian Language Journal*, XLIII, Nos. 145–146 (1989), p. 196.

8. Iyer, *Video Night in Katmandu*, p. 24.

9. Cited by A. Iu. Melvil, "Osobennosti amerikanskikh vospriatii Sovetskogo Soiuza," in *Vzaimodeistvie kul'tury SSSR i SShA, xviii–xx vekov*, ed. by O. E. Tuganova (Moskva: Nauka, 1987), pp. 79–81.

10. Susan Eisenhower, *Breaking Free: A Memoir of Love and Revolution* (New York: Farrar Straus Giroux, 1995), p. 12.

11. Sam Keen, *Faces of the Enemy: Reflections of the Hostile Imagination* (San Francisco: Harper and Row, 1986), p. 46.

12. Keen, p. 58. Women have traditionally been the spoils of war, and Americans brought back "enemy" Japanese and German war brides. Americans had access to information about these "enemies," however, for Germany and Japans were relatively open societies. Though Russia was also "the enemy," it was not an adversary with whom the U.S. was ever formally at war. During World War II we were allies; the real hostilities developed during the cold war era.

13. Robert English and Jonathan J. Halperin, "The Other Side: How Soviets and Americans Perceive Each Other," in *Beyond the Kremlin* (New Brunswick, New Jersey and Oxford: The Committee for National Security and Transaction Books, 1987), p. 18.

14. Michael Barson, *Better Dead than Red! A Nostalgic Look at the Golden Years of Russophobia, Red-Baiting, and Other Commie Madness* (New York: Hyperion, 1992), unpaged.

15. S. Frederick Starr, *Red and Hot: The Fate of Jazz in the Soviet Union 1917–1980* (New York: Limelight Editions, 1985), p. 161, and Svetlana Boym, *Common Places: Mythologies of Everyday Life in Russia* (Cambridge, Massachusetts: Harvard University Press, 1994), p. 114.

16. Barson, *op. cit.*

17. See Paula Garb, *They Came to Stay: North Americans in the USSR* (Moscow: Progress, 1987), p. 27.

18. John Scott, *Behind the Urals: An American Worker in Russia's City of Steel* (Bloomington and Indianapolis; Indiana University Press, 1989), pp. 3–5.

19. *Ibid.*, p. xvi.

20 Pearl Buck, *Talk About Russia (With Masha Scott)* (New York: John Day, 1945), p. 119.

21. *Ibid.*, pp.13–14, p. 104.

22. Buck, p. 107.

23. Scott, p. 126.

24. Ripp, p. 65; see also J.P. Murray, *Project Kuzbas: American Workers in Siberia 1921–26* (New York: International Publications, 1983), pp. 10 and 104.

25. Garb, *They Came to Stay*, pp. 18–29 and 117–121.

26. Margaret Wettlin, *Fifty Russian Winters: An American Woman's Life in the Soviet Union* (New York: Pharos Books, 1992), p. 49.

27. *Ibid.*, p. 42.

28. *Ibid.*, p. 43.

29. *Ibid.*, pp. 158 and 72.

30. *Ibid.*, p. 3.

31. In *Russia and the Negro: Blacks in Russian History and Thought* (Washington, D.C.: Howard University Press, 1986), Allison Blakely provides an excellent overview of American blacks in Russia and tells of many black American-Russian marriages. See Blakely, pp. 40 and 144, and Homer Smith, *Black Man in Red Russia* (Chicago: Johnson Publishing Company, 1964), pp. 34–46.

32. Aljean Harmetz, "U.S. And Soviet Sisters Meet at Last," *New York Times,* 11/5/85, p. 32.

33. Harry Haywood, *Black Bolshevik: Autobiography of an Afro-American Communist* (Chicago: Liberty Press, 1978), pp. 310–315, 387–390.

34. Buck, p. 126.

35. Scott, pp. 248–249.

36. See Edmund Stevens, *This is Russia Uncensored* (New York: Didier, 1950), p. 87, and Thomas P. Whitney, *Russia in My Life* (New York: Reynal & Company, 1962), pp. 215–216.

37. Wesley Andrew Fisher, *The Soviet Marriage Market: Mate-Selection in Russia and the USSR* (New York: Praeger Publishers, 1980), pp. 252–253.

38. N. Nikolaev, "Ostorozhno: Rodstvenniki za granitsei," *Argumenti i Fakty,* October 1990, #42 (523), p. 2.

39. *Ibid.*, p. 2.

Dateline Moscow

1. Whitman Bassow, *The Moscow Correspondents: Reporting on Russia from the Revolution to Glasnost* (New York: Paragon House, 1989), p. 265. Bassow provides an excellent overview of the lives, activities, and difficulties of American journalists posted to the USSR.

2. The Soviet male journalists assigned to the U.S. in these decades—there were no women among them—were married, and most of them came to the U.S. with their wives. They feared the professional and political consequences of close relationships with foreigners.

3. Peter G. Filene, *Americans and the Soviet Experiment 1917–1933* (Cambridge, Massachusetts: Harvard University Press, 1967), p. 277.

4. Louis Fischer, *Men and Politics: An Autobiography* (New York: Duell, Sloan and Pearce, 1941), pp. 46–47, 531.

5. Eddy Gilmore, *Me and My Russian Wife,* (Garden City, New Jersey: Doubleday and Co., 1954); Tamara Gilmore, *Me and My American Husband* (Garden City, New Jersey: Doubleday and Co., 1968).

6. Eddy Gilmore, p. 126.

7. Tamara Gilmore, pp. 9–10.

8. *Ibid.,* p. 11.

9. Eddy Gilmore, p. 109.

10. Tamara Gilmore, pp. 164, 10, 14.

11. *Ibid.,* p. 16.

12. *Ibid.,* p. 16.

13. Eddy Gilmore, p. 105.

14. Tamara Gilmore, p. 44.

15. *Ibid.,* pp. 45–46.

16. Eddy Gilmore, pp. 126–127.

17. Tamara Gilmore, p. 68.

18. *Ibid.,* pp. 67 and 235–237.

19. Whitney, p. 67.

20. Harrison Salisbury, *A Journey for Our Times* (New York: Carroll and Graf, 1983), p. 377.

21. Whitney, p. 68.

22. *Ibid.,* pp. 70–71.

23. *Ibid.,* pp. 75–76.

24. *Ibid.,* pp. 86–87.

25. *Ibid.,* p. 136.

26. *Ibid.,* pp. 146–147.

27. Salisbury spells her name as Juli. Salisbury, p. 392.

28. *Ibid.,* p. 399.

29. Whitney, p. 306.

30. Bassow, p. 238.

31. Conversation with the author, Geneva, 11/17/94.

Divided Houses, Divided Spouses

1. See Victoria Fyodorova and Haskel Frankel, *The Admiral's Daughter* (New York: Delacorte Press, 1979).

2. Fyodorova and Frankel, pp. 110–111, and Aleksandr Minchin, "'Teplo li nam doma?' Interv'iu s Viktoriei Fedorovoi," *Ogonek* #2, 1990 (#3300), pp. 22–26 and Minchin, "Sud'ba Zoi Fedorovoi," *Argumenty i Fakty* #35, 1990, p. 6.

3. Fyodorova and Frankel, p. 222; Peter Watson, *Nureyev: A Biography* (New York: Hodder and Stoughton, Coronet Books, 1994), p. 519.

4. Fyodorova and Frankel, pp. 277–278.

5. *Ibid.*, pp. 300–304; Minchin, "'Teplo li nam doma?'" p. 24.

6. Fyodorova and Frankel, pp. 300–304.

7. Minchin, "'Teplo li nam doma?'" p. 25.

8. *Ibid.*, p. 23. Nothing was taken, and a full police investigation was never conducted. See also Watson, *Nureyev*, pp. 515–526 for theories on Zoya Fyodorova's alleged involvement in the Russian underground art world as a reason for the murder.

9. Thomas J. Watson, Jr. and Peter Petre, *Father, Son & Co.* (New York: Bantam, 1991), p. 110.

10. Wolfgang Saxon, "Ellsworth Raymond Dies at 84; Kremlin Watcher of Stalin Era," *New York Times*, 8/23/96, p. 25.

11. Bassow, p. 282.

12. Edmund Stevens, *Russia is No Riddle* (New York: Greenberg, 1945), pp. 145–146.

13. Edmund Stevens, *This is Russia Uncensored* (New York: Didier, 1950), pp. 83–84.

14. Bassow, pp. 138–144. In 1963 Khrushchev told a Swedish diplomat's Russian wife that he was glad she had married her husband because that gave foreigners a good idea of what Russian women were like. When she retorted that for years Soviet citizens had been forbidden from marrying foreigners he replied, "Yes, that was the barbarian—Stalin." See Bassow, p. 145.

15. Yelena Khanga, *Soul to Soul: The Story of A Black Russian-American Family, 1865–1992* (New York: W. W. Norton and Company, 1992), pp. 177–180.

16. Tamara Gilmore, pp. 38–39.

17. Bassow, pp. 191–192.

18. See Ronald Kessler, *Moscow Station: How the KGB Penetrated the American Embassy* (New York: Simon and Schuster, Pocket Books, 1990).

19. *Ibid.*, p. 272. An article in *Izvestiia* reported that Violetta Seina claimed that she had really fallen in love with Lonetree. When the former Marine was released from prison in 1996, having served 9 years of a 30-year sentence,

he sent her a fax saying he forgave her everything. Later, however, he reportedly acquired a girlfriend of his own Navaho Indian background. Vladimir Skosyrev, "Inostranets v medovom kapkane," *Izvestiia*, 1/29/97, p. 3.

20. Wettlin, *Fifty Russian Winters*.

21. *New York Times*, 11/9/93, pp. B10. A 1994 documentary film by Steve Martin, "Theremin: An Electronic Odyssey," recounts the story of this unusual life.

22. *New York Times*, 11/17/85, p. 4.

23. "State Department Identifies Those Expected to Leave Soviet," *New York Times*, 1/17/85, p. 14.

24. "Soviet Said to Weigh 'Divided Spouse' Emigration," *New York Times*, 1/5/86, p. 3.

25. Irina McClellan, *Of Love and Russia* (New York: W.W. Norton and Company, 1989), p. 22.

26. *Ibid.*, p. 26.

27. *Ibid.*, p. 44, 90.

28. *Ibid.*, p. 108.

29. *Ibid.*, pp. 196, 211, 292.

30. *Ibid.*, pp. 305, 307.

31. Adi Ignatius, "The Best Part of Life For These Americans is Not Paying Taxes," *The Wall Street Journal*, 11/12/93, pp. 1, 26.

32. Richard Balmforth, "U.S. Embassy Tightens Rules on Love with Russians," Reuters World Service, BC cycle, 6/25/96.

33. "Amerikanskoe posol'stvo ofitsial'no ob"iavliaet svoim sotrudnikam ob okonchanii kholodnoi voiny," *Izvestiia*, 5/25/95, p. 1. Russians and Americans with access to classified information and the U.S. Marines guarding the Embassy were still restricted in their contacts with foreigners.

34. Stevens, *Russia is No Riddle*, p. 89.

FINDING A SPOUSE

Why Do I Love You?

1. Iyer, *Video Night in Katmandu*, p. 23.

2. Ripp, p. 22.

3. Eugene Lyons, *Assignment in Utopia* (New York: Harcourt Brace, 1937), p. 238.

4. Jo Durden-Smith, "In the Belly of the Beast," *European Travel and Life*, December–January 1992, p. 44.

5. *Ibid.*, p. 44.

6. *Ibid.*, p. 46.

7. Durden-Smith, *Russia: A Long-Shot Romance,* (New York: Alfred A. Knopf, 1994), p. 216.

8. See David Klimek, *Beneath Mate Selection and Marriage: The Unconscious Motives Behind Human Pairing* (New York: Van Nostrand Reinhold, 1979); Wen-Shing Tseng et al., *Adjustment in Intercultural Marriage* (Honolulu: University of Hawaii, 1977); and Dugan Romano, *Intercultural Marriage: Promises and Pitfalls* (Yarmouth, Maine: Intercultural Press, 1988), pp. 5–15.

9. Interview with Michael Gayle, Radio Liberty, "Russian Fiancées—American Fiancés," 6/20/94.

10. Shelley Aspaklaria, "U.S.-Soviet Couples: The Emotional Cost Continues to Surprise," *New York Times,* 1/8/85, pp. C1, C14.

11. Lois Smith Brady, "Vows: Laura Mason, Alexander Khutorsky," Weddings, *New York Times,* 1/14/96, p. 39.

12. Durden-Smith, *Russia: A Long-Shot Romance,* p. 216.

13. See Barson.

14. Mary Buckley, *Women and Ideology in the Soviet Union* (Ann Arbor: The University of Michigan Press: 1989), pp. 133–138, and report of the Ostankino Evening News Program "Vremia," 3/8/95.

15. Vassily Aksyonov, *In Search of Melancholy Baby* (New York: Vintage Books: Random House, 1989), p. 136.

16. Carola Hansson and Karen Liden, *Moscow Women* (New York: Pantheon Books, 1983), p. 77 and 36.

17. Ada Baskina, "Amerikanskie zhenshchiny usilivaiut bor'bu protiv muzhchin," *Izvestiia,* 9/7/94, p. 7.

18. Elena Khanga, "No Matryoshkas Need Apply," *New York Times,* 11/25/91, p. A19.

19. Francine du Plessix Gray, *Soviet Women: Walking the Tightrope* (New York: Doubleday, 1989), p. 178.

20. Tatyana Tolstaya, *"Notes From Underground,"* [Review of Francine du Plessix Gray *Soviet Women: Walking the Tightrope*] *New York Review of Books,* 5/31/90, pp. 3–4.

21. Ludmilla Petrushevskaya, *The Time: Night* (New York: Pantheon Books, 1994), p. 122.

22. Ronald Hingley, *The Russian Mind* (New York: Charles Scribner's Sons, 1977), p. 188.

23. Hansson and Liden, p. xvii.

24. Igor Kon, *The Sexual Revolution in Russia* (New York: The Free Press, 1995), p. 150.

25. Alessandra Stanley, "Rich or Poor, More Russian Mothers Go it Alone," *New York Times,* 10/21/95, p. 1.

26. Letter to friend of the author, July 1992.

27. Sergei Zalygin, "Women and the NTR," in Sigrid McLaughlin, ed., *The Image of Women in Contemporary Soviet Fiction* (New York: St. Martin's Press, 1989), p. 220.

28. Durden-Smith, *Russia: A Long-Shot Romance*, p. 8.

29. du Plessix Gray, p. 7.

30. "From Russia With Love: Red Beauties Want American Hubbies," *Sun*, Vol. 8, No 41, 8/9/90, p. 5.

31. *Ibid.*, p. 5.

32. "East-West Climbers Find Differences Do Exist," *New York Times*, 6/27/87, p. 12.

33. Baskina, "Amerikanskie zhenshchiny usilivaiut bor'bu protiv muzhchin," p. 7.

34. Interview, Radio Liberty, "Russian Fiancées—American Fiancés," Special Program, 6/20/94, New York.

35. Radio Liberty interview, 6/20/94, and Sullivan, p. A10.

36. Tamara Gilmore, p. 31.

37. Liesl Schillinger, "The Yupskies are Coming," *New York* Magazine, 8/2/95, p. 36, 38.

38. A. Genis, Interview with Radio Liberty, 6/20/94, New York.

39. Anton Pomeshchikov, "Natalia Vetlitskaia, 'Ia prosto krivilas,'" *Playboy* (Russian edition), July 1995, p. 103.

40. David Blum, "From Russia Without Love," *New York* Magazine, 5/11/87, pp. 46–56, 53–54.

41. *Ibid.*, pp. 46–56.

42. Sullivan, p. A10.

43. "European Journal," CUNY Cable TV, 1/13/92. Her sentiments are borne out by a survey in which, when asked if they would marry someone who had all the qualities they desired in a mate if they were not in love with the person, only 40% of the Russian women respondents said they would refuse, as opposed to 89% of the American women. Kon, *The Sexual Revolution in Russia*, p. 165, and Vladimir Shlapentokh, *Love, Marriage, and Friendship in the Soviet Union: Ideals and Practices* (New York: Praeger, 1984), pp. 40–44.

44. Scanna International, *Worldwide Correspondence* (Pittsford, New York), 1995.

45. See Janet Collins and Dmitrii Kotov, "Zanevestit'sia po-amerikanski," *Moskovskii komsomolets*, 8/30/96, p. 8.

46. Melinda Hennenberger, "From Warm Letters to Cold Warring, Romance Fades," *New York Times*, 10/28/92, p. B1.

47. Quoted in Jeannie Ralston, "Love with a Perfect Stranger," *Glamour*, September 1993, p. 284; see also Weston Rogers, *Love Letters . . . From Russia* (Dallas, Texas: Weston Rogers Productions, 1993).

48. See Rogers, p. 120.

49. Ralston, p. 311.

50. Jeannie Rawlston and Mary K. Moore, "Remember This Mail-Order Marriage?" *Glamour*, March 1996, p. 114.

51. "Love Letters," advertising brochure.

52. *Amour,* Tver, 1992.

53. Sullivan, p. A10. Another such Russian-based service, Alliance, claims to have 3,000 Russian women seeking foreign husbands, and Harmony Advertising, run by a Texan who married a Ukrainian, boasts of a catalogue circulation of 30,000. *Russian Travel Monthly*, October 1994 (Montpelier, Vermont: Russian Information Services), pp. 2–3.

54. Iyer, *Video Night in Katmandu,* p. 32.

COUPLES

1. Pico Iyer, T*he Lady and the Monk: Four Seasons in Tokyo* (New York: Knopf, 1991), p. 79.

2. Zara Witkin, *An American Engineer in Russia: The Memoirs of Zara Witkin 1932–1934,* pp. 1–2.

3. The original Russian title was *Baby ryazanskie, (Ryazan Women)*, but in English the film was entitled *Village of Sin.*

4. *Ibid.*, pp. 26–34.

5. *Ibid.*, pp. 100, 102.

6. *Ibid.*, p. 104.

7. *Ibid.*, p. 108.

8. *Ibid.*, pp. 195, 227.

9. *Ibid.*, p. 247.

10. *Ibid.*, p. 288.

11. Armand Hammer, *Witness to History* (London: Hodder and Stoughton, 1988), p. 240.

12. *Ibid.*, p. 243.

13. *Ibid.*, p. 260.

14. *Ibid.*, p. 283.

15. Homer Smith, *Black Man in Red Russia*, p. 98. Since Pushkin had African blood and is considered by some African-Americans as a black cultural figure, Smith may have been making a parallel between himself and Marie, and Pushkin and Goncharova, reputed to have been the greatest beauty of the poet's time.

16. *Ibid.*, p. 100.

17. *Ibid.*, pp. 100–101.

18. Edward Jay Epstein, *Legend: The Secret World of Lee Harvey Oswald* (New

York: Reader's Digest Press, McGraw Hill, 1978), p. 132. Norman Mailer's book *Oswald's Tale: An American Mystery* (New York: Random House, 1995) contains a great deal of interesting material on Oswald's life and marriage. Mailer was given access to papers from the KGB files on Oswald's life in Minsk, and conducted lengthy interviews with Marina Oswald Porter.

19. Mailer, pp. 169, 167.
20. *Ibid.*, p. 167.
21. See *Ibid.*, p. 176.
22. Epstein, p. 137; Gerald R. Ford and John R. Stiles, *Portrait of the Assassin* (New York: Simon and Schuster, 1965), p. 50.
23. Ford and Stiles, p. 50.
24. Mailer, p. 785.
25. See Mailer, Priscilla Johnson McMillan, *Marina and Lee* (New York: Harper and Row, 1977), Epstein, Ford and Stiles.
26. McMillan, p. 338.
27. *Ibid.*, pp. 230–231.
28. In Texas Marina became acquainted with several Russian women married to Americans. Katya Ford had married first an American soldier and then a geologist; Valentina Ray had three children with her American husband Frank.
29. Mailer, p. 486.
30. *Ibid.*, pp. 471–472.
31. Steve Salerno, "June Oswald," *New York Times Magazine*, 4/30/95, pp. 34–35.
32. McMillan, p. 452.
33. Mailer, p. 785.
34. See Glenn Fowler, "William Wesley Peters Dies at 79; A Disciple of Frank Lloyd Wright," *New York Times*, 7/18/91, and Bassow, p. 324.
35. *Time*, 10/5/92 p. 91; "Stalin's Daughter Has Fallen Upon Hard Times," *New York Times*, 9/3/92, p. B8; *Izvestiia*, 2/3/96, p. 3.
36. Henry S.F. Cooper, Jr., *New Yorker*, 6/11/90, p. 84.
37. Eisenhower, p. 25.
38. *Ibid.*, p. 59.
39. *Ibid.*, p. 12.
40. *Ibid.*, p. 80.
41. *Ibid.*, pp. 32–33.
42. *Ibid.*, p. 41.
43. *Ibid.*, p. 98.
44. *Ibid.*, p. 158.
45. *Ibid.*, p. 127.

46. *Ibid.*, p. 213.
47. *Ibid.,* p. 216.
48. *Ibid.,* p. 217.
49. *Ibid.*, p. 87.
50. *Ibid.,* p. 174.
51. *Ibid.*, p. 224.
52. Susan Eisenhower, conversation with the author, 12/3/94, Brown University, Providence, Rhode Island.
53. Eisenhower, p. 230.
54. *Ibid.*, p. 203.
55. Susan Eisenhower, conversation with the author, 12/3/94, Brown University, Providence, Rhode Island.
56. *New York Times*, 9/3/95, p. 42.
57. *New York Times,* 10/29/95, p. 48.
58. *New York Times*, 6/9/91, p. 56, 8/18/96, p. 58, and *Harvard Magazine*, October 1991, p. 94.
59. The question which these couples must answer is that of when the limit of tolerance is reached. Craig Storti pointed out that in every culture there is behavior we cannot accept even when we expect it, because such behavior violates values which are so basic to our identity that our self-respect forces us to reject it. See Craig Storti, *The Art of Crossing Cultures* (Yarmouth, Maine: Intercultural Press, 1991), pp. 65–66.
60. Annabella Bucar, conversation with the author, Moscow, 1/11/95.
61. Sara Harris, conversation with the author, Moscow, 3/6/96.
62. Sara Harris, conversation with the author, Moscow, 3/6/96.
63. Jim Vail, "Spotlight on Expatriates Who've Come to Stay," *Moscow Tribune*, 5/14/94, p. 9.
64. Conversations with Joanne Turnbull and Nikolai Formosov, Moscow, 1/9/95, and New York, 3/14/95.
65. The names and identifying details of this couple have been changed to protect privacy.
66. Conversation with Mary C., New York, 12/20/95.
67. Conversation with Dick G., Moscow, 1/9/95.
68. Conversation with Svetlana Kozlova and Robert Coalson, 1/14/95, Moscow.
69. Gelsey Kirkland, *Dancing on My Grave* (Garden City, New York: Doubleday and Company, 1986), pp. 119 and 128.
70. *Ibid.*, p. 142.
71. *Ibid.,* pp. 142, 67, 143, 35.
72. Judy Chavez with Jack Vitek, *Defector's Mistress* (New York: Dell Publishing Company, 1979).

73. *Ibid.*, p. 238.
74. *Ibid.*, pp. 78, 81, 96.

ADAPTING

1. Raymonde Carroll, *Cultural Misunderstandings: The French-American Experience* (University of Chicago Press: Chicago and London, 1988), p. 58.
2. Eva Hoffman, *Lost in Translation* (New York: Dutton, 1982), pp. 186–187, 245, 265.
3. Tamara Gilmore, pp. 89–90.
4. Buck, p. 108.
5. McClellan, p. 123.
6. Vera A., conversation with the author, Moscow, August 1991.
7. See Mailer, p. 559.
8. Minchin, *Ogonek*, #42 (1990), pp. 25–26.
9. Quoted in McVay, pp. 141, 165.
10. *Ibid.*, p. 204.
11. Tatiana Leshchenko-Sukhomilina, *Dolgoe budushchee: Vospominaniia* (Moscow: Sovetskii pisatel', 1991), pp. 32, 261.
12. Aksyonov, p. 31.
13. McClellan, *Of Love and Russia,* p. 310.
14. *Ibid.*, p. 311.
15. *Ibid.*, p. 311.
16. *Ibid.*, p. 313.
17. *Ibid.*, p. 317.
18. Numerous other factors such as age, social class and education also influence the spouse's behavior. See Craig Storti, *Cross-Cultural Dialogues* (Yarmouth, Maine: Intercultural Press, 1994), p. 8.
19. Tamara Gilmore, p. 86.
20. McClellan, p. 308.
21. Lyons, p. 239.
22. A. Minchin, "'Teplo li nam doma?'" #42, 1990, pp. 26–27.
23. Craig Storti noted that there is trouble with mail, school, language, housing, transportation, and shopping, and that the people in the new country are mostly indifferent to all these problems. The newcomer therefore sticks with his compatriots and criticizes the customs and people of the new country. See Storti, *The Art of Crossing Cultures,* p. 34.
24. Pico Iyer's comments regarding romances between Asians and Westerners are applicable to Russian-American liaisons as well. He noted that cross-cultural romances developed with all the ups and downs of any love story in which opposites continually attract and repel each other. The Westerner

is attracted to the Easterner's traditions, and practically envies his suffering, while the Easterner is attracted by precisely the opposite—the Westerner's easier life and endless possibilities for the future. Each gradually becomes more similar to the other, and less like the individual the partner previously admired. See *Video Night in Katmandu*, p. 31.

25. Whitney, p. 307.
26. Garb, *They Came to Stay*, p. 186.
27. Scott, pp. 248–249.
28. Garb, *They Came to Stay,* pp. 91–92.
29. *Ibid.*, p. 92.
30. *Ibid.*, pp. 8–9 and 93–94.
31. *Ibid.,* pp. 92, 96.
32. *Ibid.,* pp. 109, 180.
33. The American linguist Benjamin Whorff posited that man's entire perception of the world is programmed by the language he speaks.
34. Edward T. Hall, *The Silent Language* (New York: Doubleday, Anchor Books, 1981), p. 101.
35. Tamara Gilmore, p. 96.
36. Garb, *They Came to Stay,* p. 119.
37. Hoffman, p. 245.
38. See Mailer, p. 80; McMillan, p. 193.
39. See Mailer, p. 310.
40. Garb, *They Came to Stay,* p. 91.
41. *Ibid.,* p. 185.

FOR BETTER OR FOR WORSE

Passions and Psychobabble: Roles and Sex

1. Wettlin, p. 113.
2. Hedrick Smith, *The Russians* (New York, Quadrangle/The New York Times Books Co., 1976), p. 130.
3. See Rogers, p. 17.
4. Mark Popovsky, *Na drugoi storone planety,* p. 265 (Philadelphia: Poberezh'e, 1994), p. 265.
5. Ada Baskina, "Amerikanskaia sem'ia," *Izvestiia*, 12/15/94, p. 7.
6. Ripp, p. 108.
7. See James Maddock, et al, eds., *Families Before and After Perestroika* (New York: The Guilford Press, 1994), pp. 98–103.
8. Kon, p. 13.
9. *Ibid.*, p. 2.
10. Shlapentokh, p. 552.

11. Quoted in Lynne Atwood, "Sex and the Cinema," in *Sex and Russian Society*, ed. by Igor Kon and James Riordan (Bloomington and Indianapolis: Indiana University Press, 1993), p. 66. A Soviet journalist's interview in 1992, however, with the woman who said this was titled "In Russia There is Everything, Including Sex!" Quoted in Laura Engelstein, "There is Sex in Russia—and Always Was: Some Recent Contributions to Russian Erotica," *Slavic Review*, Winter 1992, vol. 51 #4, p. 726.

12. Hingley, p. 191, and Kon and Riordan, p. 20.

13. Lidiia Osheverova, "Rossiane—odna iz samykh seksual'no aktivnyx natsii, no luchshie liubovniki—frantsuzy," *Izvestiia*, 5/29/96, p. 10.

14. Kon, pp. 163, 186, 189, and Inga Prelovskaya, "Cherez sem' let posle svad'by," *Izvestiia*, 7/5/95, p. 5. In 1994 there were about 225 abortions for each 100 live births. "Po chislu abortov my po-prezhnemu lidery," *Izvestiia*, 6/24/95, p. 1; Maurice T. Maraschino, *Allez-y doucement, camarades!* (Paris, Robert Laffont, 1991), pp. 140, 153; Maddock, p. 24; Kon, p. 189. In 1995 there were 40,000 abortions performed on girls under 18. Iulia Nikolaeva, "Chto oni khoteli znat' o sekse?," *Argumenty i Fakty*, 7/12/96, p. 12.

15. du Plessix Gray, p. 17.

16. Whitney, p. 73.

17. *Ibid.*, p. 75.

18. Eisenhower, p. 95.

19. Erica Jong, *Fear of Fifty* (New York: Harper Paperbacks, 1994), p. 140.

20. Kon, p. 80.

21. Marina Ripinskaia, "Suzhenyi iz-za moria," *Novoye Russkoye Slovo*, 8/16/96, p. 49.

22. Quoted in Kon, p. 154.

23. Aksyonov, p. 137.

24. Popovsky, pp. 267–268.

25. A recent American poll showed that 71% of 1,000 male and female respondents aged 18–39 found it easy to tell their partners what they liked and didn't like during sex, and that 40% discussed their sex lives with their partners at least once a week. "Can You Talk About Sex?" *Glamour*, August 1995, p. 68.

26. Kon, p. 135.

27. McMillan, pp.120–121.

28. Mailer, p. 185.

29. Chavez, pp. 56, 129, 184.

30. Aksyonov, p. 134.

31. A recent *Izvestiia* survey showed that, despite their long-standing reputation for philandering, 80% of French males considered themselves faithful husbands, while one of every two Russians openly admitted to infidelity.

"Geroiami-liubovnikami frantsuzy byli tol'ko v epokhu Gi de Mopassana," *Izvestiia,* 9/29/94, p. 3.

32. Quoted in Andrew Nagorski, "Sex Tiger Seeks Genius," *Newsweek,* 10/2/95, p. 21.

Home, Sweet Home

1. Jo Durden-Smith, *Russia: A Long-Shot Romance,* p. 19.
2. Hansson and Liden, p. 72.
3. Whitney, p. 232.
4. Mailer, p. 192.
5. See Rogers, p. 12.
6. Kirkland, p. 215.
7. McMillan, p. 187.
8. Karen Watson, "Guess Who Came to My House," *Ladies' Home Journal,* September 1990, p. 24.
9. Aksyonov, p. 73.
10. Chavez, p. 165.
11. *Ibid.,* p. 169.

Looks and Manners

1. Kitty Kelley, *Nancy Reagan: The Unauthorized Biography* (New York: Simon and Schuster, 1991), pp. 452, 496–497.
2. *Ibid.,* p. 252.
3. Buck, p. 111.
4. Jo Durden-Smith, *Russia: A Long-Shot Romance,* p. 120.
5. Chavez, p. 88.
6. McMillan, pp 38–41.
7. du Plessix Gray, p. 160.
8. *Ibid.,* p. 164.
9. Katherine Baldwin, "The Russian Front," *New York Times Magazine,* 11/6/94, p. 69.
10. With the increase in Russian-American contacts the importance of understanding each other's manners and customs has led to courses on differences in manners and behavior. A California consulting firm claims more than 2,000 clients for its programs on Russian-American etiquette. Vladimir Mikheev, "Kak amerikanskie astronavty uchilis' russkomu etiketu," *Izvestiia,* 7/8/95, p. 2.
11. Mailer, p. 169.
12. David Owen, "Shouts and Murmurs," *The New Yorker,* 12/18/95, p. 28.
13. Jan Perkowski, quoted in Craig Storti, *The Art of Crossing Cultures,* p.19.
14. Eisenhower, p. 200.

15. Edward T. Hall and Mildred Reed Hall, *Understanding Cultural Differences: Germans, French and Americans* (Yarmouth, Maine: Intercultural Press, 1990), p. 146.
16. Edward C. Stewart and Milton J. Bennett, *American Cultural Patterns* (Yarmouth, Maine: Intercultural Press, 1991), p. 165.
17. Deborah Tannen, *You Just Don't Understand* (New York: Ballantine Books, 1991), p. 207.
18. Barbara Bush, *A Memoir* (New York: St. Martin's Paperbacks 1994), p. 228.

Two Kinds of Time

1. Eddy Gilmore, p. 105.
2. Edward T. Hall, *Understanding Cultural Differences*, pp. 13–15.
3. Hingley, p. 43.
4. Hall, *The Silent Language*, pp. 150–159.
5. Conversation with Susan Eisenhower, Providence, Rhode Island, 12/3/94.
6. Wettlin, p. 264.

On the Job

1. Maddock, pp. 158, 166.
2. Witkin, pp. 56–57.
3. Garb, "Culture Learning and Cultural Adaptation Among North Americans in the USSR," pp. 86–93.

Dollars and Rubles

1. Olga Dashkevich, "The Master and Margarita or Lessons in Capitalism," *Marina*, special issue 1994, p. 34.
2. *Moscow Tribune*, 4/2/94, p. 10.
3. Aksyonov, p. 103.
4. Olga Kondrat'eva, "Uzh zamuzh za rubezh?" *Cosmopolitan* (Russian edition), February 1996, p. 88.
5. Dashkevich, *Marina*, p. 34.
6. Chavez, pp. 39–40.
7. Popovsky, p. 284.
8. Dashkevich, p. 33.
9. Kirkland, p. 170.
10. Kondrat'eva, p. 88.
11. Garb, "Culture Learning and Cultural Adaptation Among North Americans in the USSR" (Moscow: Academy of Sciences of the USSR), p. 119.

"You Marry the Family"

1. Mailer, p. 305.
2. See Popovsky, p. 282.

3. Jim Vail, "Russians and Foreigners: Beyond the Wedding Vows," *Moscow Tribune*, 4/2/94, p. 10.

4. Shelley Aspaklaria, "US-Soviet Couples: The Emotional Cost Continues to Surprise," *New York Times*, 1/8/85, pp. C1, C14.

5. Hansson and Liden, p. xvi.

6. Mailer, p. 419.

7. Garb, *They Came to Stay*, p. 91.

8. In 1993 the maternal mortality rate for Russia was 2.5 times higher than in the rest of Europe. Kon, p. 189.

9. Buck, pp. 115–116.

10. Eddy Gilmore, p. 356.

11. Garb, *They Came to Stay*, pp. 176–177.

12. Popovsky, p. 285.

13. Kon in Maddock, pp. 62–64.

14. Garb, "Culture Learning and Cultural Adaptation Among North Americans in the USSR," pp. 113–115.

15. Garb, *They Came to Stay*, p. 178.

16. Conversation with the author, Moscow, 3/6/96.

17. Ada Baskina, "Amerikanskaia sem'ia: II," *Izvestiia*, 12/22/94, p. 7.

18. Bush, p. 363.

19. Wettlin, p. 322.

20. Garb, *They Came to Stay*, p. 189.

21. Jim Vail, "Spotlight on Expatriates Who've Come to Stay," *Moscow Tribune*, 4/14/94, p. 9.

22. Conversation with Sara Harris, Moscow, 3/6/96.

23. Vail, "Spotlight on Expatriates Who've Come to Stay," p. 9.

24. Felicity Barringer, "The Tie that Binds from a World Away," *New York Times*, 8/31/95, p. C8.

"Friend" or *"Droog"*

1. Richmond, pp. 17 and 85.

2. Eisenhower, p. 117.

3. Colette Shulman, "The Individual and the Collective," in *Women in Russia*, ed. by Dorothy Atkinson et al (Stanford California: Stanford University Press, 1977), p. 381.

4. Lois Smith Brady, "Vows: Tom Gillett and Marina Volokhonskaya," *New York Times*, 3/14/93, p. 12.

5. Khanga, pp. 177–180.

6. Quoted in Cathy Young, review of Yuri Tarnopolsky, *Memoirs of 1984* (Lanham, Maryland: University Press of America) in *New York Times Book Review*, 1/6/94, p. 37.

7. See Stewart and Bennett, pp. 101–102.

8. Quoted in du Plessix Gray, p. 177.

9. Carroll, p. 80.

10. A study of Russian émigré friendships showed that in 1979 79% of a group of Soviet Jewish emigres said that their three closest friends were other Russian immigrants, and only 3% claimed no Russians among their closest friends. In a 1984 study 84% of the immigrants said their close friends were other immigrants, and few claimed to have made American friends. See Fran Markowitz, "*Russkaia Druzhba*: Russian Friendship in American and Israeli Contexts," *Slavic Review* #50, no. 3, Fall 1991, p. 642.

11. Hammer, p. 281.

12. Wettlin, p. 299.

13. Garb, *They Came to Stay,* p. 95.

14. *Ibid.*, p. 180.

Eat, Drink and—Relax?

1. Mailer, p. 212.

2. Chavez, p. 174.

3. Popovsky, p. 282.

4. Russians avoid eating soup after seven in the evening, however, believing that it is bad for you and makes you go to the bathroom at night.

5. Chavez, p. 101.

6. Aksyonov, p. 33.

7. Popovsky, p. 264.

8. N. I. Kostomarov, *Ocherk domashnei zhizni i nravov velikorusskogo naroda v xvi i xvii stoletiiakh* (Moscow: Respublika, 1992), pp. 224 and 227.

9. Conversation with Susan Eisenhower, Brown University, Providence, Rhode Island, 12/3/94.

10. Garb, "Culture Learning and Cultural Adaptation Among North Americans in the USSR," p. 103.

11. Tom Heymann, *On An Average Day in the Soviet Union* (New York: Fawcett Columbine, 1990), pp. 13 and 29. At the time there were 10 million alcoholics in the U.S.

12. Hingley, p. 53.

How Are You Feeling?

1. James Barron, "Kleenex, Juice (Sniff), Aspirin, Fax," *New York Times*, 2/1/95, p. C1.

2. Wettlin, p. 95.

3. Kirkland, p. 145.

4· Bush, pp. 227–228.

5. Chavez, p. 115.
6. Buck, p. 113.
7. *Ibid.,* p. 120.

THE MINDSET

1. Mailer, p. 110.
2. An article in *New York* magazine on the subject of the Russian propensity for cheating on tests quoted an American professor as saying "They don't feel ill at ease because they don't see anything wrong with it. To them it's just 'helping' someone." The reaction of a Russian student to a request to copy from his test paper was "It's doubtful that I'd refuse. If you say no, people will say you're a bad person. Better I get caught than say no." Julia Gorin, "Copy Comrades," *New York* Magazine, 12/25/95–1/1/96, p. 26.
3. Garb, "Culture Learning and Cultural Adaptation Among North Americans in the USSR," p. 10.
4. Eisenhower, p. 141. Today, however, the Russian collective spirit is under assault from the rough transition to a market economy. A young Muscovite married to an American said that his Russian friends were beginning to think like Americans, and that young people who were supporting their parents or who were out for success didn't really care very much any more about their friends. Igor Kon noted that while in the past Russians thought of themselves as an intrinsic part of a social group, today people increasingly feel that the individual is the focus of his own world, and that social roles and identities are aspects of the personality which are secondary to the self. See Kon, *The Sexual Revolution in Russia,* pp. 88–89.
5. Mailer, p. 784.
6. Chavez, p. 85.
7. A content analysis of texts using words to characterize people showed that the most popular word was *dobryi*—"kind" or "good." *Russkie: Etno-sotsio-logicheskie ocherki* (Moskva: Nauka, 1992), p. 376.
8. See Maddock, p. 51.
9. Of course, Americans tell white lies to protect themselves and the feelings of others, but lying on serious subjects is not nearly as automatic a reflex as for Russians. A 1993 survey revealed that the most frequent subject of Americans' lies included their weight, age, and hair color. Bernice Kaner, "Americans Lie, or so They Say," *New York Times,* 6/2/96, pp. 43–44.
10. Tatyana Tolstaya, quoted in Yale Richmond, *From Net to Da* (Yarmouth, Maine: Intercultural Press, 1992), p. 47.
11. Vadim Burlak, "Moia Amerika ili pis'ma k amerikanskoi kuzine," unpublished manuscript, Moscow, 1990, p. 2.

12. A. Minchin, "'Teplo li nam doma?'" 1990, pp. 26–27.
13. Hedrick Smith, *The Russians,* p. 105.
14. Quoted in Richmond, p. 123.
15. Wettlin, p. 298.
16. Jo Durden-Smith, *Russia: A Long-Shot Romance,* p. 145.
17. Popovsky, pp. 239–240.
18. Deborah Tannen, *Talking from 9 to 5: Men and Women in the Workplace: Language, Sex and Power* (New York: Avon Books, 1994), p. 238.
19. Stewart and Bennett, p. 67: "The American emphasis on problem solving construes disagreement as a negative factor that must be solved . . . 'No problem' is synonymous with 'I agree.'"
20. Raymond F. Smith, *Negotiating with the Soviets* (Bloomington and Indianapolis: Indiana University Press, 1989, p. 14).
21. Chavez, p. 62.
22. Popovsky, p. 247.
23. *Ibid.*, p. 284.
24. Romano, p. 32.
25. Eleonora Rabinovich, "Letter to the Editor," *New York Times,* 7/10/90, p. 10.
26. Minchin, *Ogonek,* #42, 1990, pp. 25–26, and Fyodorova and Frankel, p. 3.
27. Iurii Kovalenko, "Elena Safonova: Teper' ia poniala, pochemu frantsuzam tak nraviatsia russkie zhenshchiny," *Izvestiia,* 12/8/95, p. 10.
28. Fyodorova and Frankel, p. 3.

LOVE AND MARRIAGE DOT-COM

1. Vita Bekker, "Lonesome Men Seek Out Local Love," *St. Petersburg Times,* #543, 2/18/00.
2. See Robert J. Scholes, "The 'Mail-Order Bride' Industry and Its Impact on US Immigration." INS, 1998. Author's telephone interview with Art Steckler, Director, European Connections, 7/9/98.
3. Frank R. Coleman, *To Russia For Love: The American Man's Best Option* (Oklahoma City, Oklahoma: Red Star Publications, 1999), p. 79.
4. During my interviews and in reading agency catalogues and postings to the Russian Women's List, I noticed that there were a very large number of computer and software professionals among the men. As several of them explained, "computer types" are by definition "global," for their work takes them all over the Internet and the virtual globe, and frequently requires travel as well. Many say they have foreign colleagues, recruited from all over the world; others commented that knowledge of computer languages could lead to greater facility with foreign languages, and lessen fear of tackling a "difficult" language such as Russian. And while conservative midwesterners and their parents might look askance at a young

Russian wife, "Computer people don't care what other people think of them . . . the informality—the jeans and T-shirt mentality—reflect a 'let's hang out with lots of different people' attitude." Though some of the men have traveled abroad, most of them have never been to Russia, do not speak the language, and have little familiarity with Russian culture.

5. Donald C. Drake, "Time to Choose," in "To Russia For Love: An 8-part serial," *The Philadelphia Inquirer,* 12/1/98, p. F1.

6. Gary Clark, *"Your Bride is in the Mail!"* (Las Vegas: Words That Work Publications, 1998), p. 6.

7. Vita Bekker, "Lonesome Men Seek Out Local Love," *St. Petersburg Times,* #543, 2/18/00.

8. Helena Goscilo, "Porn on the Cob: Some Hard Core Issues," in M. Levitt and R. Toporkov, eds., *Eros and Pornography in Russian Culture* (Moscow: Ladomir, 1999), p. 567.

9. Bekker, *St. Petersburg Times,* #543, 2/18/00.

10. Goscilo, p. 566.

11. Letter to the author from a Russian woman, 3/4/00.

12. Goscilo, p. 568.

13. Matthew Fisher, "Russians Dream of Life in The West," *Toronto Sun,* 10/18/99.

14. "Common Questions and Answers," Scanna International, Atlanta Georgia, advertising sheet.

15. Such men may be hard to find, but they do exist. Those Russian women who succeed in finding decent men in their own country, however, are not our subject here. And, as we will see later, quite a few American women have found happiness with Russian husbands.

16. See Emil Draitser, *Making War, Not Love: Gender and Sexuality in Russian Humor* (New York: St. Martin's Press, 1999), p. 118.

17. Cited in Bekker, *St. Petersburg Times,* #543, 2/18/00.

18. Interview with Nina Rubasheva, Moscow, 1/16/00.

19. Gregory Katz, "To Russia for Love," *The Dallas Morning News,* 8/23/98, pp. 1 and 34A.

20. Author's telephone interview with Art Steckler, Director, European Connections, 7/9/98.

21. Gregory Katz, "To Russia for Love," *The Dallas Morning News,* 8/23/98, pp. 1 and 34A. The owners of the firms are quite open about their goals. "While I think it's very nice to have more and more Americans and Russians getting together," one of them remarked, "the goal of my firm is to make money."

22. Yuri Kovalenko, "Kak vyiti zamuzh za frantsuza," *Novoye Russkoye Slovo,* 1/20/99, p. 7.

23. Coleman, *To Russia For Love,: The American Man's Best Option* (Oklahoma City, Oklahoma: Red Star Publications, 1999), p. 155.

24. Post to the Russian Women's List.

25. See Donald C. Drake, "Time to Choose," in "To Russia For Love: An 8-part serial," *The Philadelphia Inquirer,* 11/29–12/6/98.

26. See Scholes report for the INS.

27. CBS "48 Hours," 2/14/00; Ol'ga Zherebtsova, "Russkie Zolushki mochat amerikanskikh printsev," *Novoye Russkoye Slovo*, 10/22/99, p. 50.

PARENTS AND CHILDREN

1. There is an excellent discussion of the role of children in society and of cultural differences in raising children in a Russian work by I.S. Kon, *Rebenok i obshchestvo (istoriko-etnograficheskaia perspektiva)* (Moscow: Nauka, 1988).

2. Some of the problems faced by interracial children are similar to those of children raised in crosscultural families. See Felicia R. Lee, "Bridging a Divide," *New York Times*, The City, 4/30/00, p. 1.

3. On the admiration of Russian women for the way American men treat their stepchildren as their own sons and daughters, see Iuliia Kamenskaia, "I khochetsia, i koletsia," *Novoye Russkoye Slovo*, 3/27–3/28/98, p. 30.

4. For examples of differences in Russian and American attitudes towards raising children see Maria Knjazeva, *America Through the Eyes of a Russian Woman* (Kohtla-Jarve, Estonia: Ou Mark & Partnerid, 1999).

5. On this issue of children earning money see Gary Althen, *American Ways: A Guide for Foreigners in the United States* (Yarmouth, Maine: Intercultural Press, 1988), pp. 50–52. In the last few years, though, attitudes towards adolescents earning money have been rapidly changing in Russia.

6. For a survey of earnings, beliefs and habits of American adolescents, see Mary Lawless, "All About Kids," *Ladies' Home Journal*, May 2000, pp. 136–137. For discussion of attitudes of contemporary Russian adolescents see Irinba Pruss, "Neklassicheskii podrostok," *Itogi,* 5/16/00, pp. 48–50.

7. The Russian journal *Pedologiia: Novyi vek*, No 1, February 2000 and No 2, April 2000, contains interesting material on approaches to raising children in Russia today.

THE CULTURE CONFLICT

1. The *New York Times* marriage announcements range from a Russian and American musician who met at orchestra rehearsals—and played a duet at their wedding—to a 53-year-old New York perfume manufacturer who through the Internet met a 24-year old computer programmer from Obninsk. New couples include an American manager living in

Moscow with her retired Russian army colonel husband and two children, an American sculptor married to a Russian émigré painter, and a twice-married Jewish émigré lady mathematician who found love at age 39 and has been happily married for 16 years to a twice-divorced WASP computer expert. See Lois Smith Brady, "Vows: Pamela Holmes and Boris Astafiev," *New York Times*, 12/26/99, Styles, p. 8; Brady, "Vows: Oksana Katsuro and Douglas Hopkins," *New York Times*, 11/21/99, Styles, p. 9.

2. *Itogi*, 2/22/00 p. 5.

3. Emil Draitser, *Making War, Not Love*, 135.

4. George Steiner, *Errata: an examined life* (New York and London: Yale University Press, 1998), p. 101. Nor does the sexual revolution necessarily change deeply ingrained behavior. "Sure, we can get 'those things' now," one Russian woman commented. "But more often than not you think, well, just this time I'll risk it—I'll probably be OK. That's the time you get pregnant." While condoms are for sale at dozens of kiosks, the Russian male is in no rush to use them, particularly in a country where AIDS is not nearly as feared as in the U.S.

5. Draitser, p. 78.

6. *Cosmopolitan*, Russian edition, December 1997, p. 150.

7. Michelle Berdy, quoted in *The Russian Weekly*, David Johnson, ed., 6/19/98, Item #4.

8. Tatiana Shcherbina, "Bolshiye trudnosti s muzhchinoi," *Izvestiia*, 8/10/99, p. 6.

9. *Liza*, #4, 1/24/00, pp. 8–9.

10. Tatiana Korsakova, "Dusha moia dushechka," *Izvestiia*, 11/26/99, p. 11.

11. The English linguistic environment is winning out over her father's native Russian pronunciation and intonation.

12. Michelle Berdy, "Slovo v zashchitu russkikh muzhchin," *Literaturnaia gazeta*, (#5670), 11/17/97.

EPILOGUE

1. Kathryn Casey, "Marina's Story," *The Ladies' Home Journal*, May 1993, p. 158.

2. Wettlin, p. 321.

BIBLIOGRAPHY

WORKS IN ENGLISH

Aksyonov, Vassily. *In Search of Melancholy Baby*. New York: Vintage Books, Random House, 1989.

Althen, Gary. *American Ways: A Guide for Foreigners in the United States*. Yarmouth, Maine: Intercultural Press, 1988, pp. 50–52.

Aspaklaria, Shelley. "U.S.-Soviet Couples: The Emotional Cost Continues to Surprise." *New York Times*, 1/8/85, pp. C1, C14.

Attwood, Lynne. *Sex-Role Socialization in the USSR*. Bloomington and Indianapolis: Indiana University Press, 1990.

Baldwin, Katherine. "The Russian Front." *New York Times Magazine*, 11/6/94, pp. 68–69.

Balmforth, Richard. "U.S. Embassy Tightens Rules on Love with Russians." Reuters World Service, BC Cycle, 6/25/96.

Barringer, Felicity. "A U.S.-Soviet Venture of a Gentler Kind." *New York Times*, 1/6/90, p. 5.

———. "The Tie That Binds From a World Away." *New York Times*, 8/31/95, p. C8.

Barron, James. "Kleenex, Juice (Sniff), Aspirin, Fax." *New York Times*, 2/1/95, p. C1.

Barson, Michael. *Better Red Than Dead! A Nostalgic Look at the Golden Years of Russophobia, Red-Baiting, and Other Commie Madness*. New York: Hyperion, 1992.

Bassow, Whitman. *The Moscow Correspondents: Reporting on Russia from the Revolution to Glasnost*. New York: Paragon House, 1989.

Bauer, R. A. *The New Man in Soviet Psychology.* Cambridge: Harvard University Press, 1952.

Bekker, Vita. "Lonesome Men Seek Out Local Love." *St. Petersburg Times,* #543, 2/18/00.

Bellah, Robert N. et al. *Habits of the Heart: Individualism and Commitment in American Life.* New York: Harper and Row, 1985.

Binyon, Michael. *Life in Russia.* New York: Pantheon Books, 1983.

Blakeley, Allison. *Russia and the Negro: Blacks in Russian History and Thought.* Washington, D.C.: Howard University Press, 1986.

Blekher, Feiga. *The Soviet Woman in the Family and in Society.* New York: Halsted Press, 1979.

Blum, David. "From Russia Without Love." *New York* Magazine, 5/11/87. pp. 46–56.

Boym, Svetlana. *Common Places: Mythologies of Everyday Life in Russia.* Cambridge, Massachusetts: Harvard University Press, 1994.

Brady, Lois Smith. "Vows: Laura Mason, Alexander Khutorsky." Weddings. *New York Times,* 1/14/96, p. 39.

——. "Vows: Tom Gillett and Marina Volokhonskaya." *New York Times,* 3/14/93, p. 12.

——. "Vows: Oksana Katsuro and Douglas Hopkins." *New York Times,* 11/21/99, p. 9.

——. "Vows: Pamela Holmes and Boris Astafiev." *New York Times,* 12/26/99, p. 8.

Bochner, Stephen., ed. *Cultures in Contact: Studies in Cross-cultural Interaction.* Oxford and New York: Pergamon Press. 1982.

Brislin, Richard. *Cross-Cultural Encounters: Face-to-Face Interaction.* Elmsford, New York: Pergamon Press, 1981.

Buck, Pearl. *Talk About Russia (with Masha Scott).* New York: John Day, 1945.

Buckley, Mary. *Women and Ideology in the Soviet Union.* Ann Arbor: The University of Michigan Press, 1989.

Bulter, Juliet. "Can Russia Turn Your Children Into Bigots?" *The Moscow Times,* 1/21/00, p. 9.

Bush, Barbara. *A Memoir.* New York: St. Martin's paperbacks, 1994.

Carroll, Raymonde. Translated by Carol Volk. *Cultural Misunderstandings: The French-American Experience.* Chicago: University of Chicago Press, 1987.

Casey, Catherine. "Marina's Story." *Ladies' Home Journal,* May 1993, pp. 156–158.

Chavez, Judy, with Vitek, Jack. *Defector's Mistress.* New York: Dell Publishing Company, 1979.

Clark, Gary. *"Your Bride is in the Mail!"* Las Vegas, NV: Words That Work Publications, Inc., 1998.

Coleman, Frank R. *To Russia For Love: The American Man's Best Option.* Oklahoma City, Oklahoma: Red Star Publications, 1999.

Cooper, Ann. "Matchmaker's Dream: From Russia With Love." *New York Times*, 6/28/90, p. A4.

Costa, Alexandra. *Stepping Down From the Star: A Soviet Defector's Story*. New York: G. P. Putnam's Sons, 1986.

CUNY Cable Television. "European Journal," 1/13/92.

Dashkevich, Olga. "The Master and Margarita or Lessons in Capitalism." *Marina*, special issue, 1994, pp. 32–36.

Dick, John H. "Soviet Images of America, or Where Do We Go From Here?" *Russian Language Journal*, XLIII, Nos. 145–146 (1989), pp. 193–199.

Draitser, Emil A. *Making War, Not Love: Gender and Sexuality in Russian Humor*. New York: St. Martin's Press, 1999.

Drake, Donald C. "To Russia for Love: An 8-part serial." *The Philadelphia Inquirer*, 11/29–12/6, 1998.

du Plessix Gray, Francine. *Soviet Women: Walking the Tightrope*. New York: Doubleday, 1989.

Durden-Smith, Jo. "In the Belly of the Beast." *European Travel and Life*, December–January 1992, pp. 43–48, 114.

———. *Russia: A Long-Shot Romance*. New York: Alfred A. Knopf, 1994.

English, Robert, and Halperin, Jonathan J. "The Other Side: How Soviets and Americans Perceive Each Other." *Beyond the Kremlin*. New Brunswick, New Jersey and Oxford: The Committee for National Security and Transaction Books, 1987.

Eisenhower, Susan. *Breaking Free: A Memoir of Love and Revolution*. New York: Farrar Straus Giroux, 1995.

Engelstein, Laura. "There is Sex in Russia—and Always Was: Some Recent Contributions to Russian Erotica." *Slavic Review*, Winter 1992, vol. 51 #4, pp. 786–790.

Epstein, Edward Jay. *Legend: The Secret World of Lee Harvey Oswald*. New York: Reader's Digest Press, McGraw Hill, 1978.

Fairweather, Natasha. "Where Has All the Sex Gone?" *Moscow Times*, 2/22/97, pp. 13–14.

———. "Speaking of Questions About That." *Moscow Times*, 2/22/97, p. 14.

Filene, Peter G. *Americans and the Soviet Experiment 1917–1933*. Cambridge, Massachusetts: Harvard University Press, 1967.

Fischer, Louis. *Men and Politics: An Autobiography*. New York: Duell, Sloan and Pearce, 1941.

Fisher, Matthew. "Russians Dream of Life in The West." *Toronto Sun*, 10/18/99.

Fisher, Wesley Andrew. *The Soviet Marriage Market: Mate-Selection in Russia and the USSR*. New York: Praeger Publishers, 1980.

Ford, Gerald R., and Stiles, J. *Portrait of the Assassin*. New York: Simon and Schuster, 1965.

Fowler, Glenn. "William Wesley Peters Dies at 79; A Devotee of Frank Lloyd Wright." *New York Times*, 7/18/91, p. B8.

Fyodorova, Victoria and Frankel, Haskel. *The Admiral's Daughter.* New York: Delacorte Press, 1979.

Garb, Paula. "Culture Learning and Cultural Adaptation Among North Americans in the USSR." Moscow: Academy of Sciences of the USSR, 1990. University Microfilms International, Ann Arbor: Michigan.

———. *They Came to Stay: North Americans in the USSR.* Moscow: Progress Publishers, 1987.

Gayle, Michael. "Russian Fiancées—American Fiancés." Radio Liberty Program, 6/10/94.

Gilmore, Eddy. *Me and My Russian Wife.* Garden City, New Jersey: Doubleday and Co., 1954.

Gilmore, Tamara. *Me and My American Husband.* Garden City, New Jersey: Doubleday and Co., 1968.

Glamour. "Can You Talk About Sex?" August 1995, p. 68.

Goode, William. *The Family.* Englewood Cliffs, New Jersey: Prentice-Hall, 1964.

Gorin, Julia. "Copy Comrades." *New York* Magazine, 12/25/95, pp. 26–27.

Goscilo, Elena. "Porn on the Cob: Some Hard Core Issues." In Levitt, M. and Toporkov, R., Eds. *Eros and Pornography in Russian Culture.* Moscow: Ladomir, 1999, pp. 553–571.

Grimes, William. "Leon Theremin, Musical Inventor, is Dead at 97." *New York Times*, 11/9/93, p. B10.

Gross, Michael. "From Russia With Sex." *New York* Magazine, 8/10/98, pp. 22–32, 61, 82.

Hall, Edward T. *The Silent Language.* New York: Doubleday, Anchor Books 1981.

———, and Hall, Mildred Reed. *Understanding Cultural Differences: Germans, French and Americans.* Yarmouth, Maine: Intercultural Press, 1989.

Hammer, Armand. *Witness to History.* London: Hodder and Stoughton, 1988.

Hansson, Carola, and Liden, Karen. *Moscow Women.* New York: Pantheon Books, 1983.

Harmetz, Aljean. "U.S. And Soviet Sisters Meet At Last." *New York Times*, 11/5/85, p. 32.

Harvard Magazine, October 1991, p. 94.

Haywood, Harry. *Black Bolshevik: Autobiography of an Afro-American Communist.* Chicago: Liberty Press, 1978.

Hennenberger, Melissa. "From Warm Letters to Cold Warring, Romance Fades." *New York Times*, 10/28/92, p. B1, B5.

Heymann, Tom. *On An Average Day in the Soviet Union.* New York: Fawcett Columbine, 1990.

Hingley, Ronald. *The Russian Mind.* New York: Charles Scribner's Sons, 1977.

Hoffman, Eva. *Lost in Translation: Life in a New Language.* New York: E. P. Dutton, 1989.

Hubbs, Joanna. *Mother Russia: The Feminine Myth in Russian Culture.* Bloomington and Indianapolis: Indiana University Press, 1988.

Ignatius, Adi. "The Best Part of Life for These Americans is Not Paying Taxes." *The Wall Street Journal,* 11/12/93, pp. 1, 16.

Iyer, Pico. *The Lady and the Monk: Four Seasons in Tokyo.* New York: Knopf, 1991.

———. *Video Night in Katmandu.* London: Black Swan, 1988.

Jong, Erica. *Fear of Fifty.* New York: Harper Paperbacks, 1994.

Kaner, Bernice. "Americans Lie, or So They Say." *New York Times,* 6/26/96, pp. 43–44.

Katz, Gregory. "To Russia for Love." *The Dallas Morning News,* 8/23/98, pp. 1 and 34A.

Keen, Sam. *Faces of the Enemy: Reflections of the Hostile Imagination.* San Francisco: Harper and Row, 1986.

Kelley, Kitty. *Nancy Reagan: The Unauthorized Biography.* New York: Simon and Schuster, 1991.

Kessler, Ronald. *Moscow Station: How the KGB Penetrated the American Embassy.* New York: Simon and Schuster, Pocket Books, 1990.

Khanga, Yelena. *Soul to Soul: The Story of a Black Russian-American Family, 1865–1992.* New York: W. W. Norton and Company, 1992.

———. "No Matryoshkas Need Apply." *New York Times,* 11/25/91, p. A19.

Kirkland, Gelsey. *Dancing on My Grave.* Garden City, New York: Doubleday and Company, 1986.

Klimek, David. *Beneath Mate Selection and Marriage: The Unconscious Motives Behind Human Pairing.* New York: Van Nostrand Reinhold, 1979.

Klose, Eliza K. "Message." *Surviving Together,* Vol. 11, #3, Fall 1993, p. 2.

Knjazeva, Maria. *America Through the Eyes of a Russian Woman.* Kohtla-Jarve, Estonia: Ou Mark & Partnerid, 1999.

Kon, Igor. *The Sexual Revolution in Russia.* New York: The Free Press, 1995.

———, and Riordan, James, eds. *Sex and Russian Society.* Bloomington and Indianapolis: Indiana University Press, 1993.

Lawless, Mary. "All About Kids." *Ladies' Home Journal,* May 2000, pp. 136–137.

Lee, Felicia R. "Bridging a Divide." *New York Times,* The City, 4/30/00, p. 1.

Levitt, M. and Toporkov, R., Eds. *Eros and Pornography in Russian Culture.* Moscow: Ladomir, 1999.

Lewis, Paul. "Road to Capitalism Taking Toll on Men in the Former Soviet Bloc." *New York Times,* 8/11/99, p. 3.

Lyons, Eugene. *Assignment in Utopia.* New York: Harcourt Brace, 1937.

Mace, David. *The Soviet Family.* London: Hutchinson, 1964.

Maddock, James W., et al., ed. *Families Before and After Perestroika.* New York: The Guilford Press, 1994.

Mailer, Norman. *Oswald's Tale: An American Mystery.* New York: Random House, 1995.

Mandel, William. *Soviet Women.* New York: Anchor Books. Doubleday, 1974.

Maraschino, Maurice T. *Allez-y doucement, camarades!* Paris: Robert Laffont, 1991.

Markowitz, Fran. "Russkaia Druzhba: Russian Friendship in American and Israeli Contexts." *Slavic Review*, #50, no. 3, Fall 1991, pp. 637–645.

McClellan, Irina. *Of Love and Russia.* New York: W. W. Norton and Company, 1989.

McLaughlin, Sigrid., ed. *The Image of Women in Contemporary Soviet Fiction.* New York: St. Martin's Press, 1989.

McMillan, Priscilla Johnson. *Marina and Lee.* New York: Harper and Row, 1977.

McVay, Gordon. *Isadora and Esenin.* Ann Arbor, Michigan: Ardis, 1980.

Michael, Robert T., Gagnon, John H., Laumann, Edward O., and Kolata, Gina. *Sex in America: A Definitive Survey.* New York: Warner Books, 1995.

Murray, J. P. *Project Kuzbas: American Workers in Siberia 1921–1926.* New York: International Publications, 1983.

Nagorski, Andrew. "Sex Tiger Seeks Genius." *Newsweek*, 10/2/95, p. 21.

New York Times. "East-West Climbers Find Differences Do Exist," 1/28/87, p. 12.

——. "Stalin's Daughter Has Fallen Upon Hard Times," 9/23/92, p. B8.

——. "State Department Identifies Those Expected to Leave Soviet," 11/17/85, p. 14.

——. Russian-American wedding announcements: 9/3/95, p. 42; 10/29/95, p. 48; 2/18/90; 6/9/91, p. 56; 8/18/96, p. 58.

O'Flynn, Kevin. "American Willing to Pay Price to Find a Wife." *The Moscow Times*, 2/24/00.

Owen, David. "Shouts and Murmurs." *The New Yorker*, 12/18/95, p. 28.

Petrushevskaya, Ludmilla. *The Time: Night.* New York: Pantheon Books, 1994.

Rabinovich, Eleonora. "Letter to the Editor." *New York Times*, 7/10/90, p. 10.

Ralston, Jeannie. "Love with a Perfect Stranger." *Glamour*, September 1993, pp. 281–285, 306–311.

——, and Moore, Mary K. "Remember This Mail-Order Marriage?" *Glamour*, March 1996, p. 114.

Richmond, Yale. *From Nyet to Da.* Yarmouth, Maine: Intercultural Press, 1992.

Ripp, Victor. *Pizza in Pushkin Square.* New York: Simon and Schuster, 1990.

Robinson, John P., Andreyenkov, Vladimir G., and Patrushev, Vasily D. *The Rhythm of Everyday Life: How Soviet and American Citizens Use Time.* Boulder, Colorado: Westview Press, 1989.

Rogers, Weston. *Love Letters . . . From Russia.* Dallas, Texas: Weston Rogers Productions, 1993.

Romano, Dugan. *Intercultural Marriage: Promises and Pitfalls.* Yarmouth, Maine: Intercultural Press, 1988.

Rositzke, Harry. *The KGB: The Eyes of Russia.* London: Sidgwick & Jackson, 1981.

Salerno, Steve. "June Oswald." *New York Times Magazine,* 4/30/95, pp. 32–35.

Salisbury, Harrison. *A Journey for Our Times.* New York: Carroll and Graf, 1983.

Saxon, Wolfgang. "Elbridge Durbrow, U.S. Diplomat, Dies at 93." *New York Times,* 5/2/97, p. A25.

——. "Ellsworth Raymond Dies at 84; Kremlin Watcher of Stalin Era." *New York Times,* 8/23/96, p. 25.

Scanna International. *Worldwide Correspondence.* Pittsford, New York, 1995.

Schillinger, Liesl. "The Yupskies Are Coming." *New York Magazine,* 8/2/95, pp. 34–40.

Scholes, Robert J. *"The 'Mail-Order Bride' Industry and Its Impact on U.S. Immigration."* Immigration and Naturalization Service, 1998.

Scott, John. *Behind the Urals: An American Worker in Russia's City of Steel.* Bloomington and Indianapolis: Indiana University Press, 1989.

Sedugin, Petr Ivanovich. *New Soviet Legislation on Marriage and the Family.* Translated from the Russian by Nicholas Bobrov. Edited by Jim Riordan. Moscow: Progress Publishers, 1973.

Shlapentokh, Vladimir. *Love, Marriage, and Friendship in the Soviet Union: Ideals and Practices.* New York: Praeger, 1984.

Shtern, Mikhail. *Sex in the USSR.* New York: Times Books, 1980.

Shulman, Colette. "The Individual and the Collective." *Women in Russia.* Edited by Dorothy Atkinson *et al.* Stanford, California: Stanford University Press, 1977, pp. 375–384.

Smith, Hedrick. *The Russians.* New York: Quadrangle/New York Times Books Co., 1976.

Smith, Homer. *Black Man in Red Russia.* Chicago: Johnson Publishing Company, 1964.

Smith, Raymond. *Negotiating with the Soviets.* Bloomington and Indianapolis: Indiana University Press, 1989.

Stanley, Alessandra. "Rich or Poor, More Russian Mothers Go It Alone." *The New York Times,* 10/21/95, p. 1.

——. "Russian Wives Learn What Money Can't Buy," *New York Times,* 3/11/97, pp. A1, A 4.

——. "Valentines to Russia, Seeking Patient Brides." *New York Times,* 2/14/97, pp. A8, A28.

Starr, S. Frederick. *Red and Hot: The Fate of Jazz in the Soviet Union 1917–1980.* New York: Limelight Editions, 1985.

Stevens, Edmund. *Russia Is No Riddle.* New York: Greenberg, 1945.

———. *This is Russia Uncensored.* New York: Didier, 1950.

Stewart, Edward C., and Bennett, Milton J. *American Cultural Patterns: A Cross-Cultural Perspective,* rev. ed. Yarmouth, Maine: Intercultural Press, 1991.

Storti, Craig. *Cross-Cultural Dialogues.* Yarmouth, Maine: Intercultural Press, 1994.

———. *The Art of Crossing Cultures.* Yarmouth, Maine: Intercultural Press, 1990.

Sullivan, Kevin A. "A U.S.—Russian Formula for True Romance." *Washington Post,* 5/24/94, pp. A1, A10.

Sun. Vol. 8, No. 41, 8/9/90, p. 5.

Tannen, Deborah. *Talking From 9 to 5: Men and Women in the Workplace: Language, Sex and Power.* New York: Avon Books, 1994.

———. *You Just Don't Understand.* New York: Ballantine Books, 1991.

Taubman, Philip. "Soviet Said to Weigh 'Divided Spouses' Emigration." *New York Times,* 1/5/86, p. 3.

Taylor, S.J. Stalin's Apologist: *Walter Duranty: The New York Times's Man in Moscow.* New York and Oxford: Oxford University Press, 1990.

Tolstaya, Tatyana. "Notes From Underground." Review of Francine du Plessix Gray, *Soviet Women: Walking the Tightrope. New York Review of Books,* 5/31/90, pp. 3–7.

Tseng, Wen-Shing et al. *Adjustment in Intercultural Marriage.* Honolulu: University of Hawaii, 1977.

Vail, Jim. "Russians and Foreigners: Beyond the Wedding Vows." *Moscow Tribune,* 4/2/94, p. 10.

———. "Spotlight on Expatriates Who've Come to Stay." *Moscow Tribune,* 5/14/94, p. 9.

Visson, Lynn. "About Face: American Women Pursue Russians." *The Moscow Times,* 11/11/98, p. 9.

———. "For Better or Worse: Russian Brides Not Boring." *The Moscow Times,* 6/17/98, p. 9.

———. "Opposites Attract: The Challenges of Russian-American Marriages." *Russian Life,* October/November 1998, pp. 12–16, 45.

Washington Post. "The Search For Miss Right Takes a Turn Towards Russia." 3/8/98, p. A 01.

Watson, Karen. "Guess Who Came to My House." *Ladies' Home Journal,* September 1990, pp. 24, 221–223.

Watson, Peter. *Nureyev: A Biography.* New York: Hodder and Stoughton, Coronet Books, 1994.

Watson, Thomas J. Jr., and Petre, Peter. *Father, Son & Co.* New York: Bantam, 1991.

Welch, Liz and Brower, Alison. "How I Met My 'Marry Me' Man." *Glamour,* February 2000, p. 208.

Wettlin, Margaret. *Fifty Russian Winters: An American Woman's Life in the Soviet Union.* New York: Pharos Books, 1992.

Whitney, Tom. *Russia in My Life.* New York: Reynal & Company, 1962.

Witkin, Zara. *An American Engineer in Stalin's Russia: The Memoirs of Zara Witkin, 1932–1934.* Berkeley: University of California Press, 1991.

Wolfgang, Aaron, ed. *Nonverbal Behavior: Perspectives, Applications, Intercultural Insights.* Lewiston, New York : C. J. Hogrefe, 1984.

Womack, Helen. "It's Harder to Stay Together These Days." *Moscow Times,* 2/22/97, p. 8.

Young, Cathy. Review of Yuri Tarnopolsky, *Memoirs of 1984* (Lanham, Maryland: University Press of America). *New York Times Book Review,* 1/6/94, p. 37.

WORKS IN RUSSIAN

Baranskaia, N. "Nedelia kak nedelia." *Novyi Mir,* 11, 1969, pp. 23–55.

Baskina, Ida. "Amerikanskaia sem'ia. II." *Izvestiia,* 12/15/94, p. 7.

———. "Amerikanskaia sem'ia. III." *Izvestiia,* 12/22/94, p. 7.

———. "Amerikanskie zhenshchiny usilivaiut bor'bu protiv muzhchin." *Izvestiia,* 9/7/94, p. 7.

Binev, A. "Detektiv bez razviazki." *Argumenty i Fakty,* 1(53–54) 1991, p. 4.

Burlak, Vadim. "Moia Amerika ili pis'ma k amerikanskoi kuzine." Unpublished manuscript. Moscow, 1990.

Collins, Janet, and Kotov, Dmitrii. "Zanevestit'sia po-amerikanski." *Moskovskii Komsomolets,* 8/30/96, p. 8.

Gerasimov, Gennadii. "Demokratiia i demografiia." *Izvestiia,* 12/5/98, p. 7.

Golod, S. I. *XX vek i tendentsii seksual'nykh otnoshenii v Rossii.* Sankt-Peterburg: Aleteia, 1996.

Izvestiia. "Amerikanskoe posol'stvo ofitsial'no ob"avliaet svoim sotrudnikam ob okonchanii kholodnoi voiny." 5/25/95, p.1.

———. "Geroiami-liubovnikiami frantsuzy byli tol'ko v epokhu Gi de Mopassana." 9/29/94, p. 3.

———. "Moskvichei i moskvichek vlechet zarubezhnoe schast'e." 8/10/96, p. 1.

———. "Po chislu abortov my po-prezhnemu lidery." 6/24/95, p. 1.

Kabakov, Alexander. "Pogovorim o strannostiakh liubvi." *Moskovskie Novosti,* 2/18/90, p. 11.

Kamenskaia, Iuliia. "I khochestsia i koletsia." *Novoye Russkoye Slovo,* 3/27–3/28/98, p. 30.

Kharchev, Anatolii G. *Brak i sem'ia v SSSR: opyt sotsiologicheskogo issledovaniia.* Moscow: Mysl', 1964, and 2nd ed., 1979.

———. "Nekotorye tendentsii razvitiia sem'i v SSSR i kapitalisticheskikh stranakh." *Sotsiologiia i ideologiia.* Moscow: Nauka, 1969.

Kon, I. S. "Ne govorite potom, chto vy etogo ne znali." *Izvestiia,* 12/30/97, p. 5.

———. *Rebenok i obshcestvo (istoriko-etnograficheskaia perspektiva).* Moscow: Nauka, 1988.

———. *Seksual'naia kul'tura v Rossii: klubnika na berezke.* Moscow: O.G.I, 1997.

Kondrat'eva, Ol'ga. "Uzh zamuzh za rubezh?" *Cosmopolitan* (Russian edition), February 1996, pp. 87–90.

Kordev, Iu. A. *Brak i razvod: sovremennye tendentsii.* Moscow: Iuridicheskaia literatura, 1978.

Korsakova, Tat'iana. "Dusha moia dushechka." *Izvestiia,* 11/26/99, p. 11.

Kovalenko, Iurii. "Elena Safonova: Teper' ia poniala, pochemu frantsuzam tak nraviatsia russkie zhenshchiny." *Izvestiia,* 12/8/95, p. 10.

———. "Kak vyiti zamuzh za frantsuza." *Novoye Russkoye Slovo,* 1/20/99, p. 7.

Leshchenko-Sukhomilina, Tat'iana. *Dolgoe budushchee: Vospominaniia.* Moscow: Sovetskii pisatel', 1991.

Leviton, Lina. "Roman s grustnym prodolzheniem." *Novoye Russkoye Slovo,* 11/20/98, p. 50.

Levkovich, Valentina P. *Metodika diagnostiki supruzheskikh konfliktov v raznonatsional'nykh sem'iakh.* Moscow-Almaty: Institut psikhologii akademii nauk Rossii, 1992.

———. "Osobennosti supruzheskikh vzaimootnoshenii v raznonatsional'nykh sem'iakh." *Psikhologicheskii zhurnal,* tom 11, No 2, 1990, pp. 25–36.

———, and Zus'kova, O. E. "Uroven' moral'noi motivatsii suprugov kak faktor stabilizatsii sem'i." *Sotsial'no-psikhologicheskie aspekty izucheniia lichnosti. Shornik nauchnykh trudov.* Moscow: Akademiia Nauk SSSR, Institut psikhologii, 1963, pp.146–153.

Melvil', A. Iu., "Osobennosti amerikanskikh vospriatii Sovetskogo Soiuza." *Vzaimodeistvie kul'tury SSSR i SShA, xviii-xx vekov.* Edited by O. E. Tuganova. Moscow: Nauka, 1987, pp. 63–73.

Mikheev, Vladimir. "Kak amerikanskie astronavty uchilis' russkomu etiketu." *Izvestiia,* 7/8/95, p. 2.

Minchin, Aleksandr. "Sud'ba Viktorii Fedorovoi." *Argumenty i Fakty* #35, 1990, p. 6.

———. "'Teplo li nam doma?' Interv'iu s Viktoriei Fedorovovoi." *Ogonek* #2, #3300, 1990, pp. 22–26.

Munitsina, Aleksandra. "Vse muzhchiny utomliaiut odinakovo." *Novoye Russkoye Slovo,* 9/9/99, p. 15.

Neimark, Maria. "Bud'te muzhchinoi." *Novoye Russkoye Slovo,* 12/20/96, p. 28.

Nikolaev, N. "Ostorozhno: Rodstvenniki za granitsei." *Argumenty i Fakty.* October 1990, #42 (523), p. 2.

Orlikova, Marianna. "Moia russkaia zhena." *Cosmopolitan* (Russian edition), December 1997, pp. 146–150.

Osheverova, Lidiia. "Rossiiane—odna iz samykh seksual'no aktivnykh natsii, no luchshie liubovniki—frantsuzy." *Izvestiia*, 5/29/96, p. 10.

Pedologiia: Novyi vek. No 1, February 2000; No 2, April 2000.

Pomeshchikov, Anton. "Natalia Vetlitskaia, 'Ia prosto krivilas'." *Playboy* (Russian edition), July 1995, p. 103.

Prelovskaia, Inga. "Cherez sem' let posle svad'by v Rossii raspadaetsia kazhdyi vtoroi brak." *Izvestiia*, 7/5/95, p. 5.

Popovsky, Mark. *Na drugoi storone planety.* Philadephia: Poberezh'e, 1994.

Raskina, Sof'ia. "Chem kumushek schitat' trudit'sia . . ." *Novoye Russkoye Slovo*, 12/20/96, p. 28.

Ripinskaia, Maina. "Suzhenyi iz-za moria." *Novoye Russkoye Slovo*, 8/16/96, p. 49.

Rozin, M. *Sud'ba molodoi sem'i.* Moscow: Moskovskii rabochii, 1990.

Russkie: Etno-sotsiologicheskie ocherki. Moscow: Nauka, 1992.

Shcherbina, Tat'iana. "Bolshiye trudnosti s muzhchinoi." *Izvestiia*, 8/10/99, p. 6.

Skosyrev, Vladimir. "Inostranets v medovom kapkane." *Izvestiia*, 1/29/97, p. 3.

———. "Vstupil v intim—rasskazhi nachal'stvu." *Izvestiia*, 6/27/96, p. 3.

Startsev, Sergei. "Doch' Stalina postriglas' v monakhini." *Izvestiia*, 2/3/96, p. 3.

Susokolov, A. A. *Mezhnatsional'nye braki v SSSR.* Moscow: Mysl', 1987.

Sverdlov, Grigorii. *Sovetskie zakony o brake i sem'e.* Moscow: Znanie, 1955.

Svistunova, Svetlana. "Vyiti zamuzh za amerikantsa?" *Nezavisimaia gazeta*, 3/20/98, p. 16.

Sysenko, V. A. *Ustoichivost' braka: problemy, faktory, usloviia.* Moscow: Finansy i statistika, 1981.

Topol, Eduard. *Novaia Rossiia v posteli.* Moscow: ACT, 1998.

Uspenskaia, Tat'iana. *Ia vyshla zamuzh v Ameriku.* Moscow: FiS, 1997.

Visson, Lynn. *Chuzhie i blizkie v russko-amerikanskikh brakakh.* Moscow: Valent, 1999.

———. "Rossiisko-amerikanskie braki: pritiazhenie protivopolozhnostei." *Vy i My: Almanakh*, No 3 (15) 1997, pp. 23–26.

Yakovleva-Ustinova, Tat'iana. "Industriia schast'ia." *Izvestiia*, 11/17/99, p. 7.

Zherebtsova, Ol'ga. "Russkie Zolushki mochat amerikanskikh printsev." *Novoye Russkoye Slovo*, 10/22/99, p. 50.

INDEX

Also by Lynn Visson . . .

The Art of Uzbek Cooking

A historical crossroads in Central Asia, Uzbekistan and its cuisine reflect the range of nationalities that form the country and continue to flourish there. This collection of some 175 authentic Uzbek recipes includes chapters on Appetizers & Salads, Soups, Meat, Poultry & Fish, Plovs, Stuffed Pastries, Dumplings, Pasta & Pancakes, Vegetables, Breads, Desserts, Drinks, and even Suggested Menus.

The Art of Uzbek Cooking provides an introduction to a little known and exciting cuisine through easy-to-follow recipes that have been tested and adapted for American kitchens.

278 pages • 5½ x 8¼ • 0-7818-0669-0 • $24.95hc • (767)

Russian-interest titles from Hippocrene . . .

Hippocrene Children's Illustrated Russian Dictionary
English-Russian/Russian-English

- 500 words with full-color pictures
- specially designed for the youngest readers, ages 5–10
- commonsense phonetic pronunciation for Russian words
- Russian-English index

94 pages • 8½ x 11 • 0-7818-0772-7 • $14.95hc • (259)

Treasury of Russian Love Poems, Quotations & Proverbs
In Russian and English

Edited by Victorya Andreyeva

Filled with romantic imagery, this charming bilingual gift volume provides a glimpse into the Russian culture's unique approach to affairs of the heart. With poems from Tolstoy, Chekhov and Pushkin along with proverbs and quotations from numerous other Russian literary greats, this collection presents the works in the original Russian with side-by-side English translation. Also available in an audiocassette edition, read by native Russian speakers.

128 pages • 5 x 7 • 0-7818-0298-9 • $11.95hc • (591)

Also available as an audiobook: 0-7818-0364-0 • $12.95 • (586)

Folk Tales from Russia
Donald A. Mackenzie

From Hippocrene's classic folklore series comes this collection of short stories, each infused with the rich and varied cultural identity of Russia. Readers will be charmed by these legendary folk tales that symbolically weave magical fantasy with the historic events of Russia's past. This is an ideal gift, a learning tool, and a perfect addition to any Russian literature collection.

192 pages • 8 b/w illustrations • 5½ x 8¼ • 0-7818-0696-8 • $12.50hc • (788)

Russia: An Illustrated History
Joel Carmichael

Encompassing one-sixth of the earth's land surface—the equivalent of the whole North American continent—Russia is the largest country in the world. Renowned historian Joel Carmichael explores Russia's rich and expansive past—upheaval, reform, social change, growth—in an easily accessible and concentrated volume. From the Tatar's reign to the present, this book spans seven centuries of Russian history, highlighting the major political events, cultural accomplishments, military conflicts and economic developments that have helped to shape the tradition of modern-day Russia. Over 50 photographs and illustrations bring Russia's history to life for readers.

255 pages • 5 x 7 • 0-7818-0689-5 • $14.95hc • (781)

The Best of Russian Cooking
Alexandra Kropotkin

"Russia has a decided culinary heritage. This book reflects that heritage better than any volume I know."—Craig Claiborne

From *zavtrak* (breakfast) to *uzhin* (dinner), Russians love to eat heartily. *The Best of Russian Cooking* presents a wonderful array of Russian recipes, including invaluable cultural insights and culinary tips to help you create your own authentic Russian feast.

The 300 recipes are presented in an easy-to-read format, and the book also includes an extensive section of menu terms in Russian and English. A cookbook classic, originally published in 1964, it is as practical for the modern-day cook as it was back then.

288 pages • 5½ x 8¼ • 0-7818-0131-1 • $11.95pb • (251)

Russian Language Studies . . .

Dictionary of 1000 Russian Proverbs
Edited by Peter Mertvago

This collection of the most commonly used and understood proverbs of the day is designed for a broad readership comprised of students of both language and culture, from secondary school level to post-graduate, as well as teachers, travelers, and linguists.

A comparable or literal translation is provided for the 1,000 proverbs in this Russian-English source of Russian proverbs. This wonderful reference collection offers students insight into both the language and culture of Russia.

- Organized alphabetically by word
- Proverbs are arranged side-by-side with their English counterparts/ translations and marked to identify either literal or free translations
- Index organized by English subject

181 pages • 5½ x 8¼ • 0-7818-0564-3 • $11.95pb • (694)

Beginner's Russian
Nonna Karr and Ludmila Rodionova

This guide introduces the beginner to the Cyrillic alphabet and is a perfect stepping stone to more complex language learning.

200 pages • 5½ x 8¼ • 0-7818-0232-6 • W • $9.95pb • (61)

Mastering Russian
Erika Haber

This imaginative course, designed for both individual and classroom use, assumes no previous knowledge of the language. The unique combination of practical exercises and step-by-step grammar emphasizes a functional approach to new scripts and their vocabularies. Everyday situations and local customs are explored variously through dialogues, drawings and photos.

320 pages • 5½ x 8¼ • 0-7818-0270-9 • $14.95pb • (11)
2 Cassettes: • 0-7818-0271-7 • $12.95 • (13)

English-Russian Comprehensive Dictionary

Oleg Benyukh, *General Editor*

- Over 40,000 entries and 100,000 references with phonetic transcription, part of speech, and when appropriate, idiomatic usage of the word
- Appendix of common given names
- Appendix of weights and measures
- Appendix of geographical locations
- Tables of numbers, temperature, and Latin words and phrases

800 pages • 6 x 9 • 40,000 entries • 0-7818-0442-6 • $35.00pb • (50)

Russian-English Comprehensive Dictionary

Oleg Benyukh, *General Editor*

Containing over 40,000 entries and 100,000 references, this is the most thorough, accurate and up-to-date Russian-English dictionary in the world. It also includes phonetic transcriptions, parts of speech, appropriate idiomatic usage, and appendices of given names, geographical locations, weights and measures, Latin words and phrases, and tables of numbers and temperature. It has been described as the ultimate reference tool for students, scholars and business people.

800 pages • 6 x 9 • 40,000 entries • 0-7818-0506-6 • $60.00hc • (612)
Paperback edition: 0-7818-0560-0 • $35.00pb • (689)

Russian-English/English-Russian Standard Dictionary
With Complete Phonetics

Revised Edition with Business Terms

Oleg Benyukh and Ksana Benyukh

With over 32,000 entries, this Russian-English/English-Russian dictionary will help you speak on any topic and translate any material. The commonsense phonetics in the Russian-English section show the romanization of Russian words. Phonetics in the English-Russian section show English words in the Cyrillic alphabet to help Russians pronounce American English. To assist travelers to Russia, the dictionary includes a detailed menu from a Moscow restaurant, including the English translation.

418 pages • 5½ x 8¼ • 32,000 entries • 0-7818-0280-6 • $18.95pb • (322)

Russian-English/English-Russian Concise Dictionary

- Over 13,000 entries
- Ideal for students and travelers
- Easy-to-read format
- Transliterations for each entry

512 pages • 4 x 6 • 13,000 entries • 0-7818-0132-X • $11.95pb • (262)
Also available in COMPACT size:
512 pages • 3⅛ x 4⅝ • 10,000 entries • 0-7818-0537-6 • $9.95pb • (688)

A Dictionary of Russian Verbs

E. Daum & W. Schenk

Reliable and easy to use, this dictionary features 20,000 verbs fully declined. All verb forms are consistent with those of the authoritative Russian sources available. With its comprehensive coverage of Russian verbs and verb declension, this reference guide has become the indispensable companion of thousands of Russian language students.

750 pages • 5½ x 8¼ • 20,000 fully declined verbs • 0-7818-0371-3
• $45.00hc • (572)
Paperback edition: 0-88254-420-9 • $35.00pb • (10)

Dictionary of Russian Proverbs, Bilingual

477 pages • 5½ x 8¼ • 5,335 entries index • 0-7818-0424-8 • $35.00pb • (555)

Russian Phrasebook and Dictionary, Revised

256 pages • 5½ x 8¼ • 3,000 entries, subway maps of Moscow and St. Petersburg
• 0-7818-0190-7 • $11.95pb • (597)
2 cassettes: 120 minutes • 0-7818-0192-3 • $12.95 • (432)

Prices subject to change without notice. **To purchase Hippocrene Books** contact your local bookstore, call (718) 454-2366, or write to: HIPPOCRENE BOOKS, 171 Madison Avenue, New York, NY 10016. Please enclose check or money order, adding $5.00 shipping (UPS) for the first book and $.50 for each additional book.